JUSTIN MARTYR

JUSTIN MARTYR

HIS LIFE AND THOUGHT

BY

L. W. BARNARD

CAMBRIDGE

AT THE UNIVERSITY PRESS

1967

CAMBRIDGE UNIVERSITY PRESS

Cambridge, New York, Melbourne, Madrid, Cape Town, Singapore, São Paulo, Delhi

Cambridge University Press
The Edinburgh Building, Cambridge CB2 8RU, UK

Published in the United States of America by Cambridge University Press, New York

www.cambridge.org
Information on this title: www.cambridge.org/9780521041065

First published 1967
This digitally printed version 2008

A catalogue record for this publication is available from the British Library

Library of Congress Catalogue Card Number: 66–16665

ISBN 978-0-521-04106-5 hardback
ISBN 978-0-521-09157-2 paperback

CONTENTS

PREFACE

JUSTIN MARTYR was the most important of the second-century Greek Apologists, yet he has usually been regarded as but one of a larger group of writers who reflected, in their presentation of Christianity, the intellectual currents of the age. This treatment is reflected in the paucity of books specifically concerned with Justin. The last full treatment of his theology in English was written as long ago as 1923 and, having been published in Jena in Germany, is now almost impossible to obtain. This fact has done Justin a real injustice, for he was a pioneer Apologist and the others, such as Tatian and Athenagoras, were heavily indebted to him. It is not without justice that the doyen of German patristic scholars, Baron von Campenhausen, has said that nearly all the Greek Fathers of the Church were, consciously or unconsciously, his imitators.[1]

In this book I have attempted to give a coherent account of Justin's thought, paying special attention to his background in Greek philosophy and Judaism. Recent study has enabled this background to be portrayed with sharper accuracy and the interpretation of Justin, in these pages, takes account of this work. I have discussed many problems concerning Justin's background with the Reverend J. H. Davies and wish to acknowledge the help which this contact has given. I am also grateful to my old Oxford tutor, the Reverend L. B. Cross, who first introduced me to the Greek Fathers of the Church.

This book has been written during the odd moments which could be spared from a busy parochial ministry. I have found much food for thought and also encouragement from the example of this Apologist who rose so triumphantly above his material and who, in one bold stroke, summed up the whole history of the human race in Christ. Justin, whatever his faults and the incompleteness of his theology, was a man with a

---

[1] *The Fathers of the Greek Church* (London, 1963), p. 15.

vii

mission. His Christian philosophy was no neat academic amalgam of Plato and Christianity. For him Christianity was philosophic truth itself and to its service he devoted his life with unswerving courage, honesty and audacity. What more could be asked of any Christian?

L. W. B.

All Saints Rectory
Winchester

ABBREVIATIONS

B.J.R.L.	*Bulletin of John Rylands Library.*
C.Q.	*Classical Quarterly.*
C.Q.R.	*Church Quarterly Review.*
D.C.B.	*Dictionary of Christian Biography.*
E.R.E	*Encyclopædia of Religion and Ethics.*
J.B.L.	*Journal of Biblical Literature.*
J.Q.R.	*Jewish Quarterly Review.*
J.T.S.	*Journal of Theological Studies.*
N.T.S.	*New Testament Studies.*
R. Bén.	*Revue Bénédictine.*
R. Bibl.	*Revue Biblique.*
R.H.E.	*Revue d'histoire ecclésiastique.*
R.H.P.R.	*Revue d'histoire et de philosophie religieuses.*
R.S.R.	*Revue des sciences religieuses.*
T. & U.	*Texte und Untersuchungen.*
V.C.	*Vigiliae Christianae.*
V.T.	*Vetus Testamentum.*
Z.N.T.W.	*Zeitschrift für die neutestamentliche Wissenschaft.*

CHAPTER I

LIFE, CONVERSION AND MARTYRDOM

THE AGE OF THE APOLOGISTS

CHRISTIANITY was born within a Jewish cradle and it was natural that the earliest attempts at a theological formulation of its doctrines should have been expressed in Jewish terms. It was not long however before the Gospel had spread into the great cities of the Graeco-Roman world where it could not be assumed that converts to the new faith would be acquainted with the Jewish Scriptures or even with the monotheistic worship of Judaism. It is true that numbers of god-fearers, or religious inquirers, had attached themselves to the synagogues and that many of these had become attracted to Christianity through the medium of Hellenistic Judaism. Nevertheless, there was the wider pagan world—sometimes indifferent, sometimes avowedly hostile—which misrepresented Christian teaching and spread calumnies against Christians.

The earliest Christian writings outside the New Testament, known as the Apostolic Fathers,[1] were not concerned with this wider pagan world. Their concern was rather with the consolidation of the little Christian communities spread throughout the Graeco-Roman world. They dealt with such problems as internal schism (I Clement); pre-baptismal instruction and the ordering of Church Services (Didache); the problem of repentance (Hermas); the Unity of the Church (Ignatius); the sin of avarice (Polycarp); how the Old Testament is to be interpreted (Barnabas). These writers, for the most part conservative in outlook, were dealing with definite practical and moral problems which the Church of their day was facing. When they are judged in the light of these practical considerations, and not as speculative theologians, their achievements are impressive. However, even within the Apostolic age Christianity had come into contact with the wider Roman world, as

---

[1] The Epistle to Diognetus should not strictly be classed with the Apostolic Fathers as it is an Apology.

represented by its Governors and pro-Consuls, and the need became apparent for an *apologia*, or defence of the faith, to that world. In one aspect Luke–Acts is an attempt to provide such an *apologia* whoever Theophilus may have been. In this connection it is an interesting fact that the first *Christian* books found on rolls, in contrast to the usual Codex form, are Luke and Acts, which may point to their having been designed for a non-Christian public.[1] It was, however, one thing to write a Gospel or 'Good News' with a non-Christian audience in mind. It was another thing to face persecution and hostile misrepresentations of the faith.

Persecution in the early Church was mainly of a sporadic, local nature—certainly no 'general' persecution occurred before the time of Diocletian. Nevertheless, individual Christians, in some areas, did go in fear of their lives with the hated *delator* or informer never far away. Domitian, at the end of the first century, selected his victims one by one and disposed of them with a stealth and lack of pity worthy of Stalin's Russia. Mob violence was also always a threat whipped up, as it sometimes was, by strange distortions of Christian teaching and practice. The case of Demetrius in Acts xix shows that once the new faith opposed traditional ways and practices then trouble soon ensued. A faith which shunned popular vices and amusements provoked a hatred which took the form of blackening the character of Christians. A faith which forbad its followers to sacrifice to the State deities—and especially to the *genius* of the Emperor—could only be held, it was said, by a community of atheists capable of any crime. The Christians were therefore accused of all kinds of wickedness. Their assemblies for worship, instruction and for the celebration of the Eucharist were none other than secret gatherings for incest, child murder and cannibalism. Such calumnies no doubt came to the notice of the Roman authorities who, while not encouraging false accusations, could not totally ignore them.

The appearance of the Christian Apologists is an indication that the Church took these calumnies seriously and had decided to do something about them. Christians had to be vindicated against false accusations; the Emperor himself must hear of the

[1] C. H. Roberts, Sandars Lectures at Cambridge, February 1961, quoted in C. F. D. Moule, *The Birth of the New Testament* (London, 1962), p. 92.

2

cruel wrongs perpetrated in his name. The Christian way of life had to be shown as the highest ideal of ethical conduct which the world had yet seen. Yet *apologia*, or the case for the defence, embraced far more than the refutation of these attacks—and that was not difficult. It was based on the magnificent defence which Socrates had made at his trial before the people of Athens in which he showed the essential rationality of his position. The Christian Apologists therefore set themselves the wider task of showing how Christianity was the embodiment of the noblest conceptions of Greek philosophy and was the truth *par excellence*. In following this path the mantle of Judaism fell upon Christianity. Josephus and Philo had already under-taken the same task in defence of Judaism—Philo, in particular, had sought to bridge the gulf between the Jewish and Hellen-istic worlds. It is a fact often forgotten that following on the reconstruction of Judaism at Jamnia, when Rabbinism came to the fore, Philo's writings were in all probability not preserved by Jews[1] but by the Church.

In addition to the refutation of calumnies and the presenta-tion of Christianity as a rational faith the Apologists were also concerned with the questionings of thoughtful men. The object and form of Christian Worship and the character of the Christian life were clearly the subject of much discussion in certain circles. The introduction to the Epistle to Diognetus gives an interesting insight into these questionings:

Since I perceive, most excellent Diognetus, that you are exceedingly zealous to learn the religion of the Christians and are asking very clear and careful questions concerning them, both who is the God in whom they believe, and how they worship him, so that all disregard the world and despise death, and do not reckon as gods those who are considered to be so by the Greeks, nor keep the superstition of the Jews, and what is the love which they have for one another, and why this new race or practice has come to life at this time, and not formerly; I indeed welcome this zeal in you, and I ask from God who bestows on us the power both of speaking and of hearing, that it may be granted to me so to speak that you may benefit so much as possible by your hearing, and to you so to hear that I may not be made sorry for my speech (ch. i).

---

[1] The first Jew to mention Philo by name after his time is A. de Rossi (A.D. 1573).

I-2

The earliest Christian Apologies, those of Quadratus and Aristides, are assigned to the reign of Hadrian by Eusebius,[1] but it now seems more likely that the latter was in fact presented to Antoninus Pius some time before the year A.D. 147 when Marcus Aurelius became joint Emperor. The reign of Antoninus (A.D. 138–61) and that of his successor Marcus Aurelius (A.D. 161–80) covered a period of peace and prosperity in the history of the Empire—perhaps the happiest years the Empire had known.[2] Antoninus was a broad-minded ruler who encouraged the philosophers and literary writers of the Latin and Greek traditions who flocked to his court. His conception of Government, like that of Aurelius, was influenced by the Stoic belief in a divine Reason directing the Universe. This period was suitable for the production of Apologies. Ariston and Justin Martyr defended Christianity against Jewish attacks; Justin, followed by Tatian, Athenagoras, Theophilus of Antioch and Melito of Sardis, argued for the truth of the new religion as against polytheism and philosophy and demanded its recognition by the State. The Jewish Christian Hegesippus produced the first ecclesiastical chronicle while the growth of Gnosticism and Marcionism called forth defences of the traditional faith from within the Church. Unfortunately, many Christian writings, including not a few Apologies, have been lost from this period, and the literary productions which remain are but scattered fragments of what was once a large body of material.

The subject of this book, Justin Martyr, represents a pioneer type of Greek Apologist. He is concerned not only with the refutation of attacks against Christians and Jewish objections; he is also concerned to show that philosophy is truth, reason a spiritual power and Christianity the fulness of both.[3] Justin was not a clear thinker, if he is judged by the side of Tertullian, Origen or St Augustine. In spite of his varied contacts with leading philosophies it cannot be said that he had fully mastered

[1] *H.E.* iv. 3.

[2] Note the remarks of Gibbon, *Decline and Fall*, ch. III: 'If a man were called to fix the period in the history of the world during which the condition of the human race was most happy and prosperous, he would, without hesitation, name that which elapsed from the death of Domitian to the accession of Commodus.'

[3] Westcott, *Canon of the New Testament* (Cambridge and London, 1881), p.65.

contemporary philosophy and culture. Yet his testimony to Christianity as the true philosophy is one of the most important that has come down from the second century. Justin belonged to a generation which was still in touch with those who had known Our Lord's Apostles; but these were advanced in years and everywhere in the Church new men, new thoughts were arising to do battle for the faith.[1]

Our knowledge of the life of Justin comes almost entirely from his own writings, for Eusebius does little more than collect these notices. He was born at Flavia Neapolis,[2] a city not far from the ruins of Sychem, which had been named in honour of the Emperor Vespasian. Justin was, in consequence, a Samaritan by birth although nothing in his writings suggests that he was familiar with Samaritan traditions or religion. He did not hear of Moses and the Prophets until well on in life. He classes himself with those Gentiles to whom the Gospel was opened when the main mass of the house of Jacob rejected it.[3] He speaks of being brought up in Gentile customs, of being uncircumcised[4] and of having received a Greek education.[5] The name of his grandfather Bacchius is Greek; of his father Priscus and of himself Latin. Little can be salvaged from these details—possibly Justin's ancestors were colonists who had settled in Flavia Neapolis soon after its establishment.

We are on no firmer ground in regard to the date of his birth. According to Epiphanius[6] Justin was martyred under Hadrian when only thirty years of age; but as this date for his martyrdom is almost certainly wrong we cannot place any credence on the age given. We only know that Justin taught at Rome in the reign of Antoninus Pius[7] and that he was martyred under Marcus Aurelius,[8] from which we infer that his birth occurred either late in the first century or early in the second. Justin's writings are full of vigour and do not suggest that he was of an advanced age at the time of his death. His martyrdom seems to have been the outcome of a conflict with a certain Crescens the Cynic whom Justin had convicted of ignorance. 'Crescens,'

---

[1] Carrington, *The Early Christian Church* (2 vols. Cambridge, 1957), II, 107.

[2] *I Apol.* i.	[3] *I Apol.* liii.	[4] *Dial.* xxix.
[5] *Dial.* ii.	[6] *Haer.* xlvi. 1.	[7] Eus. *H.E.* iv. 11.
[8] *Ibid.* 16.		

Tatian writes, 'who made himself a nest in Rome, while professing to despise death, proved his fear of it by scheming to bring Justin and myself to death as to an evil thing.'[1] Tatian does not assert that Crescens succeeded, but in Justin's *Second Apology* we have ominous forebodings that this may happen.[2] Certainly the reality of his martyrdom in the cause of Christ is attested by Eusebius and also by his historic title. For an actual account of his death we are dependent on the Acts of his Martyrdom which embody the third-century tradition of the death-scene.[3] Justin and his companions, according to this account, are brought before Rusticus, the prefect of Rome, and are simply commanded to sacrifice to the gods—there is no mention of Crescens or of Justin's writings. Justin, on examination, testifies to Christianity as the truth. He confesses that he has held meetings, on his second visit to Rome, in the house of one Martinus at the baths of Timotinus—although only there. After a brave refusal to sacrifice Justin and those with him are condemned to be beaten with rods and beheaded. They pass to their death praising God and confessing Christ; later faithful Christians secretly carry off their bodies in order to give them a fit burial.

Although the actual date of Justin's birth is uncertain, as with so many other figures in early Christian history, we are on firmer ground as to the details of his later life. In the opening chapters of the *Dialogue* with Trypho he gives a graphic account of the studies through which he had passed before becoming converted to the Christian Faith. From youth Justin appears to have been of an earnest and religious type of mind intent upon finding intellectual peace and satisfaction. He reverences above all philosophers: 'for philosophy is, in fact, the greatest possession, and most honourable before God, to whom it leads us and alone commends us; and these are truly holy men who have bestowed attention on philosophy'.[4] With this hope in mind he undergoes instruction from a Stoic teacher only to be disappointed in his quest. Then he tries a Peripatetic only to find him more concerned about his fee than with the know-

---

[1] *Oratio* xxxii; cf. Eus. *H.E.* iv. 16.   [2] *II Apol.* iii.

[3] A good recent translation is that of E. R. Hardy, *Faithful Witnesses* (London, 1960), pp. 65–9. For the original see *Ausgewählte Märtyrerakten* (ed. G. Krüger) (3rd ed. Tübingen, 1929).   [4] *Dial.* ii.

ledge of the truth. Undaunted, Justin next goes to a celebrated Pythagorean teacher only to be told that a long course in music, astronomy and geometry is needed before the soul can attain to invisible realities. On learning of Justin's ignorance in these disciplines the teacher dismisses him somewhat contemptuously. Finally Justin, in a restless condition, spends much time with a Platonist 'who had lately settled in our city'.[1] The Platonic philosophy immediately impresses him: 'the perception of immaterial things quite overpowered me, and the contemplation of ideas furnished my mind with wings'.[2] He supposed that before long he would look upon God—the supreme goal of Plato's philosophy.

It was while a Platonist that Justin became a Christian. He meets an old man while meditating in a field who points him to the Hebrew prophets: 'certain men more ancient than all those who are esteemed philosophers, both righteous and beloved by God, who spoke by the Divine Spirit, and foretold events which would take place, and which are now taking place'.[3] These prophets were witnesses to the truth above all demonstration, and worthy of belief; they glorified God as Creator and Father and proclaimed his Son, the Christ. The old man concludes: 'Pray that, above all things, the gates of light may be opened to you; for these things cannot be perceived or understood by all, but only by the man to whom God and his Christ have imparted wisdom.'[4] The old man departs leaving a flame kindled in Justin's soul: 'a love of the prophets, and of those men who are friends of Christ, possessed me'.[5] Christianity was the one, sure, worthy philosophy.

This account of Justin's studies and conversion has been assailed by some scholars as an idealisation. In the opinion of E. R. Goodenough 'Justin, in the entire passage, is dramatizing the relations between Christianity and philosophy and has adopted the familiar convention of relating someone's adventures in passing from school to school, and finally in the Christian school, in order to criticize each school by the adventures related'.[6] Goodenough instances the parallel between this

---

[1] *Dial.* ii. Either Flavia Neapolis or Ephesus where the *Dialogue* with Trypho is located.   [2] *Dial.* ii.   [3] *Dial.* vii.
[4] *Dial.* vii.   [5] *Dial.* viii.
[6] *The Theology of Justin Martyr* (Jena, 1923), pp. 58–9.

account of Justin and Lucian's *Menippus* chs. iv–vi—a contemporary piece of writing.[1] In this Menippus describes how he went through several schools of philosophy and gave them up because their mutual contradictions convinced him that none could speak with authority. This is the conventionalisation of a well-known literary form. Goodenough also suggests that the same form, borrowed from the Greeks, was used by the Tannaim to describe the three types of true proselytes to Judaism, Githro, Naaman and Rahab, who go through all the heathen cults and schools without finding peace. They ultimately find their rest and peace in the haven of the Law and the Prophets.[2]

It is of course true that there was a Greek literary convention which related adventures in various schools of thought in order to criticise these schools. But Justin's account of his *actual* conversion, given in great detail with many local touches, cannot be separated from the preceding account of his experiences in different philosophic schools. On Goodenough's admission 'the two narratives are one, unbroken by any transition'.[3] And it is precisely Justin's account of his *actual* conversion at the hands of an old man which has the ring of truth about it and gives an adequate explanation of his later work as a Christian philosopher. It is true that converts to any religion tend to paint their pre-conversion life in the darkest hues. But to admit an element of idealisation and tendentiousness is something different from saying that the *whole account* is a conventional literary form taken over and later dressed up by Justin.

A different approach to this problem is that of C. Andresen in an article[4] which makes a real contribution to Justin studies. Andresen seeks to show that Justin's philosophical background can best be explained and understood by reference to Middle Platonism. We shall examine his thesis in another chapter[5] and confine ourselves here to Andresen's view of Justin's philosophical quest before his conversion[6] as recorded in the second chapter of the *Dialogue* with Trypho. Andresen believes

---

[1] Goodenough is here following Helm, *Lucian und Menipp*, pp. 40 f.
[2] Goldfahn quoted by Goodenough, *Theology of Justin Martyr*, p. 59.
[3] *Ibid.* p. 58.
[4] 'Justin und der mittlere Platonismus', *Z.N.T.W.* XLIV (1952–3), 157–95.
[5] Chapter III.   [6] *Z.N.T.W.* XLIV (1952–3), 160–3.

this to be a retrospective description which causes Justin some embarrassment and bears unmistakable signs of tendentiousness (*tendenziöser*). Thus there is no mistaking the ironic undertone when Justin describes how the Peripatetic, whom he visits, demands money 'in order that our intercourse might not be unprofitable' (*Dial.* ii. 4). This allusion to material cupidity is, as we learn from Lucian and Ailios Aristides,[1] a favourite theme in contemporary polemics against philosophers. But it is precisely these tendentious features in Justin's description which, according to Andresen, point to Middle Platonism. For it was the Platonism of the Schools (*Schulplatonismus*), with its fundamentally religious attitude, which determined the climate of the age—not least in its opinion of other philosophical systems. So Justin can speak of the great fame enjoyed by the Platonists (*Dial.* ii. 7).

Andresen next considers Justin's statement: 'I surrendered myself to a certain Stoic; and having spent a considerable time with him, when I had not acquired any further knowledge of God (for he did not know himself, and said such instruction was unnecessary) I left him...' (*Dial.* ii. 3). This description of a Stoic who did not think much of religion or piety seems incredible.[2] Andresen believes that in this description we have the judgement of Middle Platonism for whose platonist spiritualism the Stoic monistic conception of God was intolerable.[3]

It is the Peripatetic whom Justin depicts in the most unfavourable light, for he doubts whether he can be considered a philosopher at all (*Dial.* ii. 3). It is well known that in some of its representatives the philosophy of Middle Platonism is acutely opposed to the Peripatetics. Aristotle is blamed because his cosmology endangered the idea of divine providence and his theory of the fifth element the immortality of the soul.[4] These are however fundamental dogmas of *Schulplatonismus* which regarded Aristotle and Epicurus as the representatives of 'godlessness' *par excellence*.[5] Andresen thinks that through considerations of this kind Justin arrived at his opinion about the Peripatetic teachers.

---

[1] Lucian, *Dial. mort.* x. 11; A. Aristides, *Or.* 45.

[2] G. Bardy, 'Saint Justin et la philosophie stoicienne', *R.S.R.* xiii (1923), 493 f.

[3] Plutarch, *De comm. notit.* 31 f.; *De defectu* 19. 24; *De Stoic. repugn.* 31–4.

[4] Atticus-Eus. *Praep. Ev.* xv. 5, 6 f.   [5] Cf. Origen, *c.Cels.* i. 21; viii. 45.

Justin is more favourably disposed towards his Pythagorean teacher whom he describes as very celebrated and one who thought highly about wisdom (*Dial.* ii. 4). This teacher names music, astronomy and geometry as the condition for a successful study of philosophy. The sentiments which Justin, in his survey, puts into the mouth of the Pythagorean are, according to Andresen, those of Middle Platonism. Thus Theon of Smyrna puts forward in his work, 'That the fundamental sciences are useful for the study of Plato', the view that Plato largely followed the Pythagoreans.[1] And Albinus justifies the philosophical propaedeutic of the fundamental sciences by claiming that they abstract from the world of phenomena and direct thought to the world of the intelligence.[2] This favourable view of Pythagoreanism among the Middle Platonists is also responsible for Justin's statement that Plato and Pythagoras have been 'as a wall and fortress of philosophy to us' (*Dial.* v. 6), i.e. they gave philosophy its religious aim and direction. So the School Platonists equate the Platonist definition of *telos* as 'likeness to God' with the Pythagorean *telos* 'follow God'. Justin's favourable judgement of his Pythagorean teacher thus coincides with that of the Middle Platonists. Andresen believes that the opening conversation of the *Dialogue* with Trypho reflects *in toto* the beliefs of the Middle Platonism of the schools.

This approach is clearly based on the Form Critical method (*Formgeschichte*) which has been applied by many scholars to the study of the Gospel narratives. For Andresen Justin Martyr's training in the Middle Platonist schools is the *sitz-im-leben* which has shaped and determined his view of other philosophical systems and teachers and affected the account of his pre-conversion studies. There is some truth in this. All of us are affected, to a greater or lesser degree, by our immediate environment. We look at the past—and this is particularly true of the religious convert—from a particular *sitz-im-leben*. But it is worth remembering that Justin was not a 'twice born' Christian. He experienced nothing like the dramatic conversion of a St Paul or a St Augustine. Christianity was for him the true philosophy and throughout his days he retained the impress of his passage from an imperfect to a perfect philosophy.

---

[1] Ed. Hiller, 12, 10 f.   [2] *Didask.* vii. 161, 9 f.

In such cases we should expect the tendentious element to be smaller than with people who had had more dramatic experiences. We have already noted the strongly personal character of Justin's philosophical search as recorded in *Dial.* ii. It is difficult to believe that this is simply a later creation born of his experiences with the Middle Platonists. *Formgeschichte* is a valuable critical tool, but in itself it can pass no judgement on the historicity of the traditions which it handles. In our judgement the account of Justin's philosophical quest as recorded in *Dial.* ii is based on sound historical tradition—namely, that Justin *really* underwent instruction at the hands of a Stoic teacher, a Peripatetic, a Pythagorean and finally the Platonists. His was a typical experience born of the eclecticism of the age. Pupils, in those days, passed from teacher to teacher in their search for philosophic truth almost as a matter of course. But to maintain the essential historicity of Justin's account is not to deny that his views on the various philosophical schools may have been given an edge from his instruction in Middle Platonism. Is it impossible that Justin's experiences may have agreed with the criticism of the Platonist schools? To admit an element of tendentiousness is different from denying to Justin's account essential roots in his personal history. It was his varied experiences in the different schools which give an adequate explanation of his later work as a Christian philosopher. He only found the truth after much searching. It was therefore natural that he should wear the philosopher's cloak, even after his conversion, call himself a philosopher and invite men to enter his school.[1]

Justin's writings show that one other motif deeply affected his conversion. This was the steadfastness of Christians under persecution at which he never ceased to wonder: 'I myself, too, when I was delighting in the doctrines of Plato, and heard the Christians slandered, and saw them fearless of death, and of all other things which are counted fearful, perceived that it was impossible that they could be living in wickedness and pleasure.'[2] This moral steadfastness, in contrast to the lack of moral reality in so much contemporary philosophy, is mentioned elsewhere in the Apologies.[3] It clearly had a great in-

---

[1] *Dial.* i.   [2] *II Apol.* xii.

[3] *I Apol.* viii, xi *inter alia.*

fluence on Justin as is evidenced by his post-conversion emphasis on the Christian life as a sure evidence for the reality of Christian Faith.

We possess few details of Justin's life following his conversion and baptism. He seems to have come to Rome and to have stayed there some time.[1] In the Acts of his Martyrdom it is stated that he had resided twice in Rome.[2] This is consonant with what we know of the various schools of thought which Christian teachers established in the capital city of the Empire. Valentinus had connections with Alexandria and Cyprus as well as with Rome. Marcion's nickname, the 'sea-captain', suggests that he made a number of voyages. Greek philosophers such as Lucian of Samosata taught in province after province.[3] It is not therefore to be assumed that Justin established a permanent school of Christian philosophy at Rome. Most probably he taught in other cities at different times in his career.

Justin's special task was Christian apologetic or the defence of the faith. Eusebius vividly describes his work: 'But Justin was the most noted of those that flourished in those times, who, in the guise of a philosopher, preached the truth of God, and contended for the faith, also, in his writings.'[4] Again the Acts of his Martyrdom speak of him as sitting in the house of Martinus, a recognised place of meeting for Christians, and there conversing with any who visited him, imparting to them the true doctrine. The persons condemned with Justin are those whom he has gathered around him and converted. 'I took delight', says one Evelpistus, 'in listening to Justin's discourse.' This is a picture of a philosophic evangelist informally training disciples. One of the most famous of these was Tatian, the brilliant Assyrian, who came from the neighbourhood of Nisibis beyond the Euphrates; afterwards he became famous as a heretic and the author of the *Diatessaron*, the first harmony of the Gospels. Tatian is explicitly described as a hearer[5] or disciple[6] of Justin's and it would seem that he did not propagate his own peculiar views until after the death of Justin. Another pupil was

---

[1] Eus. *H.E.* iv. 11.　　　　[2] Hardy, *Faithful Witnesses*, p. 67.
[3] Carrington, *The Early Christian Church*, II, 98–9.
[4] *H.E.* iv. 11.
[5] *Iren. Adv. Haer.* i. 28. 1.　　　　[6] *Hippol. Refut.* viii. 9.

Irenaeus from Smyrna, a pupil of Polycarp. Justin's school[1] was certainly of cosmopolitan composition as was the case with other schools of thought in Rome. Pupils came from far and wide to sit at the feet of the renowned teacher and there learn the rudiments of a Christian philosophy. To judge from the writings of the master this school engaged in literary production— indeed it may have provided the literary material from which Tatian composed his *Diatessaron*. Such schools were only indirectly subject to the discipline of the Church which, at least in second-century Rome, was not much concerned with theological and philosophical matters.

Active controversy was also Justin's *métier*. The collision with Trypho in the Colonnades, as recorded in the *Dialogue*, is probably but one specimen of the intellectual debate in which Justin engaged. In Rome he engaged in public debate with the Cynic philosopher Crescens of whom he speaks with an acrimony which shows that the debate had been a sharp one.[2] Justin also distinguished himself in controversy with noted heretical teachers who had founded schools in Rome. He speaks of Marcion 'who is even at this day alive, and teaching his disciples to believe in some other god greater than the Creator'.[3]

The meagre outline of Justin's life may thus be filled in from these scattered notices. He was born probably late in the first or early in the second century at Flavia Neapolis. His conversion from Platonism to Christianity may have taken place shortly before the Bar Chochba rising in A.D. 132-5.[4] Justin came to Rome around A.D. 150 or slightly earlier—a date fixed by the date of the first Apology[5]—where he founded his school of philosophical instruction and engaged in active controversy with other philosophers and 'Christian' teachers. He was martyred for his faith in the reign of Marcus Aurelius— probably somewhere between A.D. 163 and 167. The early Roman martyrologies give the day of his death as 14 April and the Syrian chronicle gives the year as A.D. 165.[6]

---

[1] The philosophic 'school' had a long history in the Greek world. It seems probable that the early Milesian philosophers had 'schools' around them. Pythagoras himself was an Ionian: see F. C. Copleston, *A History of Philosophy*. Vol. I: *Greece and Rome* (London, 1947), p. 29.

[2] *II Apol.* iii. [3] *I Apol.* xxvi.

[4] Alluded to in *Dial.* i. [5] See p. 19.

[6] Carrington, *The Early Christian Church*, II, 173.

CHAPTER II

JUSTIN'S WORKS

⌐THE second century was an age of literary activity within the Church. Christians had to be vindicated against calumnies and the Gospel shown as the coping stone of Greek philosophy. As might have been expected of one who taught in various 'schools' at different times in his career, Justin became an author and such was his fame in the eyes of the later Church that many writings were deliberately or by mistake attributed to him (see Appendix 1). During the Middle Ages he was known only by these spurious writings, and the earliest manuscript of his works, dating from the fourteenth century, contains twelve works alleged to have been written by him.

Of the large corpus of writings preserved in Justin's name there is general agreement that only the two Apologies (addressed to Antoninus Pius and the Roman Senate) and the *Dialogue* with Trypho the Jew are genuine. The text of these three works is based on a single manuscript, Paris 450, dated 11 September A.D. 1363, which also contains most of the spurious writings of the Apologist. There is reason for thinking that the text of the *Dialogue* is more reliable than the text of the Apologies although even this shows frequent signs of carelessness.[1] The only checks on the readings of Paris 450 are the passages, few in number, where Justin is quoted by other Fathers, and a fragment of the *First Apology* chapters lxv–lxvii, which had an independent tradition in Codex *Ottobonianus Graecus* CCLXXIV of the fifteenth century in the Vatican Library at Rome.[2]

(1) THE APOLOGIES

The *First Apology* is addressed to the Emperor Antoninus Pius and to his son Verissimus the philosopher, and to Lucius the philosopher. Hellenistic Jewish writers before Justin had used

---

[1] Harnack, *T. & U.* I, 1–2 (1882), pp. 77–9. Harnack spoke of the text of Justin's works as being in a desperate condition.

[2] Goodenough, *Theology of Justin Martyr*, p. 80.

similar modes of address to ensure that their works received a sympathetic hearing by the public for whom they were designed —although it is not to be supposed that these *Apologies* never reached the Emperors.[1]

The *First Apology* opens with a bold appeal to justice—evidently in imitation of Plato's *Apology of Socrates*. Justin then goes on (3–12) to refute anti-Christian slanders. He demands (3, 4) that men should not be punished merely for a name, but only after examination of their lives and conduct. The unreasonable hatred which Christians experience is due to the instigation of daemons against the Incarnate Word—the same daemons who slew Socrates (5). Justin now (6–12) gives three of the principal charges levelled against Christians—atheism, immorality and disloyalty. He insists that Christians are not atheists, for they worship the Father of righteousness and virtue, the Son who came forth from him with his angels, and the Spirit of prophecy. They are not immoral and are willing to be punished for any crimes they commit. They are not disloyal, for the Kingdom they seek is a heavenly one.

Having made this appeal for justice and refutation of slanders Justin asserts that he has written enough to ensure a change of policy; nevertheless, he will go on to show the actual truth of Christianity and its positive worth. He begins (13) by demonstrating that Christians are monotheists who worship God, and then Jesus Christ according to his secondary rank, and then the Prophetic Spirit. Christian worship is essentially reasonable worship. Justin then gives examples (14–20) of the moral power and elevation of Christ's teaching and produces analogies between the Christian doctrines of immortality, resurrection and the end of the world and the teaching of nature and philosophy. He also gives (21–2) some of the pagan fables about the exploits of the sons of gods and shows how irrational it was for believers in these tales to persecute believers in the facts of Jesus' life. Justin's object in this part of the *First Apology* was to disarm unbelief and to show that Christianity was not contemptible nor novel but essentially rational.

He now proceeds (23) to the more theological part of his

[1] Goodenough, *ibid.* p. 82, following Heinisch, *Der Einfluss Philos auf die älteste christliche Exegese Barnabas, Justin und Clemens von Alexandria* (Münster, 1908), is I think too sceptical on this point.

work and seeks to show (a) that the teaching of Christ and the prophets is alone true and is older than all other writers; (b) that Jesus Christ is alone begotten as a Son of God, being his logos and first-born and power, and appeared on earth as teacher for the conversion and restoration of the human race; (c) that before Christ came some, influenced by the daemons, related through the poets mythological tales intended as a travesty of the future revelation. After showing (24–9) the irrationality of allowing impostors such as Simon Magus and Menander and heretics like Marcion to go unmolested, Justin passes to the main burden of his argument (30–53). This consists in elaborate proofs of the fulfilment of prophecy. The main facts of Christ's life and work and the mission of the Apostles to the world had been predicted in great detail centuries in advance. Justin here shows his liking for ingenious interpretations of the Old Testament which must strike the modern reader as pre-carious in the extreme. He also explains the different kinds of prophecy and defends it against the charge of fatalism. In a remarkable passage (46) Justin replies to the objection that since Christ came so late in time those who lived before his coming were irresponsible. Quite the opposite—the divine logos had been in the world since the beginning and those who lived according to reason, whatever their race, were really Christians though they have been thought atheists; so among the Greeks Socrates and Heraclitus and among the barbarians Abraham, Ananias, Azarias, Misael and Elias and many others. On the other hand those who lived irrationally were the enemies of Christ and wicked. From all these 'fulfilled' pre-dictions the Christian belief in Christ as the first-born of God and the universal judge of mankind is totally justified.

Justin next passes (54–8) to a demonstration that mythology was used by daemons to imitate Christ although they had failed to understand the predictions of the Cross which were also clearly evident in nature and human life. He then tries to show (59–60) that Plato was directly dependent on Moses for his account of the origin of the world and of the second and third powers in the universe. In the concluding part of his work (61–7) Justin gives an account of the Christian sacraments of baptism and the Eucharist which is of great value to students of the early liturgy. Those who are to be baptised are 'brought to the place where there is water' where they are regenerated and illuminated. Baptism is in the Name of the Trinity. In the Eucharist, after a reading from the Memoirs of the Apostles or the prophets, intercession is made for the Church and those in the world. The President or Ruler prays extemporarily over the elements, and the deacons distribute the eucharistic gifts to those present and then take them to the absent.

With a final appeal for liberty of opinion Justin concludes his *First Apology* by appending Hadrian's letter to Minucius Fundanus,[1] the pro-Consul of Asia, in which the Emperor directed that Christians should only be punished after a legal trial.

Attempts have been made[2] to find in this *Apology* an elaborate literary plan. However, it seems unlikely that Justin based his work on the Classical oration or on any other ancient literary artifice. Justin, as a philosopher and teacher, knew how to appeal to a non-Christian public and he knew what he wanted to say. But his *Apology* is his own and cannot be fitted into any predetermined plan—hence the digressions and repetitions. This is however not to deny that some of his proofs from prophecy may have been committed to writing before his time.[3] The production of testimonies based on the LXX steadily grew in bulk after the apostolic age, and transcripts of some of them probably existed although many continued to circulate orally. It was not until the monumental compilation of Cyprian or Pseudo-Cyprian that the bulk of the testimonies was committed to writing.

Justin's *Second Apology* is much shorter than the first and was apparently called into existence by his indignation at an outrage which had recently occurred—which was typical of the indignities to which Christians were subjected. A dissolute man, angry with his Christian wife for having rebuked his vices, had charged her teacher Ptolemaeus with being a Christian (2). As a result the prefect Urbicus had sentenced Ptolemaeus and two others to death simply because they were Christians. Justin then divulges (3) that he himself expects to fall a victim to the malice of Crescens, 'that lover of bravado and boasting', whom

---

[1] See Appendix 2.
[2] E. R. Goodenough, *Theology of Justin Martyr*, p. 84.
[3] See pp. 67–74.

he had publicly shown to be an ignorant demagogue. He then
goes on to discuss two popular objections to Christians: (*a*) Why
did they not kill themselves if they were so willing to face
martyrdom? Justin replies (4) that God's creation is good and
to kill themselves would prevent the spread of the divine
doctrines: (*b*) Why did their God not protect them? Justin
replies (5) by declaring that God placed the world in charge of
angels, but some of these fell and to them and their offspring
are due the evils which good men suffer. In contrast to the
daemons is the one ineffable God and his begotten logos who
became man to deliver men from the daemons (6). God in fact
spares the world for the sake of the Christians (7). In all ages
those who followed Reason have been persecuted by the
daemons (8), but the time of judgement will come (9). Christianity is superior to all other teaching because it reveals the whole
logos of God (10). Another reason why God allows men to
suffer is because of the blessedness won through discipline and
probation (11). They are as athletes who prove their virtue by
risking death. The way in which Christians regard death (12)
is a crowning proof of the truth of their religion and the falsity
of the slanders reported about them. Christianity is not hostile
to Plato (13) but the completion of what Plato and the other
philosophers taught. Each man spoke well in proportion to his
share of the Spermatic Logos or the Word disseminated among
men. Justin concludes (14) with a prayer that his book may
be authorised and remarks (15) that his writings were at least
not as injurious to public morals as some others which were
authorised.

It seems likely that the *Second Apology* was designed as a
supplement to the first although it was called into existence by
a specific injustice. This accounts for its more passionate
character and its conviction that resistance to popular hatred
without flinching is the hall-mark of the Christian. Goodenough
regards the work as a fragment of a larger work[1] and believes
that the references in it to the *First Apology* may well have their
source in the lost part of the *Second Apology*. This *Apology*,
however, does not read as a series of disconnected *membra
disjecta* but deals with specific problems, and it is surely more
plausible to take Justin at his word—that is, when he refers

[1] *Theology of Justin Martyr*, pp. 84–7.

in this work to something he has said before which is not found in it he is referring to the *First Apology*.

When were the two *Apologies* written? The first presents no problems. It is addressed to the 'Emperor Titus Aelius Adrianus Antoninus Pius, Augustus, Caesar; and to his son Verissimus the philosopher, and to Lucius the philosopher, the natural son of Caesar, and the adopted son of Pius...' This is certainly a reference to Antoninus Pius as sole Emperor with his two adopted sons, Marcus Aurelius and Lucius Verus. Antoninus reigned from A.D. 137 to 161 while Lucius was born in A.D. 130. Allowing time for the latter to earn the description of philosopher, lover of culture, we cannot place the *First Apology* earlier than *c.* A.D. 145. With this agrees the description in the *Apology* of Marcionism as the greatest type of heresy 'with a following spread over every race of men'.[1] Marcion came to Rome and taught in the reign of Hyginus, that is A.D. 139–42, and we have to allow time for his rise to pre-eminence over the other heretics. In addition we have Justin's statement[2] that he is writing 150 years after Christ's birth and his reference to a petition recently presented to Felix, the governor of Alexandria.[3] According to Sir Frederick Kenyon a Greek papyrus in the British Museum shows that this Felix was the successor of Honoratus who began his reign of office in A.D. 148 and Felix himself was succeeded by Sempronius Liberalis in A.D. 154. Felix probably held office from *c.* A.D. 150 to 154.[4] According to another papyrus, Felix's date of accession was definitely A.D. 151.[5] If these dates are correct Justin probably wrote the *First Apology* a little after A.D. 151 and certainly before A.D. 155, which would agree with the other internal evidence of the work.

The *Second Apology* is more difficult to date but cannot be long after the first. It has references to Antoninus as sole Emperor and to the Emperor and Marcus Aurelius who is saluted as the philosopher, the son of Caesar (*II Apol.* ii). Continued reference is made to the piety of these two person-

---

[1] *I Apol.* xxvi.   [2] *I Apol.* xlvi.   [3] *I Apol.* xxix.
[4] Kenyon, 'The Date of the Apology of Justin Martyr', *The Academy*, XLIX (1896), 98.
[5] Grenfell and Hunt, *The Oxyrhynchus Papyri II*, pp. 162 f. Goodenough, *Theology of Justin Martyr*, p. 81.

ages. With this cohere the references in the *Second Apology* to the first as a writing freshly remembered.

Eusebius affirms that Justin wrote two *Apologies* or defences of the faith—the one under Antoninus and the other in the time of Antoninus Verus, i.e. Marcus Aurelius: 'There is a discourse of his, addressed to Antoninus, surnamed the Pius, and his sons and the Roman senate, in defence of our doctrines. Another work, comprising a defence of our faith, which he addressed to the Emperor of the same name, Antoninus Verus, the successor of the preceding, the circumstances of whose times we are now recording.'[1] It is however doubtful whether this second defence is the same as our extant *Second Apology*. Quite apart from the difficulty of reconciling Eusebius' statement that it was addressed to Marcus Aurelius with the internal references in our *Second Apology* to Antoninus, Eusebius quite clearly gives quotations from *both* our *Apologies*, yet describes them as taken from Justin's *First Apology*.[2] The most likely deduction to be drawn from these facts is that Eusebius knew our first and second *Apologies* as the *First Apology*. The second *Apology* to which he refers is lost unless, with Harnack, we identify it with the *Supplicatio* of Athenagoras.[3] In the early Christian centuries the fusing together of different treatises into a single work is a well-known phenomenon. Thus, within the New Testament, there are indications that I Corinthians is composite, an earlier and shorter letter (chs. 10–13) having been joined to a later and lengthier one (chs. 1–9). The Epistle to Diognetus is widely regarded as two distinct documents (chs. 1–10 and 11–12) which have been joined together, just as in most extant manuscripts the latter part of the Epistle of Barnabas is attached to the former part of the Epistle of Polycarp, so as to form in appearance one work. If Dr Harrison is right,[4] as I think he is, Polycarp's Epistle to the Philippians is

---

[1] *H.E.* iv. 18.

[2] *H.E.* iv. 16, 17; cf. *H.E.* iv. 8. Note especially iv. 17. 1, ὁ δ' αὐτὸς ἀνὴρ πρὸ τοῦ κατ' αὐτὸν ἀγῶνος, ἑτέρων πρὸ αὐτοῦ μαρτυρησάντων ἐν τῇ προτέρᾳ αὐτοῦ μνημονεύει Ἀπολογίᾳ, χρησίμως τῇ ὑποθέσει καὶ ταῦτα ἱστορῶν. γράφει δὲ ὧδε · followed by a lengthy quotation from *II Apol.* ii.

[3] *T. & U.* I, 1, pp. 172 f.

[4] *Polycarp's Two Epistles to the Philippians* (Cambridge, 1936). I doubt however whether Harrison is right in dating the second letter as late as A.D. 135. See the writer's article in *C.Q.R.* CLXIII (1962), 421–30.

likewise composite, chs. 13–14 being an earlier covering letter to a collection of the Ignatian Epistles and chs. 1–12 being a later letter called into existence by a definite historical situation. Tertullian's *De Praescriptione Haereticorum* is widely recognised as consisting of an original document (chs. 1–44 and the first two sentences of ch. 45) to which has been added another work. It should therefore cause no surprise that in Eusebius' time the *First* and *Second Apologies* of Justin were fused together in the manuscript which he quoted so as to form a single work.[1] This would have been all the easier as our extant *Second Apology* contains no obvious internal dedication.

(2) THE DIALOGUE WITH TRYPHO

The *Dialogue* with Trypho, the longest of Justin's works, comes from a different background from the *Apologies*. This book, which is addressed to a certain Marcus Pompeius,[2] of whom nothing is known, is the record of a debate which Justin had with a Jew named Trypho and certain of his friends. In philosopher's cloak Justin is walking one day by the Xystus, or the cloisters of the Colonnade, in a city which Eusebius identifies as Ephesus.[3] Trypho salutes him and asks for his opinions. Justin then relates the story of his conversion which we have already discussed.[4] Christianity is for him the true philosophy and Jesus the Messiah whom the prophets have foretold. Trypho however stands his ground and urges observance of the *torah* as the true way to serve God. This leads to a long and elaborate discussion, apparently lasting two days, which is conducted for the main part in a friendly and docile spirit. In spite of the progress of the argument being interrupted with tedious repetitions and explanations of Old Testament texts three parts can be discerned in it:

The first part (chs. 11–31) deals with the Mosaic law which Trypho represents as universally binding. Justin ought to have remained a disciple of Plato and obeyed the ritual law. Justin replies that the Old Testament requires men to keep the eternal, moral decrees rather than the ceremonial laws which were only

---

[1] It should be noted that in the MS Paris 450 the *Second Apology* comes before the first.

[2] *Dial.* viii. 3, cxli. 5.   [3] *H.E.* iv. 18.   [4] Pp. 6–11.

given to the Jews because of their persistent disposition to sin. Righteousness depends on moral integrity, repentance and obedience. Christians have learnt the true righteousness from Christ who has power to deliver them from evil.

The second part (chs. 32–110) deals with the nature and significance of Jesus Christ who, Justin declares, is the fulfilment of the Old Testament prophetic witness. Justin considers the Incarnation, the existence of a second God, the Virgin Birth, the Divine and Human element in Christ's Nature, the necessity of the Crucifixion and the Resurrection. This section is wholly based on an exegesis of Old Testament texts carried out at great length and with many digressions and wanderings.

The third part (chs. 111–42) deals with the conversion of the Gentiles—God will receive, as the prophets declared, all of any race who seek him. The *Dialogue* closes with an eloquent appeal to Trypho and his friends to accept the truth: 'I urge you to enter on this greatest of all contests for your own salvation, and to endeavour to prefer to your own teachers the Christ of Almighty God.'[1]

The authorship of the *Dialogue* is not now held in question. It bears the marks of Justin's style, as known from the *Apologies*, quotes from the *First Apology*[2] and is attributed to Justin by Eusebius.[3] The arguments of E. Preuschen[4] that the author of the *Dialogue* is an unknown writer who used the writings of Tertullian and Irenaeus depends on the *a priori* assumption that, in quoting the LXX, Patristic writers were dependent on each other. Recent studies have shown[5] that a method of collecting Old Testament texts in blocks of testimony material had begun in New Testament times, and in the early Patristic period these testimonies grew in bulk and partial transcripts also came into existence. It is not to be supposed that because two writers use the same testimonies or subject-matter they are necessarily dependent on one another. Both may have used testimony material independently.

---

[1] cxlii. 2 (A. L. Williams' translation).

[2] cxx. 5. [3] *H.E.* iv. 18.

[4] 'Die Echtheit von Justins Dial. gegen Trypho', *Z.N.T.W.* (1919–20), pp. 102–26.

[5] See especially C. H. Dodd, *According to the Scriptures* (London, 1952).

There is evidence that the *Dialogue*, which is very long, was originally divided into two treatises which marked the end of the first day's discussion and the beginning of the second. John the Damascene[1] quotes ch. 82 in his *Sacra Parallela* as having been taken from the second book. It is probable, as there is no mention of the first day coming to an end, or of the meeting on the next, that some material has dropped out of the *Dialogue*. A. L. Williams has exhaustively investigated this and quotes passages to show that several pages of the *Dialogue* are missing.[2]

The date of the *Dialogue* cannot be determined with accuracy. It is certainly later than the *First Apology*, which we have dated *c.* A.D. 151–5,[3] which it quotes. Many scholars[4] are of the opinion that a date *c.* A.D. 160 best fits the background of the *Dialogue*.

Did this debate with Trypho really occur? The details of the meeting of Justin and Trypho in which Trypho says he is a refugee who has lately escaped from the Jewish War of A.D. 132–135,[5] and the emotions which move both sides, are vividly described. We gain a clear impression of the character and outlook of Trypho and his friends—which is essentially liberal and tolerant—in contrast to the fierce hatred of the Palestinian Jews against Christians which the war had inflamed. These personal references seem to rule out the view that the historical setting of the *Dialogue* is fictitious and that Trypho is a 'straw man' who is merely a tool in Justin's hands.[6] On the other hand it is unlikely that Justin remembered, nearly thirty years later, all that was said in the debate. But probably some repetitions did occur in view of the addition of further friends of Trypho on the second day. Discussions such as these must have been frequently held, as Christians sought to commend their faith openly, although not all may have been so amiable as this one. The best solution to the literary problem of the *Dialogue* is to postulate an original, historical debate with Trypho which

---

[1] K. Holl, *T. & U.* xx, ii (1899), p. 34.

[2] *The Dialogue with Trypho* (London, 1930), pp. xvii–xix. Note especially the references in *Dial.* lvi. 16, lxxviii. 6, lxxxv. 4, xcii. 5, cxviii. 4, cxxii. 4, cxxxvii. 4.   [3] P. 19.

[4] F. L. Cross, *The Early Christian Fathers* (London, 1960), p. 51.

[5] *Dial.* i. 3. In xvi. 2 the great misery which has afflicted Palestine is mentioned; in cviii. 3 Jerusalem is already taken.

[6] This is the view of Goodenough, *Theology of Justin Martyr*, pp. 90–3.

occurred soon after A.D. 132, which Justin subsequently elaborated *c.* A.D. 160, drawing on oral and written testimony material which was known and used in the Church of his day. Nevertheless to describe the *Dialogue* as 'a collection of all possible arguments rather than a report of a discussion in which each argument was actually brought up as recorded'[1] seems unduly sceptical.

Who was Trypho? Attempts have been made to identify him with Rabbi Tarphon who belonged to the second generation of Mishna teachers (*c.* A.D. 90–130). This identification has nothing to commend it apart from the fact that Trypho may be a Greek form of Tarphon. R. Tarphon was a violent anti-Christian rabbi whose disposition, as revealed by his sayings, is entirely out of keeping with that of Trypho who is a courteous and friendly opponent. Moreover the Trypho of the *Dialogue* is not a rabbi strictly trained in rabbinical methods of interpretation but a 'layman' in Jewish lore.[2] He is a hellenistic Jew with a philosophic training possessed of an open and tolerant mind which cannot be confined to mere *torah* learning—indeed he understands no Hebrew. He is eager to learn, has read the Christian Gospels—a thing forbidden to Palestinian Jews after *c.* A.D. 100—and, if convinced, is prepared to become a Christian. Trypho even sees no insuperable objections to belief in an intermediary Deity. On the other hand, although no rabbi, Trypho reproduces accurately, in his casual comments, some of the traditional sayings of the Jewish rabbis. He allows hope of salvation to morally upright heathen—which was a belief of the Tannaim.[3] He repudiates the divine character of the expected Messiah.[4] He says that there must have been both God and an angel in the flaming bush.[5] In accordance with

---

[1] Goodenough, *op. cit.* p. 90. The *Dialogue* was probably intended for Gentile Christian readers.

[2] A. L. Williams, *The Dialogue with Trypho*, p. xxv. Note that Trypho includes himself among those whom the rabbis have warned against entering into discussions with Christians; *Dial.* xxxviii. 1. B. Altaner, *Patrology* (Edinburgh–London, 1960), p. 122, accepts the identification with Tarphon.

[3] R. Joshua ben Chanonja on Ps. ix. 18.

[4] See J. Klausner, *The Messianic Idea in Israel* (London, 1956), p. 459: 'A noble King, a man of the highest moral quality, a political and spiritual leader of the Jewish people in particular and of the human race in general —this, and only this, was the Messiah of the Tannaim.'   [5] Ex. Rabba 32.

rabbinic tradition he ascribes Isa. vii. 14 to Hezekiah.[1] Good-enough says Justin 'has created in Trypho a Jew who embodies the best of both schools of Judaism, one who knows Scripture and the Rabbinic interpretations...and yet who has all the open-mindedness and cosmic sense of the Hellenistic Jews...It is useless in such a case to scatter energy in an attempt to class Trypho as either Palestinian or Hellenistic.'[2]

Recent discoveries have thrown new light on the relationship between Hellenistic and Rabbinic Judaism and this has a bearing on our immediate concern. The rigid dichotomy between the two branches of Judaism which used to be postulated is now doubted by many scholars. It was common text-book theory that Judaism, following on its reconstruction at Jamnia after the catastrophe of A.D. 70, became almost wholly Rabbinic and that Hellenistic Judaism, as known before A.D. 70 in the writings of Philo, virtually ceased to exist. The discovery of the Dead Sea Scrolls has caused a revision of this neat theory. They have shown that Hellenistic terminology and ideas were invading Palestinian soil *before* the beginning of the Christian era and that there was a far greater variety within Judaism than was previously thought.[3] In fact we should be wary of talking of a 'normative', i.e. Pharisaic, Judaism which was finally codified in the Mishna.[4] These new discoveries, to which we should add the Gnostic documents found at Nag Hammadi, throw new light on the background from which cosmopolitan Jews such as Trypho emerged. Trypho is no longer a 'curious'[5] or an 'ideal' type of Jew but one who was not unrepresentative of one facet of Judaism. Combining the culture and inquiring spirit of the Hellenistic world with a knowledge of Scripture and Haggadic interpretation he represents, not the strict Judaism of the Pharisees, nor the Judaism of the extreme hellenisers, but a mediating Judaism, perhaps native to Palestine, which has as much right to be considered 'normative' as the rest.

---

[1] *Dial.* lxvii. 1; cf. Ex. Rabba 18.

[2] *Theology of Justin Martyr*, p. 95.

[3] See W. D. Davies, *Christian Origins and Judaism* (London, 1962), pp. 108, 144.

[4] The Classic position of G. F. Moore, *Judaism in the First Three Centuries of the Christian Era* (1927–30).

[5] *D.C.B.* III, 570.

The two *Apologies* and the *Dialogue* with Trypho are the only extant works of Justin which have come down to us. They are not systematic theological treatises, for Justin is a pioneer venturing along unexamined roads rather than a wielder of the tools of disciplined precision. Justin had studied widely in pagan literature and philosophy. But he is no literary artist such as was the unknown author of the Epistle to Diognetus. Indeed he expressly denies any claim in this direction: 'I am not anxious to present a merely artistic arrangement of arguments. For I have no ability to do this.'[1] Nevertheless, Justin's writings, especially the *First Apology*, are full of vigorous thoughts expressed in the diction of common life. His tone and character are attractive by their genuineness, simplicity, high-mindedness and frank and confident energy.[2]

In his three works Justin covers a large part of the theological field. Christianity is for him the highest truth, the crown of both Greek philosophy and the Jewish scriptures. Like Bishop Butler in the *Analogy of Religion* Justin's concern is to find likenesses and agreements with, rather than differences from, his opponents although he faces questions, not asked before his day, with courage and sincerity. His writings repay careful study, for in them we are in touch with a profoundly Christian mind before the classical theological definitions had been formulated. The Apostolic Fathers had dealt with the practical day-to-day problems of the Church; speculative thought and Christian philosophy begin with Justin.

[1] *Dial.* lviii. 1.
[2] This is well brought out in *D.C.B.* iii, 566.

CHAPTER III

BACKGROUND: GREEK PHILOSOPHY

Justin Martyr made no clear distinction between theology and philosophy in the strict sense. There was, for him, but one wisdom, one philosophy, which had been revealed fully in and through Jesus Christ. This involved however no clear break with Greek philosophy, the best elements in which were a preparation for the Gospel. In so far as philosophers had divined the truth they had done so in the power of the logos and Jesus Christ was himself the logos incarnate. This sympathetic view of the function of philosophy is in marked contrast with that of the New Testament, which only once uses the word φιλοσοφία[1] and then as a probable cause of peril to Christians. It is true that St Paul shows affinities with Stoic thought in his speech at Athens, yet even then he speaks of previous ages as 'times of ignorance'[2] and shows no real understanding of, or sympathy with, the prevailing popular philosophies. In the earliest age of the Church the Old Testament, rather than pagan thought, was the sole *praeparatio evangelica*.

It was however not long before Christians felt the need of a philosophy of their own as the new religion spread throughout the Graeco-Roman world. We have already noted[3] the influence of apologetic on the growth of a Christian philosophy as the Church sought to refute attacks and false accusations. It was natural to base such an *apologia* on the magnificent defence of Socrates at his trial. Yet the Apologists also felt a desire to form a comprehensive view of the world and human life in the light of their faith and it was natural that they should turn to the prevailing philosophy. In order then to understand the thought of Justin Martyr we must first give some account of his philosophic background.

Plato and Aristotle had both been men of the Greek city-state and their philosophies were thought out against that background.

[1] Col. ii. 8.
[2] Acts xvii. 30.
[3] Pp. 2–3.

27

From the time however of the Macedonian Alexander the Great new forces were at work which merged the city-state into a larger whole; men now thought in terms of cosmopolitanism —of the world state. Yet once the individual was cast adrift from his position in the city-state, with its duties and responsibilities, he needed guidance and help if he was successfully to meet the demands of a wider cosmopolitan world. Philosophy therefore came, in the Graeco-Roman period, to display an ethical and practical trend as in Stoicism and Epicureanism. Metaphysical speculation waned and philosophers were content to borrow from the past rather than attempt independent speculations of their own. Thus the Stoics had recourse to the physics of Heraclitus and the ethics of the Cynics while the Epicureans returned to the Atomism of Democritus and the ethics of the Cyrenaics.

This ethical and practical trend was particularly marked in the Roman period when the phenomenon of the philosopher-director, who provided the individual with a code of conduct, came to the fore. This concentration on the practical led to a wide diffusion of philosophy among the cultured classes of the Graeco-Roman world and so to a kind of popular philosophy which was part of the regular course of education.

Father Copleston, in his celebrated *History of Philosophy*, distinguishes these phases in the development of Graeco-Roman philosophy:[1]

(*a*) The first period, from the end of the fourth century B.C. to the mid-first century B.C., which saw the founding of the Stoic and Epicurean philosophies. These systems emphasised conduct and the attainment of personal happiness while using pre-Socratic thought for their cosmologies. A certain eclecticism is also visible in this period which is shown in a tendency of the Middle Stoa, the Peripatetic school and the Academy to eclectic assimilation of each other's doctrines.

(*b*) A second period from the first century B.C. to the mid-third century A.D. when eclecticism and scepticism continue to be a force. A return to philosophic 'orthodoxy' is however a characteristic of this phase and a great interest is taken in the founders of the schools, their lives, works and doctrines. This eclecticism and orthodoxy are to some extent in conflict—as in

[1] I, 382-3.

Middle Platonism—which accordingly gives the impression of being an amalgam and a philosophic transition stage.

(c) The third period, from the mid-third century A.D. to the mid-sixth century A.D., is that of Neoplatonism. This final speculative effort of ancient philosophy sought to combine all the valuable elements in the philosophic and religious doctrines of east and west in one comprehensive whole and, in fact, dominated philosophic development for several centuries. Plotinus is the most outstanding figure of this period. He has been described as the greatest thinker between Aristotle and Descartes.[1]

The second period is our immediate concern in this book and, in view of the influence of Plato on Justin Martyr, to be mentioned shortly, it is necessary to indicate the particular aspects of Middle Platonism with which he was acquainted.

Eclecticism was one of the leading characteristics of Middle Platonism. Platonists, in Justin's day, did not possess the lectures of Plato but only the more popular dialogues, which do not suggest that Plato had left any systematised doctrine as a norm which had to be handed on. Indeed the Middle Platonists took over the Peripatetic logic on the grounds that this was more carefully elaborated than anything they found in the *Dialogues*. An insistence on the Divine Transcendence was taken over from Neopythagoreanism together with its theory of intermediate beings. Yet in spite of this eclecticism, and to some extent in opposition to it, the Middle Platonists emphasised the person and *dicta* of Plato as a result of their profound commentaries on the Platonic *Dialogues*. Thus there arose a tendency to stress *the differences* between Platonism and other philosophic systems, and works directed against the Peripatetics and Stoicism were written. Middle Platonism is accordingly not a unified system but an amalgam of different tendencies with the 'orthodox' Platonic element uppermost.[2]

This eclecticism is to be found in the three most distinguished exponents of Middle Platonism—Eudorus of Alexandria (c. 25

---

[1] Whittaker, *Neoplatonism*, p. 33. Neoplatonism did not simply replace Middle Platonism. Plotinus frequently discussed Middle Platonist interpretations of Plato.

[2] Cf. the judgement of Porphyry on the Enneads: ἐμμέμικται καὶ τὰ Στωικὰ λανθάνοντα δόγματα καὶ τὰ περιπατητικά (*Vit. Plot.* 14).

B.C.), Plutarch (b. A.D. 45) and Albinus, who taught in the second century A.D. We shall confine ourselves to the philosophy of Albinus which is more relevant to that of Justin Martyr and is a good representation of the Platonism of his time.

All that is known of the life of Albinus is soon told. Galen, having attended the lectures of 'a pupil of Gaius' at Pergamum,[1] went on to Smyrna in order to hear 'the Platonist Albinus'. This took place in the year A.D. 151/2 and is our sole historical reference to the philosopher's activity. Albinus was clearly a Platonist of some importance with a school at Smyrna; two treatises of his have been preserved: ΑΛΒΙΝΟΥ εἰσαγωγὴ εἰς τοὺς Πλάτωνος διαλόγους and ΑΛΚΙΝΟΟΥ[2] διδασκαλικὸς τῶν Πλάτωνος δογμάτων. His importance lies in the fact that his works—particularly the *Didaskalikos*—give a complete picture of the Platonic philosophy as it appeared to a writer separated from Plato by a period of some five hundred years.

Albinus held that God (whom he calls ὁ πρῶτος Νοῦς) is unmoved and he equates this first Νοῦς with the Demiurge;[3] he operates through a lower νοῦς or world-soul which, although not produced by God,[4] is yet moved by him. This idea of God as the unmoved mover is Aristotelian although elements of Albinus' system are derived from Plato.

It is difficult to discover how the Middle Platonists came to adopt the Aristotelian idea of God. By the beginning of the second century it was prominent in their teaching although it found no favour with the anti-Aristotelian group in the Academy itself. Most probably it was introduced into Platonism just before or soon after the turn of the Christian era. It seems likely that the first Platonist to use the Aristotelian theology was Eudorus of Alexandria who wrote a *Commentary* on the Meta-

[1] v. 41 κ. This was in A.D. 144.
[2] R. E. Witt, *Albinus and the History of Middle Platonism* (Cambridge, 1937), pp. 104–13, has shown conclusively that 'Αλκίνοος is a corruption for 'Αλβῖνος. Some older MSS give the title 'Επιτομὴ τῶν Πλάτωνος δογμάτων. See C. J. de Vogel, *Greek Philosophy*, III (Leiden, 1959), 400.   [3] Albinus XII. I.
[4] οὐχὶ ποιεῖ ὁ θεὸς ἀλλὰ κατακοσμεῖ. Albinus is not the only philosopher of his time to distinguish between a higher unmoved νοῦς and a lower which moves in response to it. Cf. Plotinus III, IX. I; Numenius *P.E.* 539 B. Albinus' hierarchy of being is as follows: (1) ὁ (πρῶτος) Νοῦς ἀκίνητος. (2) ὁ Νοῦς τοῦ σύμπαντος οὐρανοῦ (ἀεὶ ἐνεργῶν). (3) ὁ ἐν δυνάμει νοῦς. Next follow the stars (visible gods) and finally the earth with its elements, each governed by its daemons.

physics and emphasised the Transcendence of the Supreme God or τὸ ἕν.[1] From then on Aristotle's theology was generally favoured by Platonists and became part of the tradition of the school. It is this tradition which Albinus, and as we shall see Justin Martyr, reflect.

Albinus' system, if such we may call it, in addition to its Aristotelian elements, also makes use of Plato's idea of a gradual elevation to God through various degrees of beauty.[2] In his psychology and ethics Albinus reads Stoic elements into Plato: thus he identifies the Stoic ἡγεμονικόν with the Platonic λογιστικόν[3] and transfers the φυσικὴ ἔννοια of the Porch to Plato's theory of innate ideas.[4]

Albinus is a more mystical thinker than Plato although his mysticism does not approach that of Plotinus. He believes that the human body is still of value and to be trained by exercise—although not so systematically as Plato had advocated. Philosophy is for him 'the aspiration for wisdom, or the loosing and wrenching of the soul away from the body, when we turn ourselves to the Intelligible and the true Existences'.[5] This is a pure type of mysticism and other-worldly teaching and in this Albinus is at one with second-century Platonism.

Albinus is thus a typical eclectic Middle Platonist who could fuse together teaching from different sources. His philosophical theology represents a transition stage between Platonism proper and the Neoplatonism of Plotinus, that last great philosophic effort of the ancient world. As Professor E. R. Dodds has written: 'In his attempt to connect divergent views he foreshadows Plotinus: his complete failure to make anything coherent of them is one measure of Plotinus's greatness.'[6] Albinus was a product of his age and should not be blamed for his failure to distinguish the original teaching of Plato from later corruptions. Yet he is important as a precursor of Plotinus whose monumental edifice presupposed the constructive philosophical and theological thinking of the previous two centuries.

[1] Witt, *Albinus and the History of Middle Platonism*, p. 126.
[2] Such is suggested in the *Symposium*.
[3] Copleston, *History of Philosophy*, I, 455.
[4] Witt, *op. cit.*, p. 11.
[5] I, 152 l. 2, quoted by Goodenough, *Theology of Justin Martyr*, p. 31.
[6] *C.Q.* XXII, 139.

We now turn to the writings of Justin Martyr to see in what way he reflects the characteristics of the popular philosophy of his period—and, if so, how far this affected his presentation of the truth as he had found it in Jesus Christ.

In a previous chapter[1] we have described Justin's early search for truth. He is typical of the eclectic spirit of the age in going from school to school in search of the truth. He undergoes Stoic instruction, then turns to a Peripatetic, later to a Pythagorean and finally to the Platonists 'whose fame was great'. Again Justin's reverence for the person and *dicta* of the founders of the philosophic schools is characteristic of his age. Thus he describes his view of philosophy:

I will tell you [said I] what seems to me; for philosophy is, in fact, the greatest possession, and most honourable before God, to whom it leads us and alone commends us; and these are truly holy men who have bestowed attention on philosophy. What philosophy is, however, and the reason why it has been sent down to men, have escaped the observation of most; for there would be neither Platonists, nor Stoics, nor Peripatetics, nor Sceptics,[2] nor Pythagoreans, this knowledge being one. I wish to tell you why it has become many-headed. It has happened that those who first handled it, and who were therefore esteemed illustrious men, were succeeded by those who made no investigations concerning truth, but only admired the perseverance and self-discipline of the former as well as the novelty of the doctrines; and each thought that to be true which he learned from his teacher: then, moreover, those latter persons handed down to their successors such things, and others similar to them; and this system was called by the name of him who was styled the father of the doctrine (ὁ πατὴρ τοῦ λόγου).[3]

Justin's eclecticism led him to pass judgements on the various philosophic schools with which he had contact. He speaks with contempt of the Cynics: 'it is impossible for a Cynic, who makes indifference his end, to know any good but indifference'.[4] The Epicureans[5] fare no better—indeed Justin implies that philosophers of these schools are not worth seeking. His Peripatetic teacher, he tells us,[6] was more concerned with his fee than with the communication of knowledge. Justin speaks with respect

[1] Pp. 7–11.   [2] θεωρητικοί.
[3] *Dial.* ii.   [4] *II Apol.* iii.
[5] *II Apol.* vii, xii, xv.   [6] *Dial.* ii.

of the Pythagoreans,[1] but objects to the long course of intellectual discipline which they require before their scholars could behold the beautiful and the good.

Justin's view of Stoicism was more favourable in spite of his unhappy experience with a Stoic teacher. He admired the Stoic ethics and appeals to Heraclitus and to Musonius Rufus, who was banished by Nero, as examples of those who were hated and put to death because the logos dwelt in them.[2] Justin points out the correspondence between the Stoic and Christian view of the future destruction of the world by fire, although he carefully distinguishes the Stoic doctrine as a natural and necessary process (including God himself) from the Christian belief in a divine act of judgement.[3] Although he admires aspects of Stoicism Justin nevertheless objects strongly to Stoic materialism and especially to their doctrine of fate, which he believes is destructive of spiritual ideas, blurring the distinction between virtue and vice.[4] It also seems unlikely that Justin took his idea of the *Logos Spermatikos* from the Stoa.

Justin's esteem for Plato and Platonism is evident from his works, although in becoming a Christian he had passed beyond Platonism. Plato, Justin says, like the Christians taught a future judgement and derived his doctrines of creation, of human responsibility and of the Second and Third Powers in the universe from Moses. Justin sees no inconsistency in holding the Platonic doctrine that God made the world from formless matter[5] as he believes this to be the teaching of Moses in Gen. i. 2.[6] He also quotes from the *Timaeus* the statement that the World-soul was placed like a χ (Chi) in the universe, and declares that Plato referred to the Second Power and took the idea from the biblical account of the brazen serpent.[7] Plato's world-soul was, for Justin, an attempt to teach the doctrine of a personal logos. It is clear that he is here reading Christian ideas into Plato. Justin certainly prized the Platonic doctrine of the

[1] *Ibid.*

[2] *II Apol.* viii. There is, however, no evidence that these philosophers were martyred. This appears to be an error on Justin's part.

[3] *I Apol.* xx; *II Apol.* vii.

[4] *II Apol.* vii.

[5] We have discussed this fully in chapter IX.

[6] *I Apol.* lix; Justin seems to feel no necessity for the doctrine of creation *ex nihilo.*   [7] *I Apol.* lx.

immaterial world and of the being beyond essence, yet he is no uncritical advocate. Plato, he says, teaches the punishment of the wicked for only a limited period of time and in bodies other than their own, while Christians teach the *eternal* punishment of the wicked in the *same* bodies as they now possess. The introduction to the *Dialogue* shows that Justin now conceives that something more than intellectual discipline is needed if the individual is to apprehend God.[1] He no longer believes in the pre-existence of souls nor in their natural immortality.[2] The latter he denies on the principle that whatever is created is perishable. Hence Justin refers immortality solely to the will of God[3]—a view which Plato approaches in the *Timaeus* but which was not his main argument for immortality.

Justin's admiration for Socrates is everywhere evident in his works and he sees a close correspondence between the treatment of the philosopher and that accorded to Jesus Christ and his followers. When Socrates, in the power of reason (logos), or as its instrument, sought to bring men to the truth evil men put him to death as an atheist; so Christians who follow the incarnate logos are falsely termed atheists. In other words, just as the work of Socrates was a preparation for the Work of Christ so his condemnation was a condemnation of Christ and his followers.[4]

Where did Justin get his knowledge of Plato and Platonism? His works certainly show an acquaintance with the Master's works and especially with the *Timaeus*. Yet it seems likely that Justin would understand Platonic words and ideas in the light of his own philosophic training with the school Platonists. We shall seek to show that Justin reflects the eclecticism of Middle Platonism,[5] and especially that of Albinus,[6] while retaining that school's reverence for the person and *dicta* of Plato:

(*a*) Justin's transcendental conception of God, found in his extant works, is similar to that of Plato. Yet Justin also fre-

---

[1] *Dial.* iii.   [2] *Dial.* iv, v, cxli.
[3] *Dial.* vi.   [4] *I Apol.* v.

[5] I am much indebted to the important discussion of Andresen, *Z.N.T.W.* XLIV (1952–3), 167–8, although adding points of my own.

[6] Tertullian makes explicit reference to Albinus, *An.* 28–9. According to Geffcken the pale Platonism of the Christian Apologists 'gehört in vielen Fällen unmittelbar an die seite eines Albinus, Maximus, v.a.' (quoted in Witt, *Albinus and the History of Middle Platonism*, p. 144).

quently states that God is ineffable and unnameable.[1] To substantiate this idea Justin, in a remarkable passage (*II Apol.* x. 6), refers to a famous passage in *Timaeus* 28 c: 'That it is neither easy to find the Father and Demiurge of all, nor, having found him, is it safe to declare him to all.' Yet Plato only speaks of the Demiurge and not of the ineffability of God. How then could Justin use this passage? Andresen shows that the Middle Platonists interpreted the *Timaeus* passage in the same way as Justin; thus Apuleius,[2] no doubt because of the significance of the passage, first paraphrases it in Latin and then, possibly from memory, quotes it in Greek and even transmits the change in the meaning of the *Timaeus* text. Furthermore it can be shown that the actual wording of this passage was taken, not from the original text of Plato, but from a version of the text current among the Middle Platonists which Albinus knew.

Justin *II Apol.* x. 6	Albinus *Didask.* XXVII
τὸν δὲ πατέρα καὶ δημιουργὸν πάντων οὔθ' εὑρεῖν ῥᾴδιον οὔθ' εὑρόντα εἰς πάντας εἰπεῖν ἀσφαλές.	τὸ μὲν δὴ τιμιώτατον ἀγαθὸν οὔτε εὑρεῖν ῥᾴδιον οὔτε εὑρόντα ἀσφαλὲς εἰς πάντας ἐκφέρειν.

A further indication that Justin's philosophic background lies in an eclectic Middle Platonism is provided by his reproduction of the Aristotelian idea of God[3] as the Unmoved Mover which, as we have seen,[4] probably entered Platonism just before or soon after the beginning of the Christian era.

For the ineffable Father and Lord of all neither has come to any place, nor walks, nor sleeps, nor rises up, but remains in His own place, wherever that is, quick to behold and quick to hear, having neither eyes nor ears, but being of indescribable might; and He sees all things, and knows all things, and none of us escapes His observation; and He is not moved (οὔτε κινούμενος) or confined to a spot in the whole world, for He existed before the world was made.[5]

---

[1] *I Apol.* ix. 3, x. 1, lxi. 11; *II Apol.* vi. 1 f., xi. 4, xiii. 4; *Dial.* cxxvi. 2, cxxvii. 2–4.

[2] *De Plat.* I, 5.

[3] The Greek-Christian Apologists were not much interested in Aristotle although Athenagoras (*Resurr.* xxi–xxii) quotes the Aristotelian doctrine of the mean. In this they reflect the Platonic background of early Christian philosophy.

[4] Pp. 30–1.

[5] *Dial.* cxxvii.

This is very similar to Albinus' teaching on God (ὁ πρῶτος Νοῦς) which we have already noted.[1] Both Justin and Albinus combine Platonic and Aristotelian elements in their systems, which strongly suggests the eclecticism of Middle Platonism.

(b) This background of Justin is further illustrated by the conversation he had with an old Christian recorded in *Dial.* iii–vii. In *Dial.* v, when the question of the immortality of the soul is being considered, the problem as to whether the world is begotten or unbegotten is also discussed. Justin states that Plato in the *Timaeus* has hinted that the world is subject to decay inasmuch as it has been created. The fact that nevertheless the cosmos does not fall prey to dissolution is due to the divine will to preserve it. What Justin says in *Dial.* v corresponds exactly with *Timaeus* 41 A B. What is interesting is that Justin interprets the passage in a special way. The words which the Demiurge in the *Timaeus* addresses to the gods are taken out of their context and applied to the cosmological problem. Andresen points out that this interpretation is found among the Middle Platonists. So Atticus argues when he quotes the words of the Demiurge and justifies his view that one must understand the *Timaeus* passage literally in the sense that the world is begotten.[2] The thesis: 'Begotten, yes, but intransient', is known from Celsus,[3] Plutarch and Atticus.[4] It is also significant that although Justin belongs to that branch of school Platonism which held firmly to a belief in the created world and divine providence he also knows of contrary opinions held by some Platonists[5]—much as Atticus did.[6] Justin thus witnesses to the eclectic character of the Platonism of his day.

(c) A further confirmation of Justin's background is provided by his understanding of the purpose of philosophy. His conversion to Christianity, at the hands of the old Christian (*Dial.* viii), was the conclusion of his philosophical development, Christianity being recognised as the true philosophy. But Justin describes the act of knowing the Christian God in the same

---

[1] P. 30. Justin's use of the term Demiurge (Δημιουργός) for God is similar to Albinus' identification of the First Νοῦς with the Demiurge. *Didask.* XII. 1.

[2] Eus. *Praep. Ev.* xv. 6. 4 f.   [3] *Fr.* VI. 52 a.

[4] *De animae procreatione* (1012^A–1030^C); cf. Diog. Laert. III. 71 f.; Andresen, *Z.N.T.W.* XLIV (1952–3), p. 163 n. 23.   [5] *Dial.* v. 1.

[6] Eus. *Praep. Ev.* xv. 6. 3, 10.

words as he has used shortly before to describe the act of knowing philosophical truth.[1] Both passages are based on a famous
passage in Plato[2] which is also quoted by Celsus[3] in order to
describe the Platonic knowledge of God. In Andresen's opinion
both Justin and Celsus are using a common text of this passage
which was a favourite one of the Middle Platonists.[4] This pre-
dilection for Plato's seventh Epistle is connected with the
religious aims of the school philosophy—for it the experience of the highest good in the intelligible world of ideas was
central. Justin's interpretation of Plato is in line with Middle
Platonism when he designates the experience of the Ideas as the
telos of the Platonic philosophy.[5]

In the conversation with the old Christian the question is also
discussed[6] how one can know God according to Plato. The
conclusion is reached that God is not to be seen with the eyes
but is discernible to the mind alone. Albinus speaks in the same
way about the possibility of knowing God.[7] The foundation of
this, for both Justin and Albinus, is in *Phaedrus* 247 c, and
both apply the passage which deals with the knowledge of the
intelligible world of the True and the Good to the knowledge of
God. Celsus uses *Phaedrus* 247 c in a similar way.[8] It is therefore
no independent idea of Justin when he understands Plato's
ontological sentences as being theological. This is rather an
interpretation well known in Middle Platonism.

Our conclusion from the above discussion is that Justin's
philosophical background is predominantly that of eclectic
Middle Platonism, although it is well to remember that this
was not a philosophical system, as such, but rather a philosophical transition stage. In many respects Justin is a better mirror
to the intellectual forces to which he was exposed than any
other Christian writer of the second century. He was not an
original genius who wished to construct a logical, unifying,
philosophic system of his own. But he was a genuine seeker after
the truth who brought into the Church the intellectual strivings

[1] *Dial.* iv. 1.
[2] *Ep.* VII. 341 CD. [3] *Fr.* VI. 3.
[4] Albinus, *Didask.* x; Maximus Tyre *Or.* 29. 5; Plut. *De Iside,* 77.
[5] See Atticus–Eus. *Praep. Ev.* xv. 13 f. [6] *Dial.* iii. 6 f.
[7] *Didask.* x; cf. Athenagoras *Suppl.* x. 1. [8] *Fr.* VI. 64.

of his age. And in his search Platonism, as understood by the contemporary Middle Platonist schools, was a predominating influence.

Yet to isolate Justin's philosophical background could do him a disservice and merely perpetuate his memory as a second-century eclectic. It was above all his acceptance of the Christian Faith which proved to be the goal of his philosophical journey. Now he knew that he had found the one 'true' philosophy.

Justin's reverence for philosophy, as finding its consummation in Christ, was of great importance for the Church, for it meant that educated pagan converts were no longer obliged to deny the insights of their philosophical backgrounds. Platonism was now seen to be as valid a preparation for the Gospel as Judaism had been. The Church, at least in its more sensitive minds, came to see that all apprehensions of truth in Greek philosophy and in the intellectual searchings of men were due to the power of the same logos who had become incarnate in Jesus Christ. Justin faithfully reflects the eclectic Platonism of his age. What is remarkable is his clear grasp of Christianity as the one, true philosophy.

CHAPTER IV

BACKGROUND: JUDAISM

<u>JUSTIN MARTYR was born in Samaria, but he was brought</u> up as a Gentile and had a Greek education. He tells us that he was uncircumcised[1] and had no knowledge of Judaism until he was an adult when he came to know Moses and the prophets. From this we may infer either that he left Palestine at an early age or that there were no contacts, on a theoretical level, with Judaism in Hellenistic-Samaritan cities.

What kind of Judaism did Justin know later in life? Our only source of information about this is the *Dialogue* with Trypho which Justin probably composed *c.* A.D. 160. We have already suggested[2] that this *Dialogue* has behind it an original historical debate between Justin and a Jew, Trypho, which occurred soon after A.D. 132—which Justin has subsequently elaborated from oral and written material known to him. <u>Any discussion of the Jewish background of the Christian Apologist must take its start from Trypho himself.</u>

Trypho was a Jew who had fled from the war in Palestine,[3] no doubt in company with many of his compatriots. He was apparently spending much time in Greece and Corinth[4] although, at the time of the debate with Justin, he was in Ephesus.[5] His culture was Gentile, for he states that he was taught in Argos by Corinthus of the School of Socrates.[6] Trypho distinguishes himself from 'our teachers'[7] and includes himself among those who have been warned against entering into discussions with Christians.[8] He was therefore a layman and not a Jewish rabbi—a fact corroborated by his lack of knowledge of Hebrew. It is thus very improbable that he was the learned R. Tarphon who was of the second generation of Mishna teachers—and in any case R. Tarphon was strongly anti-Christian while Trypho argues from a real desire to ascertain the truth.[9] It is all the more interesting that Trypho was a

---

[1] *Dial.* xxviii.   [2] Pp. 23–4.   [3] *Dial.* i. 3, ix. 3, xvi. 2, cviii. 3.
[4] *Dial.* i. 3.   [5] *Dial.* i. 1.   [6] *Dial.* i. 2.
[7] *Dial.* xciv. 4.   [8] *Dial.* xxxviii. 1.
[9] *Dial.* lxxxvii. 1. See pp. 24–5.

layman as his conception of Judaism will represent a position different from the strict Palestinian Pharisaic orthodoxy which was being enforced following on the reconstruction of Judaism at Jamnia after A.D. 70.

Trypho's character is only too human. His manners are genial and better than those of his friends.[1] Yet he thinks that Justin is deranged[2] and accuses him, not without justice, of quoting only Old Testament passages which support his arguments.[3] He loses his temper[4] and says roundly that Justin's explanations are artificial and even blasphemous. Yet the debate finishes on a friendly note.[5] These personal touches preclude, I believe, the view that the figure of Trypho is an ideal construction which Justin has created to embody the best of both schools of Judaism.[6] If this was the case we should have expected the picture of Trypho to have been more uniform.

On the whole the Debate, as recorded in the *Dialogue*, was conducted in an amicable spirit which says much, considering what was at stake, for both the characters of Justin and Trypho. It is superior in tone to the majority of Christian writings in the *Corpus Anti-Judaicum*.

The *Dialogue* with Trypho is an important source for Jewish knowledge of Christianity as well as for Christian knowledge of Judaism and implies a closer intercourse between Christians and Jews in the first half of the second century than has usually been supposed. It would appear that the rabbis of Jamnia were not wholly successful in enforcing on the diaspora the pattern of Pharisaic orthodoxy which forbad contacts with the *Minim*, i.e. Christians.[7]

Trypho's arguments against Christianity reveal by contrast his conception of Judaism. In general he is anti-Christian (viii. 3 f.) and finds in the moral teaching of Jesus too high a standard to keep (x. 2). Trypho particularly objects to Justin's arguments about the *torah* and asks whether Justin thinks that the *torah* unfits men for salvation (xlv. 1 f.). He is surprised that

---

[1] *Dial.* i. 1, ii. 6, viii. 3, ix. 2 f.   [2] *Dial.* xxxix. 3.
[3] *Dial.* xxvii. 1.   [4] *Dial.* lxxix. 1.
[5] *Dial.* cxlii. 1.   [6] The view of Goodenough: see p. 23.
[7] See the benediction composed by Samuel the Small at Jamnia *c.* A.D. 100 given in H. Strack, *Jesus, die Häretiker und die Christen*, pp. 66 f., and G. D. Kilpatrick, *The Origins of the Gospel According to St Matthew*, p. 109. Justin knew of this—see *Dial.* xvi. 4.

Christians do not separate themselves from the heathen[1] and eat things offered to idols (viii. 4, x. 3, xix. 1, xx. 2, xlvi. 2, xxxv. 1). He asks whether Christians are allowed to keep the sabbath and to be circumcised (xlvi. 1–4, xlvii. 1), although he realises that certain precepts of the *torah* can only be observed in Palestine. Trypho and his friends are worried by Justin's remark that Gentile Christians are the children of God (cxxiv. 1) and Israel itself (cxxiii. 7). They assert that Isa. xlii. 6 f. refers to proselytes and not to Gentile Christians (cxii. 4). Trypho even infers that Justin means that no Jew shall have an inheritance in the holy mountain of God, which Justin corrects by making this dependent on repentance (xxv. 6).

Trypho particularly objects to the Incarnation on the grounds that it is incredible (lxviii. 1). The pre-existence of Jesus he asserts is impossible as he lacked the powers of the Holy Spirit at first (lxxxvii. 1 f.). He wants proof that there is another God (lxv. 1) and that he was born of a virgin (lxiii. 1).

Trypho disputes the use made by Justin of certain passages in the LXX such as Gen. xviii, Ps. xcvi, Isa. vii. 14, Isa. xi. 1–3, Isa. xl. 1–17. He is even shocked when Justin says that Christ spoke to Moses at the burning bush (xxxviii. 1, lx. 1, 3).

The Christian doctrine of the Messiah is a major stumbling block. Trypho says that the Christians 'shape a kind of Messiah for themselves' (viii. 4). He agrees, however, that the Messiah is to be born of the race of David (lxviii. 5), but is to be only a man who will *become* Messiah (xlix. 1, lxvii. 2). And even if the Messiah is to suffer he cannot suffer by crucifixion (lxxxix. 2, xc. 1). Justin, in any case, has first to prove that Jesus was called a Stone (xxxvi. 1).

It is significant for the understanding of Trypho's conception of Judaism that he accepts many of Justin's statements. Thus: 'All our race expects the Messiah, and we acknowledge that all the passages of scripture which you have cited have been spoken of him' (lxxxix. 1). Trypho holds that it is right to look for a reason in God's commands (xxviii. 1) and states that the *torah* was, in fact, given because of the hardness of Israel's heart. It was not necessary to salvation as is seen from the case of the patriarchs (lxvii. 7 f.). He grants that Justin's LXX

---

[1] Note the difference between Justin and Ep. Barnabas which is more Jewish in ethos and outlook.

quotations are such as to point to his interpretation, but he wants more information—especially concerning Isa. vii. 14 (lxxvii. 1). Such is Trypho's liberalism that he confesses that he is charmed with the debate, having found more than he expected (cxlii. 1).

Trypho's interpretations of certain passages in the LXX are interesting. He regards the 'Son of Man' mentioned in Dan. vii. 13 as the Messiah (xxxii. 1). With regard to the 'three men' in Gen. xviii. 2 he grants that God appeared to Abraham, though before the three 'men', who were really angels, came (lvi. 4 f.); but he afterwards acknowledges that they were not angels, though the passage does not show that there was another God (lvi. 9). Yet the third angel was God, and yet not the God in heaven, although his 'eating' is difficult, if not metaphorical (lvii. 1, 3). Trypho accepts Justin's explanation of Isa. xlii. 8 'My glory will I not give to another' (lxv. 7). He agrees that a new Covenant is foretold (lxvii. 9–11) and that Isa. xi. 1–3 *does* refer to the Messiah, although not to Jesus (lxxxvii. 1 f.). A friend of Trypho's who joins in the debate on the second day says he can give no reason against Justin's interpretation of the incident of the Brazen Serpent—and neither could his teachers: 'So say what you will, for we are paying heed to you as you reveal the mystery of things that cause even the precepts of the prophets to be attacked' (xciv. 4).

Trypho was a Hellenistic-Jewish layman who combined the culture and inquiring spirit of the Hellenistic world with a knowledge of traditional Jewish exegesis and haggadah. He has no knowledge of the Hebrew language but knows accurately the Septuagint version of the Old Testament. His is not the Judaism of Philo and Alexandrian-Hellenistic Judaism, nor that of the Palestinian rabbinic schools. Trypho represents a mediating Judaism, perhaps having Palestinian roots, which cannot be strictly classified. Judaism, even after A.D. 70, was not a mono-lithic structure and had a number of facets, as recent discoveries have shown.[1] Trypho represents one of these facets. He warns us against identifying the linguistic frontier between the Greek and Semitic worlds with the cultural frontier between Hellenism and Judaism.

What of Justin Martyr himself? Was he qualified to conduct

[1] See p. 25.

a controversy with such a Jew as Trypho? What knowledge did he possess of Jewish post-biblical traditions and haggadah? Again we should be in error if we assumed that Justin, because he wrote in Greek, only knew the Hellenistic Judaism of Alexandria. Indeed, as will be seen in the chapters discussing his doctrine of God and the logos, it is very doubtful if Justin was familiar with Philo, although he certainly knew the Jewish Wisdom literature. His knowledge of Judaism was derived directly from the LXX and from post-biblical practices, doctrines and exegetical methods with which he was apparently familiar. We must now discuss this in more detail.

(a) Justin's dependence on Greek version(s) of the Old Testament

It will be as well to give three examples which show his ignorance of the Hebrew text of the Bible:

(i) In *Dial.* xlix his argument based on Exod. xvii. 16 'A hand upon the throne of the Lord' is derived from the LXX which has a reading different from the Hebrew text.

(ii) Justin's quotation in *Dial.* l from Isa. xxxix. 8–xl. 18 presents several verbal variants from the LXX, yet it agrees with the LXX and Vulgate, and differs from the Hebrew, in adopting the masculine, instead of the feminine, gender in verse 9, ὁ εὐαγγελιζόμενος.

(iii) In *Dial.* cxiii Justin states that the Jews, although taking no account of the change of Oshea into Joshua, yet made it a theological question why *a* was added to the name of Abraham ('Αβραάμ for "Αβραμ) and a second *r* inserted in the name of Sarah (Σάῤῥα for Σάρα). It is difficult to imagine that this could have been said by anyone who knew that the real change in Hebrew was the addition of the letter (h) in the name of Abraham and the change of (i) into (h) in that of Sarah (i.e. Sarah for Sarai).

It is interesting that Justin not only in general follows the LXX in his quotations[1] but he charges the Jews with corrupting those copies of the LXX which, it appears, were in use in some synagogues. In *Dial.* lxviii. 7 he says that the Jewish teachers

[1] Recent study has shown that Justin pre-dates any general norms for judging types of LXX text. See the important work of D. Barthélemy, *Les Devanciers d'Aquila*: Suppl. to *V.T.* x (1963) for Justin's text of the Minor Prophets. See further Appendix 3.

'presumed to affirm that the translation made by the seventy elders in the time of Ptolemy, the King of Egypt, was in some respects untrue'. In *Dial.* lxxi Justin repeats the same charge and alleges that the Jewish teachers did not allow that the translation of the LXX was well done, and that they endeavoured to make a translation (or to give interpretations) themselves (ἀλλ' αὐτοὶ ἐξηγεῖσθαι πειρῶνται). It is just possible that this is an allusion to the version of Theodotion who, according to Irenaeus (*Adv. Haer.* iii. 24), was a Jewish proselyte and whose version was made in the first half of the second century.[1]

More interesting are the references which Justin makes in *Dial.* lxxii to certain expurgations from the LXX text alleged to have been made by the Jews. There is no certain evidence that these in fact ever existed—indeed in the case of one passage, the quotation from Jer. xi. 19, all MSS both Greek and Hebrew retain it.[2] Justin himself acknowledges that the quotation still existed in some copies found in the synagogues of the Jews (lxxii. 3). It is remarkable that Trypho, whom Eusebius describes as 'the most distinguished of the Hebrews of his time' (*H.E.* iv. 18), instead of insisting on direct evidence for so grave an accusation, was content to regard it as merely incredible.

The almost certain conclusion is that neither Justin nor Trypho knew Hebrew nor the Hebrew version of the scriptures and this led them into errors of interpretation. But in this ignorance they were joined by large numbers of Greek-speaking Jews who heard the LXX read in the synagogue service.

(b) Jewish post-biblical practices

Justin was acquainted with certain Jewish practices which are not found in the Old Testament. In *Dial.* xvi. 4, cf. xlvii. 4, cviii. 3, he refers to the cursing of Christians in the synagogues. This accords with the Palestinian form of the Twelfth Benedic-

---

[1] It is still an open question whether Theodotion's adaptation was based on the LXX or on another Greek version. See B. J. Roberts in Peake's *Commentary* on the Bible (revised ed.), p. 81. It is interesting that Justin himself, in his quotations from Daniel in *Dial.* xxxi, shows a knowledge of Theodotion's readings.

[2] This text seems to have been used in the Christian testimony collections, for both Lactantius (iv. 18), Cyprian (*Test.* ii. 15, 20), Gregory Nyssa (*Test. adv. Jud.* vi) and Dionysius Bar Ṣalibi (iv. 19, vi. 8) have it.

tion in the *Shemoneh 'Esreh* which prayed that Christians (*nôtzrim*) may perish and be wiped out of the book of life.[1] It is arguable that *nôtzrim* strictly refers to Nazarenes, i.e. Jewish Christians, but Justin assumes that it refers to *all* Christians, Gentile as well as Jewish. There is no reason to doubt the correctness of his information, although equally many Jews seemed to have remained in friendly contact with Christians in spite of the command of the rabbis not to hold discussions with Christians, to which Justin refers in *Dial.* xxxviii. 1 and which is confirmed by T.B. Aboda Zara 27 B: 'Let a man have no dealings with the heretics (*mînim*) nor get healing of bodily diseases from them—for heresy (*mînûth*) attracts.'

In *Dial.* xl. 4–5 Justin refers to the scapegoat in the ritual of the Day of Atonement:

And the two goats at the Fast that are commanded at the Fast, which by God's command must be alike, of which one became the Scapegoat, and the other an offering, were an announcement of the two Advents of Christ;[2] of one Advent, in which the elders of your people and the priests, laying their hands on him and putting him to death, sent him off as a scapegoat; and of his second Advent, because in the same place of Jerusalem you will recognise him who was dishonoured by you...Now that there is no permission for the offering of the two goats which were commanded to be brought at the Fast to take place anywhere save in Jerusalem, you are fully aware.

The basis of this account is to be found in Lev. xvi. 5–10, 21–2. But it is significant that in these passages there is no mention that the goats are to be alike nor that the elders and priests laid hands on the scapegoat—according to Lev. xvi. 21 the goat is sent into the wilderness by the hand of *one* man after Aaron, the High Priest, had laid his hands on the goat's head confessing the sins of Israel. Neither is there any mention of Jerusalem. Justin's additions to the biblical account are not merely due to his obvious desire to find typological fulfilments of the ritual of the Day of Atonement in the Advent of Christ. They also appear to reflect fresh details concerning the ceremonies observed on that Day found in the Mishna Tractate *Yoma* which in its present form dates from *c.* A.D. 200. This Tractate may well reflect genuine earlier traditions as the

---

[1] See T. B. Berakoth 29 A.   [2] So Tertullian, *Adv. Jud.* xiv.

Temple ritual, at the time *Yoma* was written, was no longer applicable to Jewish life and therefore had been less overlaid with comment by later tannaim and less exposed to the possibility of revision (cf. *Yoma* xvi a).

In *Yoma* vi. 1 f. we are explicitly told that the two goats are to resemble one another as closely as possible. The words of the High Priest's confession over the goat were: 'O God, thy people, the house of Israel, have committed iniquity, transgressed, and sinned before thee. O God, forgive, I pray, the iniquities and transgressions and sins which thy people, the house of Israel, have committed and transgressed and sinned before thee; as it is written in the law of thy servant Moses. For on this day shall atonement be made for you to cleanse you: from all your sins shall ye be clean before the Lord.' The goat was then led away, accompanied by some of the nobles of Jerusalem and later by a single man, to a place called Ṣuḳ where it was thrown backwards over a cliff and dashed to pieces among the rocks. It is also interesting that, according to *Yoma* iii. 9, the two goats used in the ritual were solemnly chosen by lot in the temple area, and this practice seems to be alluded to by Justin who clearly has a knowledge of these post-biblical Jewish practices in this passage.[1]

In *Dial.* cxxxiv. 1 Justin refers to Jewish teachers who permit Jews to have four and even five wives apiece. This is attested by Josephus who says that it is an ancient practice for the Jews to have many wives at the same time (*Ant.* xvii. 1. 2–3). In the Talmud polygamy is not ruled out: 'While one rabbi says that a man may take as many wives as he can support—Raba in *Yeb.* 65 A—it was recommended that no one should marry more than four women—*ibid.* 44 A.'[2]

(c) Jewish post-biblical beliefs

Justin, in a number of passages, shows a knowledge of beliefs held by the rabbis but not found in scripture. Thus in *Dial.* viii. 4 Trypho is recorded as saying: 'But Messiah, if indeed he has ever been and now exists anywhere, is unknown, and does

---

[1] Ep. Barn. vii. 6–11 likewise shows familiarity with the Mishnaic account. Barnabas also alludes to the thread of scarlet wool tied to the head of one of the goats. See my article in *Folklore*, LXX (1959), 443–9.

[2] *Jewish Encyclopaedia*, x, 121. Western Jews have been monogamists since the time of R. Gershom ben Judah, *c.* A.D. 1000.

not even know himself at all nor has any power, until Elijah shall have come and anointed him, and shall have made him manifest to all.' The doctrine of a Messiah as existing on earth, although unknown, is attested by IV Esdras xiii. 52, by R. Nachman (fourth century A.D.) and by Rab (T.B. Sanh. 98 B). According to T.B. Sanh. 98 A, the Messiah might even be among the lepers at the gates of Rome. The details concerning the relationship of Elijah to the Messiah are also significant.[1] According to later Jewish traditions Elijah, in the Messianic age, will restore to Israel a flask of oil for anointing the King Messiah [Kerithoth 5 ab; Horayyoth 11 b; Siphra, Tsav. 1. 9 (ed. Weiss 41 a)].[2] In several Talmudic traditions Elijah is not only a prophet but also a High Priest whose custom it was to anoint the kings. Justin's reference to the anointing of the Messiah by Elijah in the Messianic age is, in Klausner's opinion, the earliest reference to this Jewish belief.[3]

In *Dial.* xliv. 1 Justin refers to the belief that the Jewish nation is sure of salvation because they are Abraham's seed.[4] And in *Dial.* lxiv. 1 Trypho says that only Gentiles need Christ— not the Jews. In lxix. 7 there appears the Jewish belief that Jesus was a magician and a deceiver—a belief held by Celsus[5] and referred to in T.B. Sanh. 43 A, 'On the eve of Passover they hanged Jesus, and a herald went out before him for forty days, (crying) let him be stoned, for he has committed sorcery, and has deceived Israel, and led it astray.'

In *Dial.* cxxiii. 1 Justin speaks of a proselyte who undergoes circumcision 'with the object of joining the people is like one who is native-born'. This is an undoubted reference to the Jewish belief that a proselyte is like a newborn child[6] in that his former family connections had ended and that he had begun a new life.

(d) *Jewish post-biblical exegesis*

In a number of passages Justin shows a knowledge of Jewish methods of exegesis and interpretation although these are not

---

[1] Cf. also *Dial.* xlix. [2] Cf. also the Ethiopic book *Kebra Nagast* 98.
[3] *Messianic Idea in Israel*, p. 456.
[4] See Strack–Billerbeck on Matt. iii. 9.
[5] Orig. *c*.Cels. i. 28, ii. 48; cf. Clem. Rec. I. 58; Lact. *Inst. Div.* v. 3.
[6] T.B. Yeb. 62 A.

so prominent as in the Epistle of Barnabas. Justin sometimes quotes passages of scripture in an ascending order of importance, for instance, Hagiographa, Prophets and finally the Law. A good example of this is found in *Dial*. xxix. 2: 'For the words have not been fitted together by me, nor adorned by human art, but they were sung by David, proclaimed as good news by Isaiah, preached by Zechariah, written down by Moses. You recognise them, Trypho? They are laid up in your scriptures, or rather not in yours but in ours, for we obey them, but you, when you read, do not understand their sense.' The order David, Isaiah, Zechariah and Moses no doubt would have appealed to Trypho.

In *Dial*. xxxii. 1 Trypho accepts the Son of Man of Dan. vii. 13 as the Messiah. This exegesis was well known among the Jews; cf. Similitudes of Enoch xxxvii–lxxi, II Esdras xiii. R. Akiba spoke of the 'thrones' of Dan. vii. 9 as prepared for God and for David (T.B. Sanh. 38B—apparently alluding to this exegesis).

In *Dial*. xxxvi. 2–6 Ps. xxiv is referred to Solomon. This was common among the Jews; e.g. T.B. Sabb. 30A reads: 'when Solomon built the sanctuary he sought to bring the ark into the Holy of Holies. The gates clave together. Solomon said twenty-four forms of prayer, but no answer was given. He began to say, Lift up your heads, O ye gates...'

Further illustrations of Jewish exegesis occur in *Dial*. lvi. 5 (the interpretation of Gen. xviii. 2, xix. 1); in *Dial*. lvii. 2 (the question how one of the angels could be God when he ate); in *Dial*. lxii. 2 f. (the interpretation of Gen. i. 26); in lxv. 1 (Isa. xlii. 8); in lxvii. 1 (Isa. vii. 14); in cxii. 4 (the camels), *inter alia*.

Justin also appears to have been familiar with a quantity of syncretistic exegesis of Gen. i. This is shown in *I Apol*. lxiv:

From what has been said you can understand why the daemons contrived to have the image of the so-called Kore erected at the springs of waters, saying that she was a daughter of Zeus, imitating what was said through Moses. For Moses said, as I have quoted: 'In the beginning God made the heaven and the earth. And the earth was invisible and unfurnished, and the Spirit of God was borne over the waters.' In imitation of the Spirit of God, spoken of as borne over the water, they spoke of Kore, daughter of Zeus.

This linking of Gen. i with the pagan goddess of springs is compared by Professor H. Chadwick with Numenius of Apamea who links the same text with Egyptian representations of the gods as sea-borne.[1] It would seem that both Justin and Numenius drew on a Jewish syncretistic tradition of Gen. i possibly Syrian in origin.[2]

(e) Justin's knowledge of Jewish sects

Justin's knowledge of Judaism is, in the main, revealed in his discussion and controversy with the Jew Trypho—and particularly in their respective uses of the LXX; only incidentally does Justin refer to aspects of Jewish life not strictly germane to the controversy. But in *Dial.* lxii. 1–3 he refers to a heretical party among the Jews which held that in Gen. i. 26 ('Let us make man') God was speaking to the angels and that the human body was the creation of angels. There is a good Tannaitic tradition which states that God spoke to the angels at the creation[3] and Goldfahn states that such passages are frequently found—but in no orthodox Jewish tradition were the angels represented as creators of the human body. This belief was undoubtedly the crux of the heresy to which Justin refers and it would seem that this was some form of Jewish gnosticism. Certainly Philo knew of this belief, for, in speaking of the angel of Gen. xlviii. 16, he says Moses 'mentions man alone as having been made by God in conjunction with other assistance (Gen. i. 26). Here, therefore, the Father is conversing with his own powers, to whom he has assigned the task of making the mortal part of our soul…He thought it necessary to assign the origin of evil to other workmen than himself.'[4] Recent discoveries have shown that gnosticism was allied to Judaism at an early date and fragments of Jewish syncretistic interpretation appear to have been known.

---

[1] *J.T.S.* xiv (1963), 495–6. The reference is to Numenius ap. Porph. *de Antro Nympharum* 10.

[2] See C. C. Richardson, *Early Christian Fathers* (London, 1953), p. 285.

[3] Mish. Gen. Rabba 8, from A. H. Goldfahn, *Justinus Martyr und die Agada* (Breslau, 1873), p. 245.

[4] *De Fuga* xiii. 68–70; cf. *De Opif. Mundi* xxiv. No other Jewish writer seems to know of this belief. Justin does, however, refer to the orthodox Jewish belief that the permanent angels were rays from the Glory of God which it was the will of God not to recall. See *Dial.* cxxviii; cf. T.B. Chagiga 14A.

Justin makes another mention of Jewish groups in *Dial.* lxxx. 4 when he enumerates seven heretical Jewish sects which no orthodox Jew would acknowledge. After referring vaguely to certain Christian heresies, presumably Marcionism, Justin adds: '...do not suppose that they are Christians, any more than if one examined the matter rightly he would acknowledge as Jews those who are Sadducees, or similar sects of Genistae, and Meristae, and Galileans, and Hellenians, and Pharisees and Baptists (pray, do not be vexed with me as I say all I think), but (would say) that though called Jews and children of Abraham, and acknowledging God with their lips, as God Himself has cried aloud, yet their heart is far from Him.'

This list is difficult to interpret. Certainly Justin believed himself to be describing Jewish *heresies*, and not respectable Jews. It is just possible that Genistae is a Greek translation of the Hebrew word *minim* which was a term for all heretics and not only for the Jewish Christians who had been banned from the synagogues since the time of the Birkath-ha-Minim *c.* A.D. 100. The Meristae may be Jewish Gnostics who 'divided' the person of the deity—perhaps the same group as that referred to in *Dial.* lxii. 1–3 and mentioned above. The Galileans are unlikely to have been Jewish Christians, as Père Milik thought[1] (Justin is not describing *Christian* heretical groups in this passage), but a Jewish schismatic group which originated with Judas of Galilee and his revolt against the Romans in A.D. 6 or 7. This movement of revolt became quite widespread if Josephus' frequent references to it are any guide.[2] Justin's mention of the Hellenians as a Jewish heretical sect is difficult to interpret unless this is a mistake for the followers of Hillel ('Ελληνιανῶν being read for 'Ελληλιαλῶν).[3]

The *crux interpretum* of the list is however the inclusion of the Sadducees and Pharisees. It seems totally incomprehensible that Justin, in view of his knowledge of biblical and post-biblical Judaism, could describe these as heresies. Perhaps that is why he inserts the parenthesis (pray, do not be vexed with me as I say all I think). Is it significant that the Sadducees are placed first in his list and the Pharisees near, or at the end, as if the

---

[1] R. Bibl. LX. 4, pp. 526 f., quoted in M. Black, 'The Patristic Accounts of Jewish Sectarianism', *B.J.R.L.* XLI (1959), 287.

[2] *Ant.* XVIII. i. 6; XX. 5. 2; *B.J.* II. 8. 1; 17. 8, 9; VII. 8. 1.

[3] Cf. Epiph. Pan. 30.4.

word Pharisees is to be taken with Baptists, i.e. Pharisee-Baptists? The Sadducees of history seem to have disappeared with the destruction of the Temple in A.D. 70, yet Justin is describing *Jewish* heresies as is indicated by the phrase 'or similar sects of Genistae, etc.'. Professor M. Black[1] holds that Justin by Sadducees means Zadokites or Qumran Essenes and he quotes good Jewish tradition for this identification. Thus Maimonides, in his Commentary on *Pirke Aboth* I, states that the Karaites called themselves Saddoukim and were known by this name to their rabbis. The strength of this theory lies in the fact that Justin nowhere mentions the Essenes in his list—which is rather strange in a list of this kind. On the other hand Justin must have known (from the New Testament if nowhere else) of the historical Sadducees. Possibly there has been some corruption in the text.

Justin's references to the Pharisees and Baptists present great difficulties. If the link word καί is retained then the Baptists are presumably the Hemero-baptists or 'morning bathers'—a division of the Essenes who bathed every morning before the hour of prayer in order to pronounce the name of God with a clean body.[2] Professor Black has however made the brilliant suggestion[3] that the καί before βαπτιστῶν is a conjectural insertion and that the two words Pharisees, Baptists should be taken together, the second in opposition to and qualifying the first. This Jewish sect, Black believes, was one of 'baptizing-Pharisees'. Recent investigations have shown that the baptismal cult was widespread in Judaism in the first two Christian centuries, especially in the diaspora, and that it had spread into the ranks of the Pharisaic teachers, some of whom were prepared to accept proselyte baptism as alone constituting a convert Jew. One argument was that as baptism was the decisive rite in the case of a woman it ought to be in the case of a man.[4] Such views were bound to be pronounced heretical by the main body of Pharisaic orthodoxy in the period after A.D. 70.

The merit of Professor Black's theory is that he manages to

---

[1] 'The Patristic Accounts of Jewish Sectarianism', p. 290.

[2] Tosef. Yad., end.

[3] 'The Patristic Accounts of Jewish Sectarianism', p. 289.

[4] See D. Daube, *The New Testament and Rabbinic Judaism*, p. 109, quoted in Black, 'The Patristic Accounts of Jewish Sectarianism', p. 289.

4-2

explain Justin's list as six (and not seven)[1] known Jewish heretical groups. His explanation, with the possible exception of the Sadducees which may reflect textual corruption, may be accepted as the best explanation of this difficult passage which has yet been given.

The evidence assembled in this chapter will have shown that Justin had a good working knowledge of post-biblical Judaism such as would stand him in good stead in his controversy with a Jew who also knew no Hebrew and, like Justin, apparently used the Old Testament in its Greek form. Justin's errors are, on the whole, remarkably few. Trypho represented a liberal, mediating type of Judaism not strictly Philonic nor Palestinian-rabbinic in character. Justin, with his cosmopolitan culture and wide interests and footing in the Greek world, was well able to cope with the arguments of his adversary—indeed the *Dialogue* is proof that, in certain circles, there was a close intercourse between Christians and Jews even after the promulgation of the Birkhath-ha-Minim which forbad such contacts. Justin's knowledge of Judaism is in general accurate. He has a good knowledge of the LXX, and of Jewish post-biblical practices, beliefs and exegetical methods, and also is familiar with Jewish-Gnostic syncretistic exegesis of Gen. i. There is surprisingly little in Justin to suggest a close acquaintance with Philo and Hellenistic Judaism. It is, I believe, not now possible to ascertain when or how Justin acquired his knowledge of Judaism, although this was probably, in the main, before his confrontation with Trypho.

[1] But note that Hegesippus gives a list of *seven* sects 'opposed to the tribe of Judah and the Christ' (Eus. *H.E.* iv. 22). This, however, may be a catalogue of heresies *of the Church*. Lietzmann, *The Beginnings of the Christian Church*, pp. 181–2, believes that the Jewish Christians who fled to Pella before the catastrophe of A.D. 70 came into contact with Jewish sects of various kinds in the region east of the Jordan as well as east and south of the Dead Sea.

CHAPTER V

BACKGROUND:
THE CHRISTIAN TRADITION

JUSTIN wrote primarily as a Christian. His acquaintance with Greek philosophy—and especially with Middle Platonism—his familiarity with post-biblical Judaism and his obvious desire to share common ground with his readers should not blind us to this fact. For Justin, Christianity was the highest truth to which the Old Testament prophetic writers, as well as the Greek philosophers, dimly bore witness. It was then natural that he should appeal to the basic documents of the Christian religion in the cause of his *apologia* for the faith. Yet these documents themselves presuppose the continuous worshipping life of the Church, as recent study has been concerned to emphasise,[1] as well as preserving catechetical and paraenetical material used in the instruction of converts. Moreover, in the earliest age of the Church a strong oral tradition existed in some centres, which preserved sayings and narratives of Jesus which are not found in the Canonical Gospels. In addition *testimonia*, or collections of proof texts from the Old Testament, were collected which were thought to find fulfilment in the Person and Work of Jesus Christ. Some of these *testimonia* are found embedded in the New Testament. Yet the process of selecting and collecting *testimonia* was not limited to the New Testament period and continued for some centuries. Cyprian's or Pseudo-Cyprian's monumental *Testimonia*, divided into headings, is in a sense the final stage of this process.

Justin Martyr is of great importance for the understanding of the second-century Church. He is the first post-apostolic author whose writings are of any considerable size. He was acquainted with the Church at Rome, as well as with other Christian centres, at a time when Christian oral and written tradition still existed side by side although slowly the written documents alone were coming to be held as authoritative. As a witness to what was a transition stage Justin Martyr's Christian

[1] See especially: C. F. D. Moule, *The Birth of the New Testament*, pp. 11–32.

background, as far as it can be recovered from his writings, is of
no little interest. Our investigation in this chapter will be concerned with (i) his use of the New Testament; (ii) his use of oral
tradition and an uncanonical Gospel or Gospels; and (iii) his use
of *testimonia*.

JUSTIN AND THE NEW TESTAMENT

The problem of Justin's knowledge of the New Testament is
closely bound up with the formation of the Canon of New
Testament writings. If it could be shown that an authoritative
list of books of the New Testament, or groups of books, did not
come into existence until the last quarter of the second century,
i.e. until the time of Irenaeus and the author of the Muratorian
Canon (*c.* A.D. 200), then clearly Justin antedates the process
of forming a Canon. And in any case he may have written
before or around the time that Marcion drew up a collection of
books witnessing to *his* version of the Gospel which, it used to
be held, was the *first* attempt to form a Canon.[1] If it was Marcion
who stimulated the Church to form its own Canon of the New
Testament then Justin pre-dates this attempt. However, recent
discoveries have radically changed this picture, and the assumption that Marcion was the stimulus to the Church's occupation
with a Canon of authoritative writings is now seen to be
precarious in the extreme. Dr R. P. C. Hanson, in his fully
documented *Tradition in the Early Church* (London, 1962), has
discussed the early stages in the drawing up of the Canon[2] and
he shows that II Peter iii. 16 (which is to be dated between
A.D. 120 and 150) refers to a collection of St Paul's letters and
to 'other writings'. He also shows that the recently discovered
Gnostic *Gospel of Truth*, found at Nag Hammadi, which is
probably the work of Valentinus, used the four Canonical
Gospels, the Pauline Epistles, the Epistle to the Hebrews, and
the Book of Revelation, although not the Pastoral Epistles. As
this Gospel is to be dated between A.D. 140 and 145, and eman-
ated from Rome, it is probable that the author drew on an
already existing list of Christian writings.[3] Marcion was then

[1] The formation of Marcion's collection is usually dated A.D. 150–60.

[2] Pp. 187–236.

[3] Hanson hazards the opinion that this was the collection to which
II Pet. iii. 16 refers (*ibid.* p. 190).

not the first to draw up an authoritative list. This fact, as we shall see, has a direct bearing on the question of Justin's knowledge of the Gospels. The suggestion that Justin could *not* have quoted the Canonical Gospels but *only* used the Uncanonical Gospel of Peter or the Gospel according to the Hebrews, because our Gospels were not widely known in his day, is very unlikely.[1]

An interesting fact which has emerged from recent study is that the four Gospels were not the earliest books of the New Testament to be recognised and collected together. This honour belongs rather to the Pauline Epistles. The reason for this was that the Fourth Gospel had to overcome considerable suspicion and even opposition before it was accepted without question. The earliest grouping of the four Gospels, as we know them today, took place in Gnostic circles perhaps as early as A.D. 130–140. On the Catholic side Irenaeus, in a famous passage, is the first to recognise the authority of the four Gospels and *only* four.[2] It would seem that although four Gospels were known and used well before the middle of the second century what held back orthodox recognition longer than the heretical was uncertainty as to the apostolic authorship of the Fourth Gospel and its congeniality to the heretics. Perhaps that is why *direct* quotations from that Gospel are so few in early Christian literature.

We now turn to Justin's knowledge of the Gospels. He refers frequently to certain books which he describes as *memoirs* or *records* of the Apostles [τὰ ἀπομνημονεύματα τῶν ἀποστόλων (αὐτοῦ)] which, he says, were called Gospels[3] and were read in the weekly assembly of Christians interchangeably with 'the prophets' for as long as time permitted.[4] Once in the *First Apology* and seven times in the *Dialogue* Justin mentions these *memoirs* of the (or his) Apostles.[5] Four times in the *Dialogue* he simply speaks of the *memoirs*.[6] Elsewhere he uses other expressions which seem to refer to these books. Speaking of the Annuncia-

---

[1] This was the view of the German critic Schwegler, *Nachapost Zeitalter* (1846). Schwegler identified the Gospel of Peter with that to the Hebrews.

[2] *Adv. Haer.* III. 11. 11. The anonymous anti-Montanist writer who wrote to Abercius Marcellus *c.* A.D. 192 seems to refer to a written collection of New Testament writings.   [3] *I Apol.* lxvi.   [4] *I Apol.* lxvii.

[5] *I Apol.* lxvii; *Dial.* c–civ, cvi (twice).   [6] *Dial.* cv (3 times), cvii.

tion he says 'as those who related all things concerning our Saviour Jesus Christ taught'.[1] He refers to 'the Apostles, in the memoirs composed by them, which are called Gospels, thus handed down'.[2] Again: 'The Apostles wrote that the Holy Spirit as a dove flew upon' Jesus after his baptism.[3] Furthermore: 'In the memoirs which I say were composed by his Apostles and those who followed them.'[4] Finally, speaking of the change of Simon's name to Peter, Justin says 'It is written in his memoirs that it so happened'[5] which, if the text is correct, seems to refer to Peter's *memoirs*.

Much ink has been spilt over the interpretation of the term *memoirs*. Certainly for Justin the term was a descriptive one. The term Gospels or Gospel was well established in his day while the term *Memoirs* was not. R. G. Heard, in a posthumous article, held that Justin took over Papias' terminology in describing the Gospels as *Memoirs*.[6] Papias had said that Mark, being Peter's interpreter, followed Peter, listened to his teaching about Christ and wrote down some things as he recalled them (ἀπεμνημόνευσεν).[7] The argument that Justin's ἀπομνημονεύματα presuppose Papias' use of the verb is not conclusive as Justin nowhere else quotes Papias—and their respective approaches to Christianity are quite different. More to the point is Justin's interest in Xenophon. He quotes from his well-known *Memoirs* in *II Apol.* xi (cf. also *I Apol.* v; *II Apol.* x) and, as we have already noted,[8] points the parallel between the death of Socrates and that of Jesus Christ. It would seem probable, against R. G. Heard's opinion, that Justin consciously took the phrase from Xenophon's well-known Ἀπομνημονεύματα Σωκράτους, which other writers knew. This was apposite as it would give to Justin's non-Christian readers an indication of the type of narrative that the Christian Gospels contained. Yet the fact that Justin also used the phrase in the *Dialogue* shows that it was his own favourite term—quite apart from its apologetic usefulness. The *Memoirs* of the (or his) Apostles was not a title but

---

[1] *I Apol.* xxxiii.   [2] *I Apol.* lxvi.   [3] *Dial.* lxxxviii.
[4] *Dial.* ciii.   [5] *Dial.* cvi.   [6] *N.T.S.* I (Nov. 1954), 122–34.
[7] Eus. *H.E.* iii. 39; cf. Clem. Rec. II. 1, where Peter says: 'In consuetudine habui, verba Domini mei, quae ab ipso audieram, revocare in memoriam.' The term is also used by Eusebius (*H.E.* v. 8; vi. 25), though not of the Gospels.   [8] P. 34.

Justin's description of the Gospels which he knew—the *Memoirs* called Gospels. The plural 'Gospels' was no doubt the term used by the Church in Justin's day, although it is to be noted that he does also use the singular 'Gospel'. Thus in *Dial.* x Trypho says that he had 'read the precepts in the so-called Gospel'; and Justin himself says[1] that 'in the Gospel it is written that Christ said, "All things are delivered unto me by my Father"'. This seems to refer to a *collection* of written memoirs as is the case with Irenaeus[2] and many subsequent writers.

The *Memoirs* were then for Justin several evangelical narratives which, according to *Dial.* ciii, were composed by Apostles or their followers.[3] Justin does not say how many Gospels there were nor how many were written by the Apostles and how many by their followers. He nowhere gives the names of their authors unless he refers to Peter's *Memoirs*. In *Dial.* cvi Justin says, 'It is written ἐν τοῖς ἀπομνημονεύμασιν αὐτοῦ that this happened', where αὐτοῦ may conceivably refer to Peter although this is not quite certain. In any case for Justin the Gospels or *Memoirs* related information about Jesus and to them he appealed for examples of Christ's teaching[4] and for the events of his life.[5] They were regularly read in public worship and were commented upon by the chief officer or ruler of the brethren,[6] which suggests that they were well known and generally accepted reliable public documents. Both Justin and the Church used them as apostolic narratives of the life and teaching of Jesus.

What were these *Memoirs* or Records called Gospels? Were they identical with our Synoptic Gospels or with the fourfold Canon or did they also include non-Canonical Gospels? This question can only be answered after an examination of Justin's writings, bearing in mind the fact that he does not always quote his sources exactly but apparently sometimes relies on memory. Such is the case, as has long been recognised, with Justin's quotations from the LXX. It is true that Justin gives long extracts from the LXX, especially in the *Dialogue*, without

---

[1] *Dial.* c.   [2] *Adv. Haer.* iii. 5. 1; iii. 11. 7.

[3] ἐν γὰρ τοῖς ἀπομνημονεύμασιν, ἅ φημι ὑπὸ τῶν ἀποστόλων αὐτοῦ καὶ τῶν ἐκείνοις παρακολουθησάντων συντετάχθαι.

[4] *I Apol.* xv–xvii, lxvi; *Dial.* cv, cvii.

[5] *I Apol.* xxxiii; *Dial.* lxxxviii, c–civ, cvi.   [6] *I Apol.* lxvii.

break or interpolated matter—more than once quoting an entire Psalm no doubt copied from the LXX text which he had before him. But on other occasions he quotes very freely[1] and sometimes gives a free combination of different passages.[2] Other variations occur.[3] Swete, after a detailed investigation, states that Justin knew an eclectic text of the LXX and even on occasions felt obliged to criticise the LXX reading.[4]

This freedom in quotation is also a characteristic of Justin's quotations from Classical authors. In the two *Apologies* there are nine classical quotations—six from Plato, two from Xenophon and one from Euripides. Five of these[5] are short, familiar phrases which Justin repeats fairly accurately. Another, a passage from Plato, is quoted very freely and its author called 'a certain one of the ancients'.[6] Even a passage from the *Timaeus*, one of Justin's favourite writings, is quoted only loosely.[7] The familiar opening of Xenophon's *Memoirs* is cited inaccurately[8] while from the same book Justin gives a condensed account of 'Hercules' choice'.[9] If therefore there is considerable freedom in quotations from the LXX (which Justin declared to be inspired) and from Classical authors we shall not expect quotations from the Gospels to be any more exact.

We must now examine Justin's account of Jesus' life and teaching, as given in his lengthy writings, with the account given in the Canonical Gospels. It has often been remarked that Justin's account is remarkably full. He is the first post-apostolic writer to record at any length *details* of Our Lord's life and teaching. He records his birth from the Virgin[10] and the

---

[1] E.g. *I Apol.* xxxvii (Isa. lviii. 6, 7); *I Apol.* xliv (Deut. xxx. 15, 19); *I Apol.* xlvii (Isa. i. 7); *I Apol.* lx (Deut. xxxii. 22); *I Apol.* lxii (Exod. iii. 5) *inter alia*.

[2] *I Apol.* xxxii (Isa. xi. 1; Num. xxiv. 17); *I Apol.* lii (Ez. xxxvii. 7; Isa. xlv. 23) *inter alia*.

[3] *I Apol.* xxxv, the reference of Zech. ix. 9 ascribed to Zephaniah; *I Apol.* li (Dan. vii. 13 to Jeremiah) *inter alia*. But these may be due to a previous history in the Church's *pesher* tradition.

[4] *Introduction to the Old Testament in Greek* (Cambridge, 1902), p. 423.

[5] *I Apol.* v, Xen. *Mem.* i. 1; *I Apol.* xxxix, Eur. *Hipp.* 607; *I Apol.* xliv. *De Rep.* x, 617E; *II Apol.* iii, *De Rep.* x, 595C; *I Apol.* lx, *Tim.* 36.

[6] *I Apol.* iii.   [7] *II Apol.* x.

[8] *II Apol.* x. Justin alters the order and tense of the clauses, and for οὐ νομίζειν substitutes μὴ ἡγεῖσθαι.   [9] *II Apol.* xi.

[10] *I Apol.* xxi, xxii, xlvi; *Dial.* xliii, lxxxiv, c, *inter alia*.

events of the infancy.[1] Jesus, Justin says, waited in obscurity until he was about thirty years of age.[2] He records the mission of John the Baptist,[3] the baptism[4] and temptation[5] of Jesus; the characteristic features of his teaching;[6] the fact and variety of his miracles.[7] Justin gives quotations from, or references to, the accounts of the healing of the centurion's servant[8] and Matthew's feast;[9] the choosing of the twelve apostles;[10] the naming of Zebedee's sons;[11] the commissioning of the apostles;[12] Jesus' words after the departure of John the Baptist's messengers;[13] the sign of the prophet Jonah;[14] the parable of the Sower;[15] the Messianic confession of Peter;[16] and the prediction of the Passion.[17] The events of the Passion and resurrection are particularly fully recorded and documented. Justin gives passages which substantially correspond to parts of every chapter of St Matthew's Gospel—sometimes to narratives of considerable size—and to all but seven of the chapters of St Luke's Gospel. It is however to be noted that no words from the discourses of the Fourth Gospel appear in his writings.

The agreement between Justin's account of Jesus' life and teaching taken from the *Memoirs* and our Synoptic Gospels often extends to small particulars—and this is of significance. Thus his account of Jesus' infancy is identical with the Synoptic account apart from the statement that Christ was born in a cave and that the Magi came from Araþia.[18] The soberness of Justin's narrative is in marked contrast to the accounts in the second-century Apocryphal Gospels which go in for many embellishments. Justin refers to the enrolment under Cyrenius;[19] Jesus' growth from infancy to manhood;[20] he names the sons of Zebedee;[21] he records Jesus' silence at his trial;[22] Pilate's sending

---

[1] *I Apol.* xlvi; *Dial.* lxxviii, cii, cvi.
[2] *Dial.* lxxxviii.
[3] *Dial.* xlix, li, lxxxviii.
[4] *Dial.* lxxxviii.
[5] *Dial.* ciii, cxxv.
[6] *I Apol.* xiv; *Dial.* cii.
[7] *Dial.* xlix; *I Apol.* xxii, xxx, xxxi, xlviii; *Dial.* lxix.
[8] *Dial.* lxxvi, cxx, cxl.
[9] *I Apol.* xv.
[10] *I Apol.* xxxix; *Dial.* xlii.
[11] *Dial.* cvi.
[12] *I Apol.* xvi, xix, lxiii; *Dial.* xxxv, lxxxii.
[13] *I Apol.* lxiii; *Dial.* li, c, cvi.
[14] *Dial.* cvii.
[15] *Dial.* cxxv.
[16] *Dial.* c.
[17] *Dial.* li, cvi.
[18] *Dial.* lxxviii.
[19] *I Apol.* xxxiv, xlvi.
[20] *Dial.* lxxxviii.
[21] *Dial.* cvi.
[22] *Dial.* cii, ciii.

of him to Herod;[1] and the Jewish story that his body was stolen from the tomb by his disciples.[2] These coincidences in details, together with the general tenor of his account, suggest that Justin's *Memoirs* were in substance identical with our Synoptic Gospels whatever else they may have contained. Whether Justin knew the first three Gospels in the form of a primitive synopsis must however be left an open question.

What of the Fourth Gospel? Did Justin know and quote the Gospel composed nearest to his own time? We have already noted that uncertainty as to its apostolic authority on the part of Catholics apparently held back its recognition for some decades. We should not therefore expect, and do not find, any *direct* quotations from this Gospel in Justin's writings. Nevertheless, there are indications that Justin knew it or at the very least the theological background from which it emerged. In the first place Justin's use of the logos, strongly influenced though it is by the Middle Platonist philosophy, presupposes an earlier *Christian* use of the logos doctrine. Justin nowhere suggests he is introducing a *new* element into Christian thought. The very fact that St John's Gospel lacks the philosophical emphasis found in Justin's writings furnishes the presumption that Justin is working on an earlier Christian basis which had found previous expression in the Fourth Gospel.

This supposition would not however carry weight unless there are other considerations which suggest a tentative use by Justin of the Fourth Gospel or the tradition underlying it. J. N. Sanders, in *The Fourth Gospel in the Early Church*,[3] notes the following parallels between Justin and the Fourth Gospel.

Justin	Fourth Gospel
I Apol. xxxii. 10	John i. 14
xxxiii. 2	xiv. 29
lxi. 4	iii. 3, 5
lxiii. 15	i. 1
lxvi. 2	The Eucharistic teaching in John vi
Dial. xiv. 1	iv. 10
xiv. 8	xix. 37; cf. Rev. i. 7
xxvii. 5	vii. 22
xxxix. 5	xvi. 13

[1] *Dial.* ciii.   [2] *Dial.* cviii.   [3] (Cambridge, 1943), pp. 27–32.

Justin	Fourth Gospel
lvi. 11	v. 19
lxiii. 2	i. 13
lxix. 6	iv. 10, 14
lxix. 7	vii. 12
lxxxviii. 7	i. 20
xci. 4	iii. 14; cf. Barn. xii. 7
xcvii. 3	xix. 24
cvi. 1	xiii. 3
cx. 1	vii. 27
cx. 4	xv
cxxiii. 9	i. 12
cxxvii. 4	i. 18
cxxxv. 6	i. 13
cxxxvi. 3	xiii. 20, v. 46–7

Not all of these parallels are convincing, as Sanders notes, and nowhere is there a *direct* citation from the Fourth Gospel. The nearest is provided by *I Apol.* lxi. 4, 'For Christ said, "Unless you are born again (ἀναγεννηθῆτε) you will not enter into the Kingdom of heaven"', which seems to be a paraphrase or conflation of John iii. 3, 5. *Dial.* lxxxviii. 7, which represents John the Baptist as crying out 'I am not the Christ, but the voice of one crying...', is closer to John i. 20 than to the accounts in the Synoptic Gospels which do not make John deny that he is the Christ. However, the cumulative effect of these parallels is impressive and would support the cautious conclusion of Sanders:

The most reasonable conclusion from this examination of the passages from the writings of Justin which appear to show traces of the influence of the Fourth Gospel seems to be that on the whole one may say that certain passages are most naturally explained as reminiscences of the Fourth Gospel, while there are few, if any, which can certainly be said to be dependent upon it. It is therefore going farther than the evidence warrants to say that the theology of Justin is based upon the teaching of the Fourth Gospel. Justin's writings illustrate rather the first tentative use which was made of the Fourth Gospel by an orthodox writer, and this tentativeness makes it difficult to believe that Justin regarded the Fourth Gospel as Scripture or as the work of an apostle.[1]

[1] *The Fourth Gospel in the Early Church*, p. 31. This is substantially the view of H. Chadwick, *Early Christian Thought and the Classical Tradition* (Oxford, 1966), pp. 124–5.

It is however unlikely that Justin included the Fourth Gospel in his *Memoirs*, for in passages stated as coming from the *Memoirs* he never quotes or refers to a passage which could be attributed to that Gospel. Justin is tentatively feeling his way towards a recognition of the Fourth Gospel and in later Apologists this recognition becomes more explicit. Tatian, when he wrote his *Oratio*, c. A.D. 160–5, knew the Gospel which he quotes directly four times and later he included it in his *Diatessaron*. Irenaeus and Theophilus both recognised the Gospel as authoritative and as scripture in the full sense. Justin, however, wrote at a time when uncertainty still prevailed.

Justin's knowledge of the New Testament writings, outside the Gospels, can be described briefly. He mentions the Apocalypse by name: 'And further, there was a certain man with us, whose name was John, one of the apostles of Christ, who prophesied, by a revelation that was made to him, that those who believed in our Christ would dwell a thousand years in Jerusalem; and that thereafter the general, and, in short, the eternal resurrection and judgement of all men would likewise take place.'[1] This corresponds closely with Rev. xx. 2. Justin mentions the author by name as an instance of prophetic power at work in the Church although the status and authorship of the Apocalypse was clearly the subject of dispute in some circles. Dionysius of Alexandria says that even in his day there were people who discredited the Apocalypse because it predicted a literal reign of Christ on earth for a thousand years and in any case was written by Cerinthus the heretic.[2] Justin has no doubts that the Apocalypse is the work of John, the apostle and prophet.

Justin's writings contain no certain *quotations* from the rest of the New Testament writings although incidental allusions appear. He has contacts with Acts,[3] the Epistle to the Romans (Justin's argument about Abraham's circumcision in *Dial.* xxiii undoubtedly echoes Rom. iv. 10, 11),[4] I Corinthians,[5]

---

[1] *Dial.* lxxxi.   [2] *On the Gospels*, 3.

[3] *I Apol.* xlix, cf. Acts xiii. 27, 28, 48; *I Apol.* l, cf. Acts i. 8, 9, ii. 33; *Dial.* xvi, cf. Acts vii. 52; *I Apol.* xl, cf. Acts iv. 27.

[4] Cf. also *Dial.* xliv with Rom. ix. 7.

[5] Cf. *Dial.* xiv and cxi with I Cor. v. 8. Cf. also *Dial.* xxxix with I Cor. xii. 7–10.

II Thessalonians,[1] and the Epistles to the Galatians,[2] Colossians[3] and Hebrews.[4] Especially noticeable is the constant reiteration oι the Pauline phrase πρωτότοκος πάσης κτίσεως. The fact that Justin knew of Marcion's work and activity and was prepared to take issue with him is an indication that he was familiar with the Pauline Epistles. He has contacts with I John[5] and possibly with I Peter.[6] Only the Pastoral Epistles appear to have left no impression on Justin's writings.[7]

We conclude that Justin was familiar with the four Canonical Gospels. His *Memoirs* were in substance identical with our Synoptic Gospels; he valued St John's Gospel chiefly for doctrinal reasons and he was perhaps conscious that its apostolic authority was not everywhere accepted. Justin also knew most of the Epistles, with the exception of the Pastorals, although he nowhere cites them directly. This, no doubt, is to be explained by his apologetic purpose which prevented his appealing to purely *Christian* teachers and writings as authorities. For Justin the incarnation of the logos was the central fact of human history and it was therefore natural that he should give the original Christian teaching in the words of the logos, rather than in those of his followers.

JUSTIN, ORAL TRADITION AND UNCANONICAL GOSPELS

As is well known the early Fathers of the Church saw no incongruity in quoting from apocryphal books which they must have known were not accepted as authoritative by the Church.[8] Ignatius of Antioch quotes from the Gospel according to the

---

[1] Cf. *Dial.* xxxii with II Thess. ii. 3, 4, 8.

[2] Cf. *Dial.* xliv with Gal. iii.

[3] For references to πρωτότοκος see *I Apol.* xxiii, xxxiii, xlvi, liii, lxiii, *Dial.* lxxxiv, c, cxxv, cxxxviii. These seem to reflect Col. i. 15.

[4] In *I Apol.* xii, lxiii Christ is called ἀπόστολος; cf. Heb. iii. 1 only in New Testament.   [5] Cf. *Dial.* cxxiii with I John iii. 1–3.

[6] Cf. *Dial.* cxxxix with I Pet. iii. 9.

[7] Is it significant that the Gospel of Truth likewise shows no knowledge of the Pastorals?

[8] See R. P. C. Hanson, *Tradition in the Early Church*, pp. 224–34 for a good discussion.

Hebrews[1] and reproduces a saying 'near the sword is near to God' which also reappears in the Gospel of Thomas and is quoted by Origen.[2] The homily of unknown authorship known as II Clement quotes five sayings from apocryphal works or traditions one of which appears in the Gospel of Thomas.[3]

Justin gives several sayings, facts and details not found in the Canonical Gospels. He says that Cyrenius was the first procurator of Judaea;[4] that Joseph was 'of Bethlehem';[5] that Jesus was born in a cave near Bethlehem;[6] that the Magi were from Arabia;[7] and that Jesus was deformed, or not of a comely aspect, as had been predicted.[8] He speaks of John the Baptist 'sitting' by the Jordan[9] and states that when Jesus went down to the water to be baptised, a fire was kindled in the Jordan,[10] and that the voice from heaven repeated the words of Ps. ii. 7, 'Thou art my son; this day have I begotten thee.'[11] Justin states that Christ healed those who from birth were blind, dumb and lame[12] although the Jews ascribed these miracles to magic;[13] the ass's colt used in the Palm Sunday entry was found 'bound to a vine at the entrance of a village'.[14] He states that Pilate sent Jesus bound to Herod as a compliment;[15] and represents Herod Antipas as a successor of Archelaus in the dominion of Herod the Great.[16] At the crucifixion the mocking bystanders not only shook their heads and shot out their lips[17] but 'twisted their noses to each other'[18] and cried, 'Let Him who raised the dead deliver Himself'.[19] Moreover, Justin quotes two sayings of Christ not found in the Canonical Gospels, that is, 'In whatsoever I find you, in this will I also judge you';[20] and, 'there shall be schisms and heresies'.[21]

These are the only substantial deviations from the Canonical Gospels found in Justin's writings and it will be noted how few they are compared with the large area of agreement, even in small matters, between Justin and our Gospels. If Justin, as has

---

[1] *Ad Smyrn.* iii. 2, iv. 2.   [2] Logion 82; Origen. *Hom. in Jer.* xx. 3.
[3] II Clem. viii. 5, iv. 5, v. 3, ix. 11, xii. 2. Cf. Thomas logion 22.
[4] *I Apol.* xxxiv.   [5] *Dial.* lxxviii.   [6] *Dial.* lxxviii.
[7] *Dial.* lxxviii.   [8] *Dial.* xiv, xlix, lxxxi, lxxxviii, c, cx, cxxi.
[9] *Dial.* li, lxxxviii.   [10] *Dial.* lxxxviii.   [11] *Dial.* lxxxviii, ciii.
[12] *I Apol.* xxii.   [13] *Dial.* lxix.   [14] *I Apol.* xxxii.
[15] *Dial.* ciii.   [16] *Dial.* ciii.   [17] *I Apol.* xxxviii; *Dial.* ci.
[18] *Dial.* ciii.   [19] *I Apol.* xxxviii.   [20] *Dial.* xlvii.
[21] *Dial.* xxxv.

sometimes been supposed, was drawing widely on an Un-canonical Gospel or Gospels then we must suppose that this Gospel was more or less identical with the Synoptic Gospels.[1]

What, then, is the explanation of these differences? It is significant that Justin nowhere cites the authority of the *Memoirs* for these uncanonical details. In fact he is careful to avoid doing so as may be seen from his account of the fire kindled in the Jordan at Jesus' baptism where he explicitly makes the Apostles responsible *only* for the descent of the Spirit in the form of a dove. As to the differences some are obvious mistakes—such as the reference to Cyrenius as first procurator of Judaea—and his ignorance of the civil position of the Herods in Roman Palestine. Others are inferences drawn from the Gospels such as the description of Joseph as 'of Bethlehem' and Pilate's sending of Jesus bound to Herod as a compliment. Others are general summarising statements, no doubt coloured by tricks of memory, such as when Justin says that Christ healed not only the blind from birth, but also those born dumb and lame. In other instances a desire to show the fulfilment of prophecy has coloured Justin's words as in the description of Christ as deformed based on Isa. liii. 2, 'He was without form or comeliness.' In one case Justin reflects a textual difference found in certain MSS of the Gospels. The words of the Divine voice at the baptism, 'Thou art my Son, this day have I be-gotten thee', are found in D and the old Latin versions and may possibly represent a piece of floating tradition or a traditional interpretation. The detail about the fire kindled in the Jordan at Christ's baptism is also found in several Jewish-Christian works and in a fragment of Egerton Papyrus 2[2] and is akin to the great light on the Jordan at the baptism which is mentioned in Tatian's *Diatessaron* and in the Gospel of Thomas.[3] It seems to represent a traditional Jewish-Christian interpretation.

[1] This is the position adopted by E. R. Buckley, *J.T.S.* (April 1935), pp. 173–6, who believes that Justin first became acquainted with the sayings of Jesus in a single Gospel (now lost) from which he quotes; only later did he read our Synoptic Gospels. This 'solution' raises more difficulties than it solves.

[2] *Fr.* 2, verso, which also speaks of Jesus sprinkling something on the water, and as a result people are amazed. Cf. the anonymous *De Rebaptis-mate* 17(90) which says that the *Preaching of Paul* described a fire upon the water at Jesus' baptism. See Hanson, *Tradition in the Early Church*, p. 225.

[3] Hanson, *ibid.* p. 230.

The two extra-canonical sayings which Justin attributes to Jesus present difficult problems. The first, 'In whatsoever I find you, in this will I also judge you', is very well attested, but no writer, apart from Justin, attributes it to Jesus. Usually it is quoted without any indication of source, and if a source is mentioned it is ascribed to Ezekiel[1] or one of the prophets. Jeremias[2] points out that it is difficult to conceive that the dominical origin of such a frequently quoted saying should have been entirely forgotten if the saying is genuine, and he concludes that Justin took it from the apocryphal Book of Ezekiel but mistakenly attributed it to Jesus.

The second saying 'there shall be schisms and heresies' is also found in the Syrian *Didascalia* VI. 5, and the Pseudo-Clementine *Homilies* also contain two references to dominical prophecies about party strife.[3] As these sources appear to be independent of one another it is possible that the saying represents a very early floating tradition which was known to Justin. On the other hand it could be a free rendering of Matt. x. 35 f. reflecting the Church's own experience of party strife or an expression, in St Paul's language,[4] of Christ's warning against false prophets. In any case there is little to indicate that Justin is quoting from an Uncanonical Gospel.[5]

The uncanonical material found in Justin is of small compass compared with his agreements with the Canonical Gospels. The marvel is that so little legendary material appears in his works when we compare them with the fanciful accounts of the second-century apocryphal Gospels and even with traditions contained in other of the early Fathers. To compare Justin's sober account of the Magi with the account given by Ignatius of the Star of Bethlehem[6] some forty years before is most instructive. Justin always gives the simple, unadorned story rather than fanciful embellishments. His few differences from our Gospels are due to lapses of memory, a desire to show a fulfilment of prophecy, the use of traditional Jewish-Christian oral material and possibly certain apocryphal books.

---

[1] Athanasius, *Vita S. Antonii* 15; Joh. Climacus, *Scala paradisi* 7.

[2] *Unknown Sayings of Jesus* (London, 1964), pp. 28–9.

[3] Clem. *Hom.* II. 17, XVI. 21. [4] I Cor. xi. 18–19.

[5] Justin also knew the spurious *Acta Pilati* (*I Apol.* xxxv. 9, xlviii. 3) which he used to prove the correctness of his information about Jesus.

[6] *Ad. Eph.* xix.

JUSTIN'S USE OF TESTIMONIA

The phenomenon of quotations from the Old Testament which appear in the New Testament and Patristic writers has been the subject of much scholarly investigation in the last fifty years. While not the originator of this study[1] it was J. Rendel Harris who first put forward the theory, in his pioneer work *Testimonies*,[2] that there once existed a single collection of Old Testament texts which bore witness to Christ and Christianity and which existed *before* the composition of the Canonical Gospels. This 'apostolic work' was a *vade mecum* for all who wished to answer Jewish objections to the Gospel—it was the propaganda material of the new religion. Rendel Harris believed that this Book of Testimonies continued in existence throughout the first, second and third centuries and indeed was known as late as the twelfth, and perhaps even to the time of the invention of printing, although it received certain expansions and modifications in the course of the centuries.

This theory has now been generally abandoned, at least in the form in which Rendel Harris propounded it. Professor C. H. Dodd[3] has shown that the Testimonies from the Old Testament found in the New Testament were not drawn out at random but certain key passages were widely known and used and these belong together. These passages form the substructure of Christian theology and when a particular quotation is made the whole passage from which it was selected was in the mind of the writer. The discovery of the Dead Sea Scrolls has also provided evidence of a continuous work of biblical exegesis within Judaism which differed from rabbinical interpretation and exegesis. This employed the *pesher* method by which a series of historical events, contemporary with the writer, is regarded as the reality to which the Old Testament testimonies pointed forward. This sometimes involved, for the Qumran exegetes, alterations and modifications to the original texts to bring them into line with their beliefs.

[1] This belongs to E. Hatch. See his *Essays in Biblical Greek* (1889), p. 203. See also Sanday and Headlam, *I.C.C. Commentary on Romans* (1895), pp. 264, 282.

[2] 2 vols. (Cambridge, 1916 and 1920).

[3] *According to the Scriptures*. This book is of fundamental importance.

K. Stendahl[1] and B. Lindars[2] have carefully studied the Church's own version of the *midrash pesher*. The latter particularly emphasises the shift of application and modification of the text which sometimes occurred in quotations from well-known basic passages. This is most frequent in the Old Testament quotations found in Matthew and John although it also occurs elsewhere. According to Lindars a varied work of biblical exegesis went on in the early Church in the principal Church centres rather similar to the Qumran *Pesharim*.[3] This theory has received some criticisms but in general may be accepted. It is clear that no, one, fixed, stereotyped Testimony Book ever existed. Probably what we have to envisage is a series of Old Testament passages known in various centres, and interpreted according to a common method, which were drawn on *orally* by catechists, teachers and those engaged in anti-Jewish apologetic, together with a variety of partial transcripts committed to writing.[4] The early Church thus had access to a *corpus* of traditional interpretation of the Old Testament.

Recent study has not however considered questions which are germane to this book. Did the original basic *testimonia* continue to exert an influence on Patristic writers *after* New Testament times? How far in fact was the early Church's *pesher* method known and used? Were *new* testimonies drawn out from existing interpretation? By the time of Cyprian the Testimonies are found collected together and grouped under specific headings in written form. The real problem is the period between the New Testament and Cyprian and here the witness of Justin Martyr is crucial.

Justin's use of Old Testament Testimonies presents complicated problems. The very length of his quotations in the *Dialogue* with Trypho, in comparison with those in the New Testament, shows how the Testimonies grew in bulk and rules out the possibility that he is *only* carrying on the method found in the New Testament. Justin uses the Old Testament in a way which would appeal to educated Jews. He is not simply repro-

---

[1] *The School of St Matthew* (Uppsala, 1954).

[2] *New Testament Apologetic* (London, 1961).   [3] *Ibid.* p. 285.

[4] A similar situation is to be found in the Mission Field today where the catechist will sometimes deliver his teaching orally and sometimes from notes.

ducing texts in the manner of the New Testament or the *Dialogue* of Jason and Papiscus. The main burden of his argument is as follows:

(i) The Old Testament itself looks forward to the *torah* being superseded.

(ii) The Old Testament foretells the coming of the Messiah and predicts details about him which are fulfilled in Jesus. It tells of his two advents; of his pre-existence and divine nature; of his life on earth. Justin deals particularly with the coming of Elijah; the Virgin Birth; the descent of the Holy Spirit at the baptism; Jesus' humiliation, crucifixion and resurrection.

(iii) Justin believes in the millennium in a Jerusalem rebuilt, adorned and enlarged as foretold by Ezekiel, Isaiah and other prophets.

(iv) He dwells at some length on the Call of the Gentiles, God's present relation to the Jews and their behaviour towards him as foretold in the Old Testament.

In producing his massive catena of Old Testament texts in support of (i)–(iv) Justin passes far beyond the restrained use found in the New Testament. The *Dialogue* was too complicated a work to pass on 'the method' of testimony quotation easily and naturally. Justin is throughout dominated by his own theories as to how small incidents in the story of Christ were predicted in advance in the Old Testament. Typology, and the argument for literal fulfilment, are not distinguished, as in the New Testament, but merge into one another. Nevertheless, it would be an error to assume, and *a priori* unlikely, that Justin was totally ignorant of the *corpus* of traditional interpretation of the Old Testament known in the first century. We now give some examples of this:

(*a*) He knew some of the Church's *pesher* texts which he apparently quotes from memory reproducing variations found elsewhere. Thus in *I Apol.* xxxv. 11 he cites the testimony of the Triumphal Entry (Zech. ix. 9) in a form similar to that of Matt. xxi. 5 although including the introductory words of Zech. ix. 9 instead of substituting Isa. lxii. 11 for them. Yet Justin ascribes the text to Zephaniah. Lindars has acutely pointed out[1] that the opening words of Zech. ix. 9 are identical with Zeph. iii.

---

[1] *New Testament Apologetic*, p. 26 n. 2. This is a very valuable footnote.

14 in the LXX and that the briefer form of Zech. ix. 9 in John xii. 15 takes its opening words from Zeph. iii. 16 (M.T.). This suggests that Justin is dealing with a *pesher* text based on a correlation of Zechariah and Zephaniah. It would seem unlikely that Justin is borrowing *directly* from Matt. xxi. 5 in view of the differences between them; rather it looks as if he is quoting traditional interpretation from memory. It is interesting that he quotes this testimony again in *Dial.* liii. 3, this time closer to the LXX, and ascribes it correctly to Zechariah. This suggests he has looked it up in his copy of the LXX—no doubt in view of the knowledge of Trypho. It is indeed possible that many of Justin's erroneous attributions may have had a previous history in the Church's *midrash pesher*.[1]

(*b*) Justin knew certain of the Old Testament passages which Professor Dodd classifies as *primary* testimonia, i.e. passages which were understood as *wholes* although only particular verses from them might be quoted by the various New Testament writers. A good example of this is Justin's use of the famous Stone testimonium (and we shall deal mainly with this) which shows how a testimonium, originating with Jesus, had drawn to itself other testimonies by Justin's time. As is well known this testimony had its origin in the *verba Christi* Mark xii. 10–11; cf. Matt. xxi. 42, Luke xx. 7, 'Have ye not read even this scripture; the stone which the builders rejected, the same was made the cornerstone: This was from the Lord, and it is marvellous in our eyes?' This is an exact quotation of Ps. cxviii. 22–3 and it became one of

---

[1] Cf. *I Apol.* li. 8 f. (Dan. vii. 13 ascribed to Jeremiah); liii. 10 f. (Jer. ix. 26 ascribed to Isaiah); *Dial.* xii. 2 (Isa. vi. 10 ascribed to Jeremiah); xiv. 8 (Zech. xii. 10 ascribed to Hosea); xlix. 2 (Mal. iv. 5 ascribed to Zechariah). See further Lindars, *New Testament Apologetic*, p. 26. J. S. Sibinga's work on the Old Testament Text of Justin (see Appendix 3) is of great importance for the study of the testimony material in Justin. See also the important work of P. Prigent, *Justin et l'Ancien Testament* (Paris, 1964). Prigent identifies the reference in *I Apol.* xxvi. 8 to a lost treatise against all the heresies (the *Syntagma*) with a work used not only by Justin but by Irenaeus, Tertullian and other writers and which circulated widely in the early Church. This theory seems to be a return, in another form, to Rendel Harris' theory of a single testimony source. Dr R. A. Kraft points out to me (in a letter) that it is significant that the sections of Justin's writings which Prigent believes were originally in the *Syntagma* also rest heavily on the Testimonia and other school traditions. These are the important matters rather than the name of a particular stage in their history of growth and use. See further the review of Prigent by R. M. Grant in *J.T.S.* XVII (1966), 167–70.

'the sheet anchors of the early Church'.[1] From this basis other texts containing the word 'stone' soon became attached to the original testimonium—in particular Isa. viii. 14 and xxviii. 16. Thus I Pet. ii. 6–8 quotes Isa. xxviii. 16, Ps. cxviii. 22, Isa. viii. 14 in that order while Rom. ix. 33 conflates the two Isaianic passages—both writers quoting the testimonia in a version close to the Hebrew text. To this catena was added Dan. ii. 34, 44–5, which mentions the stone cut out of the mountain without hands which smites and breaks in pieces the feet of the great image. Luke xx. 18 appears to be the first to equate the Stone of Daniel with the earlier stone testimonia. There are therefore indications within the New Testament that the testimonies concerning the stone were growing in bulk, although how far, in the early stage, they remained in an oral stage of development cannot be ascertained with certainty. Certainly the *cento* Isa. xxviii. 16, Ps. cxviii. 22 and Isa. viii. 14 existed in writing in some areas in a version different from the LXX, although there is no indication of their inclusion in a written testimony book.

A later stage of the development of these stone testimonia occurs in Ep. Barn. vi. 2–4 (*c.* A.D. 120) where they occur as part of a series of proof texts which are referred to the plotting of the Jews against Jesus, the entry into Christ through baptism, the second creation and Christian worship. Barnabas has this sequence: Isa. vii. 14 or Dan. ii. 34, 45; Isa. xxviii. 16; Isa. xxviii. 17; Isa. l. 7; Ps. cxviii. 22; Ps. cxviii. 24. He clearly felt free to adapt and supplement the original testimonia in accordance with local needs—bringing in references to Isa. xxviii. 17, l. 7 and Ps. cxviii. 24 not found in the New Testament. This procedure does not suggest he was using a written Greek testimony book or directly quoting the New Testament Epistles.

This somewhat lengthy background is essential for the understanding of Justin Martyr's references to Christ as the Stone. This equation is very important for him as he frequently alludes to it and, in two passages, it appears among a series of headings:

For Christ is proclaimed as King and Priest and God and Lord and Angel and Man and Chief Captain and *Stone* and Child Born, and liable to suffering at first, then as going up to heaven and coming again with glory and having his Kingdom for ever, as I prove from all the scriptures (*Dial.* xxxiv. 2).

[1] E. G. Selwyn, *The First Epistle of St Peter*, p. 269.

He also is termed both Wisdom and Day and Dayspring and Sword and *Stone* and Rod and Jacob and Israel in this fashion or in that, in the words of the prophets...(*Dial.* c. 4).

In a remarkable passage Justin[1] says that the rock from which Mithra was born (and at which converts to Mithraism were initiated) was a deliberate imitation of the prophecy in Dan. ii. 34 f. 'a stone cut without hands out of a great mountain'. This passage from Daniel was of significance for Justin, for he quotes it again in *Dial.* lxxvi. 1: 'And his saying a stone cut without hands proclaims the same thing in a mystery. For saying that it has been cut out without hands means that it is not a human work, but of the will of God, the Father of the universe, who brought it forward',[2] i.e. the Messiah was not of human but of divine origin. This is the only Old Testament passage actually quoted by Justin in support of the testimonium Christ = the Stone, although twice he refers to other passages: 'And that Christ was proclaimed in figure as a Stone by many passages of Scripture we have likewise proved' (*Dial.* lxxxvi. 3); cf. *Dial.* cxxvi. 1, 'Christ and Stone by many'. Justin is certainly familiar with the earlier stone testimonia found in the New Testament such as Ps. cxviii. 22, Isa. viii. 14, xxviii. 16 (in any case he would have found them in the *Memoirs*), although he only quotes the Daniel prophecy.

In several passages Justin produces a new testimony to Christ as the Stone. He does not limit himself to this image but says that the circumcision by knives of stone (Josh. v. 2) suggests the same equation. True circumcision of the heart is only brought about by the true stone, Jesus Christ.

Jesus Christ circumcises all them who will, with knives of stone, as was proclaimed from of old...(*Dial.* xxiv. 2).

He (Joshua) is said to have circumcised the people with knives of stone as their second circumcision (which was a proclamation of that circumcision wherewith Jesus himself circumcises us, thus cleansing us from stones and all other idols) and making heaps of them who in every place were circumcised from their uncircumcision, that is to say from the error of the world, with knives of stone, (namely) the words of our Lord Jesus (*Dial.* cxiii. 6; cf. cxiv. 4).

[1] *Dial.* lxx. 1.

[2] The rabbis held that the great mountain is the King Messiah; see *Tanchuma* (Buber, Beresh. p. 140).

This testimonium to Christ as the Stone and New Circumciser is found later in the *Dialogue* of Athanasius and Zacchaeus 125 and in Aphraat *Hom.* xi on Circumcision 12. It may have originated with Justin himself in opposition to the Midrashic explanation which sees in the 'stone' the merits of the Fathers.[1]

We have dealt in some detail with this important primitive testimonium as it shows how, by Justin's day, references to Christ as the Stone were growing in bulk. Justin knows the early tradition, although he never quotes the primary testimonia found in the New Testament apart from Dan. ii. 34 f. which appealed to him. To these he has added Josh. v. 2. It is possible, although it cannot be proved, that in Justin's time the stone testimonia had been collected together under the heading 'Christ = the Stone'.

(*c*) Certain testimonies, which appear frequently in later Patristic writers, originated with Justin. A good example of this is Isa. viii. 14, 'The riches of Damascus and the spoil of Samaria shall be carried away before the King of Assyria.' According to Justin this is fulfilled in the coming of the Wise Men from the East to acknowledge Christ.

We cannot grant you [Justin says to Trypho], as you desire to expound it, that Hezekiah made war on the men in Damascus, or in Samaria, in the presence of the King of Assyria...And you cannot prove that this has ever happened to anyone among the Jews, but we can prove that it took place in the case of our Christ. For at the very time that he was born wise men came from Arabia and worshipped him, after they had first been to Herod who was king at that time in your land, whom the word calls the King of Assyria because of his godless and wicked mind.

And again:

That saying, also of Isaiah, 'He shall take the power of Damascus and the spoils of Samaria', meant that the power of the devil, who dwelt in Damascus, should be overcome by Christ at his very birth. And this proved to have taken place. For the Wise Men, who had been carried off as spoils for all kinds of evil actions, which were wrought in them by that daemon, by coming and worshipping

---

[1] Ex. R. on Exod. xii. 2.

Christ are shown to have departed from that power which had taken them as spoil, which (power) the word signified to us in a mystery as dwelling in Damascus.

Justin continues:

And that selfsame power, as being sinful and wicked, he rightly calls Samaria in parable. Now that Damascus did and does belong to the land of Arabia, even though it is now allotted to that which is called Syrophoenicia, not even any of you can deny. So that it would be well, Gentlemen, if you were to learn the things that you do not understand from them who have received grace from God, even us Christians, and not to be always striving to prop up your own doctrines, and do despite to those of God.[1]

We may briefly summarise our conclusions in this chapter. Justin frequently refers to the Memoirs of the Apostles. These Memoirs were in substance identical with our Synoptic Gospels. He also shows a tentative use of the Fourth Gospel although he was conscious that its authority was not everywhere accepted. Justin knew most of the other New Testament writings with the exception of the Pastoral Epistles, although nowhere quoting directly from them. Justin's uncanonical material probably came to him by way of traditional Jewish-Christian oral tradition and certain Apocryphal books. There is little to indicate that he was using any Uncanonical Gospel(s). In his use of Old Testament testimonies Justin follows the earlier *pesher* method of quotation, quoting some texts from memory and reproducing variations found elsewhere. He also knew certain of the primary testimonia, as classified by Professor Dodd, such as the stone testimonium, although he supplements these by new texts and interpretations. New testimonies also originate with him. The *Dialogue* was however too complicated a literary work to pass on the 'method' of testimony quotation easily and naturally. Justin is throughout strongly influenced by his own theories as to how small incidents in the life and work of Christ were predicted in advance in the Old Testament. Earlier testimonia are in fact immersed in a mass of prophecies which Justin believed had been literally fulfilled.

[1] *Dial.* lxxvii–lxxviii. 9–10.

CHAPTER VI

DOCTRINE OF GOD

As an Apologist Justin Martyr was required to set forth and defend the Christian doctrine of God. As a philosopher he had to show, amidst the eclecticism of his age, that he had truly found God.

Once Christianity had burst forth from its Jewish cradle and had gained a footing in the wider Gentile world the question of the unity and power of God, as against the vagaries of pagan worship, became a major consideration. So St Paul rejoiced in reminding the Thessalonians 'how they had turned to God from idols to serve a living and true God' (I Thess. i. 9). At Lystra he urged those who would have sacrificed to him 'to turn from these vanities unto the living God who made heaven and earth, and the sea, and all things that are therein' (Acts xiv. 15); and at Athens he spoke to his hearers of 'God that made the world and all things that are therein' and described him as 'Lord of heaven and earth' (Acts xvii. 24). This conception of God as the living Creator had first to be accepted before a Gentile could grasp the doctrine of the Incarnation; accordingly one great object of the Christian Apologists was to displace the current belief of the inhabitants of the Graeco-Roman world in a divine pantheon and to lead them on to a belief in one God, the Creator and Ruler of the universe. It was this constructive effort which met with bitter opposition and brought on the Christians persecution. Again and again the *Acts of the Martyrs* record that this was the searching question put to them: 'Would they submit to serve the daemons as all the nations did?' The reply was usually this: 'There is one God who made heaven and earth, and the sea, and all things therein, and one Lord Jesus Christ, the only Son of God: I will not sacrifice to any man; I will not sacrifice to daemons.' Tertullian, in *Apology* xvii–xviii, tried to show that underlying the popular phrases 'Which God grant', 'If God will', was a deeper belief in one God, to whom all power belongs, and to whose will all men look. But in general the Christians refused to attribute any

75

power or will to the pagan deities, let alone the *genius* of the Emperor, and for this refusal they were sometimes tortured and put to death.

The doctrine of God, in the pages of the New Testament, presupposed the monotheistic faith of Israel. But in the teaching of Jesus this assumed a form at once more deep and profound. Whereas in the Old Testament God was regarded as Father of the Universe, i.e. the Creator and Sustainer of the physical world, and in a moral and physical sense 'Father of Israel and the Israelites'—the sense of Fatherhood was limited by other conceptions.[1] In the teaching of Jesus this one idea of God as Father controls and determines everything else. 'My Father'[2] was a characteristic form of address—a conviction at once personal to himself. Yet Jesus also spoke to his disciples of God as 'your Father'[3] and so the close intimate communion he realised was to be theirs also. This Fatherhood of God extended to the good and evil alike, the just and the unjust; and God was Father of all animate things from the plants to the fowls of the air. The Fatherhood of God gave personal content to the Jewish monotheism which had been inherited from the Bible and which was essentially expressed in the idea of God as Creator and Sustainer of the universe.

The earliest Christian writers were much concerned with God as Creator and far less with his attribute of Fatherhood. This was quite natural in the face of the popular eclecticism of the age which addressed its worship to many deities. Thus, according to Hermas, the first commandment is to believe 'that God is one, who made all things and perfected them, and made all things to be out of that which was not, and contains all things, and is himself alone uncontained' (*Mand.* i. 1). For Clement of Rome God is 'the Father and Creator of the entire cosmos' (I Clem. xix. 2), and for the writers of the Epistle of Barnabas and the *Didache* 'our Maker' (Barn. xix. 2, *Did.* i. 2). A frequent designation, suggesting his universal sovereignty, was

[1] See J. F. Bethune-Baker, *An Introduction to the Early History of Christian Doctrine* (London, 1949), p. 12.

[2] Matt. xi. 27, vi. 4, 6, 8; John ii. 16, v. 17. Cf. St Paul's frequent use of the phrase 'The Father of our Lord Jesus Christ', Col. i. 3; Eph. i. 3; II Cor. i. 3, xi. 31.

[3] Matt. vi. 8, 15, x. 20; Luke vi. 36; cf. Matt. vi. 9; John xx. 17.

'the Lord Almighty',[1] 'the Lord who governs the whole universe',[2] and 'the Master of all things'.[3]

Although most of these ideas derive from the biblical background of the early Church they also reflect contemporary philosophic speculation. Thus Clement of Rome's references to God's ordering the cosmos[4] echo later Stoic beliefs. This influence becomes more pronounced in the writings of the Greek Apologists as would be expected in view of their philosophic training. Aristides of Athens opens his *Apology*[5] with an outline demonstration of God's existence based on Aristotle's well-known argument from motion. Although God is himself uncreated he has created everything for man; the heavens do not contain him—rather he contains them as he contains everything visible and invisible. Hence Christians acknowledge God as Creator and Demiurge of all things, and apart from him worship no other God.

This twofold background is also evident in the writings of Justin Martyr. As a result of his conversion to the Christian Faith and his subsequent life in the Church Justin had inherited the rich biblical doctrine of God. God had become a living reality to him and also a living factor in human history and life. Jesus Christ, the Son of God, had revealed God's character and will and through his gracious gift had brought him near to men. God was thus no impassive observer of human life but actively concerned in the conduct of his creatures as a gracious Father. Yet Justin remained a Platonist even after his conversion to Christianity. He retained the idea of God as unknowable and transcendent, the Unmoved first cause, Nameless and Unutterable, far removed from the struggles of day-to-day existence. Indeed it would be fair to say that this philosophic idea of God remained uppermost in his mind and threatened, at times, to overwhelm the more biblical and Christian idea which Justin knew as a fact of experience. We must now consider these two conceptions of Deity more fully:

(a) Justin's biblical and Christian background: This is shown

---

[1] *Did.* x. 3.   [2] Barn. xxi. 5.
[3] I Clem. viii. 2. See the discussion in J. N. D. Kelly, *Early Christian Doctrines*, p. 83.   [4] Chs. xx, xxxiii.
[5] i. 4. See the full discussion in Kelly, *Early Christian Doctrines*, p. 84.

in his insistence that God is not to be worshipped as if he needed anything[1] like the gods of the polytheists. On the other hand he is a living God, the most true,[2] the real,[3] alone having life in himself.[4] God exercises every noble quality—he is 'the Father of righteousness and temperance and other virtues'.[5] He is 'good',[6] especially towards men—the righteous observer of all things[7]—compassionate and long-suffering.[8] Thus he is 'the Father and Maker of all',[9] 'the Father and Lord of all',[10] 'the Father and King of the heavens',[11] or more simply 'the Father of all',[12] including Christ and man as well as the universe. According to Justin God knows both the actions and the thoughts of all his creatures[13] and can do whatever he wills.[14] He foreknows everything—not because events are necessary, nor because he has decreed that men shall act as they do or be what they are; but foreseeing all events he ordains reward or punishment accordingly.[15] God's interest in man is unceasing; he is no far away observer of human life[16] but is actively concerned in the conduct of his rational creatures,[17] requiring their obedience and enforcing his moral law.[18] He spares the wicked world that more people may be saved[19] and so that the hopes of the Christians may be fulfilled.[20] Indeed he created the world out of goodness for man's sake[21] and it was in accordance with his counsel that Christ came.[22] God cares not merely for the universe in general but for each individual in particular.[23]

It will be seen from these quotations—and more could have been given—that Justin is drawing on the biblical and Christian conception of God as a living Creator, a compassionate and long-suffering Father who in Christ has drawn near to his creation and who is concerned with the welfare of every individual soul. This was the God to whom Justin prayed and, with his fellow Christians, worshipped.

[1] *I Apol.* x. [2] *I Apol.* vi. [3] *I Apol.* xiii.
[4] *Dial.* vi. [5] *I Apol.* vi. [6] *I Apol.* xiv, xvi.
[7] *II Apol.* xii. [8] *Dial.* cviii. [9] *I Apol.* viii; *Dial.* cxl.
[10] *I Apol.* xii, xxxii. [11] *II Apol.* xii.
[12] *I Apol.* xii, xlv, lxv; *II Apol.* vi, ix; *Dial.* vii, xxxii, lvi, cv.
[13] *I Apol.* xii; *II Apol.* xii. [14] *I Apol.* xix; *Dial.* v, vi, xvi, cxlii.
[15] *I Apol.* xii, xliii, xliv; *II Apol.* vii. [16] *I Apol.* xxviii.
[17] *I Apol.* xxxvii. [18] *II Apol.* vii, ix. [19] *I Apol.* xxviii.
[20] *II Apol.* vii. [21] *I Apol.* x; *II Apol.* iv. [22] *II Apol.* vi.
[23] *Dial.* i.

(*b*) Justin's philosophical conception of Deity: Yet side by side with this idea of God is another which derives from his philosophical training and background. Justin particularly emphasises God's transcendence and rejects emphatically the Stoic idea of immanence which involved God in the process of flux and consequently in a change of nature.

For if they (i.e. the Stoics) say that human actions come to pass by fate, they will maintain either that God is nothing else than the things which are ever turning, and altering, and dissolving into the same things, and will appear to have had a comprehension only of things that are destructible, and to have looked on God himself as emerging both in part and in whole in every wickedness; or that neither vice nor virtue is anything; which is contrary to every sound idea, reason and sense.[1]

In opposition to this immanence Justin asserts that God cannot be identified with change or with motion in space.[2] He is transcendent, unchangeable,[3] eternal, passionless,[4] the incorruptible one.[5] Justin denies that God is in any way spatially determined whether by the universe as a whole or by a single place in the universe.[6] He attacks the Stoic identification of the Deity with the world precisely on the grounds of God's stability and freedom from change and motion in space.[7]

A corollary to this emphasis on the Divine Transcendence, far removed from this world, is Justin's assertion that God has no name.[8] The terms 'Father', 'God', 'Creator', 'Lord' and 'Master' do not describe what he is but are mere appellations to set forth his manifested activities.[9] In essence God is nameless because he came into existence from no external impulse and had no antecedents; hence there was no one to give him a name[10] as only a name given to a person by an elder is properly a name. Justin can even say that although there is pronounced over a person to be baptised the name of God the Father and Lord of the Universe, yet 'no one can utter the name of the ineffable God; and if anyone dares to say that there is a name, he raves with hopeless madness'.[11] Justin assumes that this idea of the

[1] *II Apol.* vii. [2] *Dial.* cxxvii. [3] *I Apol.* xiii.
[4] ἀπαθής. *I Apol.* xii; *II Apol.* xii. [5] *Dial.* v.
[6] *Dial.* cxxvii. [7] *II Apol.* vii, ix. [8] *I Apol.* x.
[9] *II Apol.* vi. [10] *Ibid.* [11] *I Apol.* lxi.

namelessness of God will be familiar to some of his readers: 'all the Jews even now teach that the nameless God spoke to Moses'.[1]

The unutterableness of God was another of Justin's emphases and on one occasion he combines this with the concept of namelessness,[2] although usually it appears alone. The term is intended to convey the immense chasm between God and man; God is beyond human reason and what little we comprehend of him is quite inexpressible. Only by revelation can man find the truth—and this revelation is enshrined in the teaching of the prophets and Jesus Christ.

We have noted earlier[3] that Justin reproduces the Aristotelian idea of God as Unmoved Mover who existed before the world was made. Yet as Aristotle insisted that the Deity must have activity so Justin says that God carries on the same ordering of the universe during the Sabbath as during all other days.[4]

A favourite term which Justin uses to describe the transcendence of God is *unbegotten* (ἀγέννητος). Goodenough[5] has pointed out that Justin consistently uses ἀγέννητος rather than ἀγένητος, which is the philosophical term expressing the fact that the Deity has no beginning and, as such, is superior to the exigencies of change and decay to which all other created beings are subject. ἀγέννητος, used by Justin, means unbegotten and is found more rarely than the other term. It signifies uncaused, not brought into existence from anything outside itself, and is properly applied to a self-caused being. So Aristotle: 'If there is nothing eternal, neither can there be any coming into existence; for any real thing which comes into existence necessarily presupposes some real thing from which it came into existence, and the last term of such a series must be unbegotten' (ἀγέννητος).[6] ἀγένητος, on the other hand, could only be applied to something which never had a beginning of any kind and is a more expressive term than ἀγέννητος for explaining the eternal nature of God. Christians, however, found ἀγέννητος useful in distinguishing God the Father from God the Son; the former was unbegotten, uncaused, while Christ was begotten, albeit eternally. Goodenough doubts whether Justin is using the correct term when he uses ἀγέννητος as the antithesis of

---

[1] *I Apol.* lxiii.   [2] *I Apol.* lxi.   [3] Pp. 30–1, 35–6. *Dial.* cxxvii.
[4] *Dial.* xxix.   [5] *Op. cit.* p. 129.   [6] *Metaph.* B 4, 999 b, 7 f.

ἀθάνατος and states blandly that Justin was a philosophical dilettante who confused the two words because he knew them largely from hearsay.[1]

If we could sum up Justin's philosophic idea of God we should say that God is for him the eternal, immovable, unchanging Cause and Ruler of the Universe, nameless and unutterable, unbegotten, residing far above the heavens, and is incapable of coming into immediate contact with any of his creatures, yet is observant of them although removed from them and unapproachable by them. God is the Universal Father, transcendent in his nature, who can act only through an intermediate being.

Where did Justin obtain this philosophic conception of the Deity? Goodenough is quite sure that his God is the God of Hellenistic Judaism and particularly that of Philo. 'The phrases and shreds of philosophical speculation about God are still recognisably a Christian adaptation of those of the Greek-Jewish school, and show no trace of an immediate borrowing from the pages or even the traditions of the schools of Greece.'[2] Thus Goodenough can quote Philonic parallels to many of Justin's statements: e.g. Justin's denial that God is spatially determined finds a parallel in Philo's argument in *Conf. Ling.* 136, 139: 'For who does not know that he who comes down must necessarily leave one place and occupy another?...God generated space and location along with bodies, and we may not assert that the Maker is contained in any of the things produced...Accordingly all terms of motion involving change of place are inapplicable to God in his true nature.'[3] Similarly Justin's coupling of the namelessness and unutterableness of God[4] is remarkably like a passage in Philo, *De Mutat. Nom.* 13 f., where Philo urges, in commenting on the incident of the burning bush, that God is unutterable and nameless. Any name which we use of God is not a name but only an appellation (πρόσρησις), for a name properly so called describes or limits the one named, while God has only revealed himself to man as 'the Existent' and is not more accurately to be described. Goodenough thinks that this passage is the origin of Justin's idea of God as unutterable and nameless. He believes this to be

---

[1] *Theology of Justin Martyr*, p. 130.
[2] *Ibid.* p. 124.   [3] *Ibid.* p. 125 n. 4.   [4] *I Apol.* lxi.

proved by Philo's further explanation that names are a symbol of created things; wherefore God, as the eldest of all beings, and as such having no predecessor who could have created or begotten him, is the nameless God.[1]

Goodenough's theory is, on the surface, attractive. We know that Philo's works were not preserved by his fellow Jews[2]— no doubt owing to the resurgence of Pharisaic Judaism following on the reconstruction of Judaism at Jamnia after A.D. 70 which looked with disfavour on Philo's attempt to bridge the gulf between the Greek and Jewish worlds. Philo's works were, it seems, preserved by the Church and influenced some early Christian writers such as the author of the Epistle of Barnabas, Clement of Alexandria, Origen and Eusebius. Yet caution is needed before we find in Philo the *primary* influence on Justin's philosophical conception of God. It is significant that nowhere else does Justin reflect any of Philo's typical views such as his allegorism and doctrine of the divine powers in the universe.[3] Nowhere does Justin show any *direct* acquaintance with Hellenistic Judaism other than with the Wisdom literature. I believe that full weight must be given to Justin's own account of his studies before becoming a Christian. He passed, as he says,[4] from contemporary Platonism into Christianity and he tells us that he was favourably disposed towards the former which was a true *praeparatio evangelica*. It is therefore *a priori* likely that his philosophical idea of God was at least influenced by the Middle Platonist *milieu* and teaching in which, Justin says, he progressed and made the greatest improvement daily.[5] We have shown in a previous chapter[6] that this was in fact the case in respect of his general philosophical approach. It is a

---

[1] Goodenough, *Theology of Justin Martyr*, p. 131.

[2] The first Jew to mention Philo by name after his time was A. de Rossi (A.D. 1573).

[3] E. A. Abbott, *Modern Review* (July 1882), was one of the first to claim direct literary dependence of Justin on Philo. His examples seem to me to be doubtful. Thus Justin uses the phrase λόγος σπερματικός in a way different from Philo; the description of the logos as ἕτερος (*Dial.* lv) than God is surely not dependent on Philo's δεύτερος θεός—it was a natural description to use in view of Justin's theology. Moreover, the illustration of the generation of the logos by the kindling of fire from fire may have been quite widespread. Far too much has been made of Philo's influence on Early Christian theology.

[4] *Dial.* ii.   [5] *Ibid.*   [6] Ch. III.

failing of Goodenough's approach when he states that Justin's origins lie in Hellenistic Judaism simply because his idea of God cannot be fitted into *Classical* Platonism. Contemporary Platonism, as we have seen,[1] was an eclectic amalgam of different, and at times contradictory, streams of philosophy and it is this which accounts for the particular emphases in Justin's idea of God. This is the source of his seeming inconsistencies rather than his being a philosophical dilettante.

Thus Justin's use of the Aristotelian idea of the non-spatial Unmoved Mover coupled with a Platonic emphasis on God's utter transcendence find their origin and background, as already noted,[2] in the system of Albinus the Middle Platonist. It is quite unnecessary to bring in Philo who, in any case, knew Plato and Aristotle only through the medium of Middle Platonism. Similarly, Justin's conception of God as nameless and unutterable, based on a passage in *Timaeus* 28c, reflects the ecclecticism of the Middle Platonists who interpreted this passage in the same way as Justin.[3]

Our conclusion is that two conceptions of the Deity existed in Justin's mind. On the one hand was his acceptance of the biblical and Christian idea of God as a living Creator, a compassionate Father who in Christ had drawn near to men and who was concerned with the welfare of each soul. On the other hand Justin retained the Middle Platonist emphasis on God as the unknowable and transcendent Cause far removed from the world and disconnected with it. Justin, as a Christian, knew the living God, yet it would seem that he could not formulate the divine indwelling in intellectual terms. In the *Dialogue* he defines God as 'that which always maintains the same nature, and in the same manner, and is the cause of all other things'.[4] He also appeals to Plato's description of that 'Being who is the cause of all discerned by the mind, having no colour, nor form, nor magnitude, nor anything visible to the eye; but it is something of this sort, that is beyond all essence, unutterable, and inexplicable, but alone beautiful and good, coming suddenly to souls that are naturally well-dispositioned on account of their affinity with, and desire to see, him'.[5] Justin had no real theory

---

[1] *Ibid.*   [2] Pp. 29–37.   [3] See more fully p. 35.
[4] *Dial.* iii.   [5] *Dial.* iv.

    6-2

of divine immanence to complement his emphasis on divine transcendence. His doctrine of the logos, soon to be discussed,[1] in fact kept the supreme Deity at a safe distance from intercourse with men and left the Platonic transcendence in all its bareness. God for Justin operated through the logos whose existence alone bridged the gulf which would have otherwise proved impassable. Justin worshipped the Father of Our Lord Jesus Christ; he prayed to the living God who had brought salvation in Christ; but it was not given to him, as a pioneer second-century Apologist, to unite transcendence and immanence in a system at once rational and biblical.

[1] Ch. VII.

CHAPTER VII

THE LOGOS

THE doctrine of the divine logos played an important part in the thought of the second-century Christian Apologists. By its use they were able to claim as 'Christian' anything that was good or noble in pagan literature and philosophy and to meet the pagan contention that what was good in Christianity was already to be found in paganism. Yet we should err if we said that the apologists had no aim but to use the logos as an apologetic convenience. It was also a theological necessity. It enabled them to solve, according to their own lights, the cosmological problem and to show that Christianity itself was as old as the creation. So Athenagoras can say: 'Our doctrine considers one God the creator of this universe, who himself has not come into being (for it is not that which is but that which is not that comes into being), but who has created all things through the logos who is beside him.'[1] Theophilus writes in similar vein: 'God created all things through his logos and wisdom, for by his Word were the heavens established, and all their power by his breath'[2] (Ps. xxxiii. 6).

Finally the logos doctrine provided a basis for the rather intellectual view of salvation that the Apologists put forward in their writings, viz. that Christ as the logos was primarily a teacher whose *words* brought salvation to men. Justin puts this succinctly: 'Jesus Christ is the only son begotten properly by God, since he is by nature his Logos and first-born and power; and by his counsel he became man and taught us these things for the relief and elevation of the human race.'[3]

Before considering Justin's idea of the logos in detail we must give a brief description of its wide background in Graeco-Roman thought and in Judaism. The doctrine of the logos, in

---

[1] *Supplicatio pro Christianis* iv. 2.

[2] *ad Autolycum* I. vii. I owe this and the previous reference to J. N. Sanders, *The Fourth Gospel in the Early Church*, p. 24.

[3] *I Apol.* xxiii. On the other hand it is only fair to state that in the *Dialogue* Justin emphasises that salvation is effected through the death of Christ. E.g. *Dial.* xii, xiii.

various forms, was widely held in the Graeco-Roman world. The word itself has many meanings most of which are subsumed under the two heads of inward thought and the outward expression of thought in speech. In any form of Theism logos could easily be used to account for a divine revelation, God's Word being communicated by his speech. But in Stoicism logos had lent itself to pantheistic use and was equated with the rational principle in accordance with which the universe existed, i.e. with God.[1] Human beings, for the Stoics, were endowed in varying degrees with seed forces (σπερματικοὶ λόγοι) which were part of this rational principle or logos of God. In the fusion of Stoicism and Platonism found among the Middle Platonists the rational principle of the Stoic Universe was the logos of God.

In the Greek Old Testament logos is frequently used of the Word of God in Creation[2] and of the message of the prophets by means of which God communicates his will to his people.[3] In all Septuagint passages the meaning is not abstract, but spoken, active communication. In later Judaism, as a result of an emphasis on Divine Transcendence, the doctrine of the Word took on a new emphasis. In the Targums of the Old Testament the Aramaic word *Memra* or Word is frequently used. It is doubtful if this was a hypostasis; rather it seems to be a way of speaking about God without using his name and thus avoiding the anthropomorphisms of the Old Testament.[4] It is largely a phenomenon of translation. A more significant approach is found in the Wisdom literature where the concept of Wisdom (*hokhmah*) was not simply 'being wise', but seems to be in some degree a personification which stood by the side of God and was concerned with the created world.[5]

[1] 'In the Stoic doctrine the λόγος is not an emanation or hypostasis of God. It is the supreme principle. The Stoic does not have a God, one of whose attributes is λόγος. He has one God who can be called indifferently νοῦς, εἱμαρμένη, Ζεύς, and many other names including λόγος. These are just names for one and the same being.' T. W. Manson, *On Paul and John* (London, 1963), p. 139.

[2] Gen. i. 3, 6, 9; Ps. xxxiii. 6. [3] Jer. i. 4; Ezek. i. 3; Amos iii. 1.

[4] Cf. Gen. iii. 8, 'They heard the voice of the Lord God', which is rendered by Targ. Onqelos, 'They heard the voice of the *memra* of the Lord God'.

[5] Prov. viii. 22; Wisd. vii. 22, 27. We cannot tell how far these passages imply a separate existence of Wisdom or whether they are poetic language.

In speculative Judaism Wisdom had two successors. The first, Philo, introduced the Stoic-Platonic logos of Middle Platonism into Judaism. It is a profitless task to seek for a consistent doctrine of the logos in Philo's voluminous writings. He identifies the logos with Old Testament *personalia*, such as the High Priest, by means of allegorical interpretation and particularly emphasises its cosmological functions much as Wisdom had cosmological associations in the Wisdom literature. He also refers to the ideal world, of which the present world is a copy, as ὁ θεοῦ λόγος.[1] The logos is also the ideal, primal Man, the image of God from whom spring and decline all mortal men. The essence of Philo's view of the logos appears to derive from Greek thought (especially Plato's *Timaeus*) as interpreted by the Middle Platonism of his day.[2] The second successor to speculative Judaism was the rabbinic emphasis on the *torah* as the equivalent to the divine wisdom. The *torah* came to be described in personal terms and to have a cosmological and soteriological role.

This widespread background to the idea of the logos lies behind the use of the term in the early Church. C. K. Barrett has well said: 'It is however an error to think that early Christian theologians (such as St John) made a neat amalgam of Hellenistic and Jewish speculation on the subject of mediation and applied it to Christ.'[3] Rather they begin with Jesus as the fulfilment of God's purposes, the logos which God has spoken and who lived a historical life on earth. The logos had become flesh—that was the line which divided Christian speculation from the speculations of Hellenistic and Rabbinic Judaism and Philo. However, in using the idea of the logos early Christian writers no doubt were appealing obliquely to the contemporary world so that both Jewish and Greek readers would understand their meaning.

The second-century Apologists had behind them earlier Jewish and Greek speculation, the logos theory of St John as well as subsequent Christian speculation. Ignatius of Antioch, in incidental references, states that Jesus Christ is the logos who

---

[1] *De Opif. Mundi*, xxiv f.
[2] But note W. Scott, *Hermetica*, II, 14 f.: 'Philo's Logos may be regarded as the Stoic God dematerialized, with a supracosmic God set up above him.'
[3] *The Gospel According to St John*, p. 129.

came forth from silence,[1] the only utterance of God, the unlying mouth by which the Father spake truly;[2] he is God made manifest in human wise.[3] The unknown author of the Epistle to Diognetus[4] declares the logos to be no servant or angel or prince, but the Artificer and Creator to whom all things are placed in subjection. He was sent as a king sends his son with a view to saving men—not by constraint but by persuasion. Yet neither of these writers really deals with the relationship of Christ to the Father in the Godhead or explains how this is related to his manifestation in space and time. They affirm by incidental allusion rather than explain.

The second-century Apologists were called to defend their faith to a wider pagan world. They were the first to give an intellectual explanation as to the relation of Christ to the Father and his coming from the Godhead into the world of time, for they could not assume that their readers accepted this as a fact of experience. This was no easy task as the Apologists, accepting the biblical faith, were as ardent monotheists as the Jews. Justin Martyr, as a pioneer Apologist, takes over and develops the earlier Christian use of the logos. He introduces the term as a familiar one to both Christian and non-Christian. But, unlike St John, and as with his doctrine of God, Justin admits a larger element of philosophical speculation into his conception of the logos. Indeed Goodenough believes that Justin is wholly dependent on Philo in this connection;[5] other scholars have pointed to Stoicism as the *fons et origo* of his doctrine while, more recently, Andresen[6] has pointed to Middle Platonism as a decisive influence on Justin. But before considering these views it is necessary to give an account of Justin's teaching on the logos.

Justin uses the term in the *Apologies* to explain the divine nature of Jesus Christ—why he is called Son of God and worshipped by Christians—as well as to explain the relation of Christianity to other truth. In the *Dialogue* with Trypho Justin uses it to show that Christ was the God who appeared to the

---

[1] *Ad Magn.* viii. The concept of Σιγή seems to owe something to Valentinian speculation. [2] *Ad Rom.* viii.
[3] *Ad Eph.* xix. [4] *Ad Diogn.* vii–x.
[5] *The Theology of Justin Martyr*, pp. 139–75.
[6] *Z.N.T.W.* xliv (1952–3), 157–95.

Jewish patriarchs in the theophanies recorded in the Old Testament.

Justin's starting point is that the logos is the personal Reason of God in which all men partake. So he states: 'For not only among the Greeks did logos prevail to condemn these things through Socrates, but also among the barbarians were they condemned by the logos himself, who took form, and became man, and was called Jesus Christ.'[1] Hence there were Christians before Christ—men who possessed seeds of the logos and so arrived at facets of the truth: 'We have declared above that he (i.e. Christ) is the logos of whom every race of men were partakers; and that those who lived reasonably (μετὰ λόγου) are Christians though they have been thought atheists; as, among the Greeks, Socrates and Heraclitus, and men like them; and among the barbarians Abraham, Ananias, Azarias, Misael and Elias and many others whose nations and names we now decline to recount, because we know it would be tedious.'[2] Justin, however, emphasises that the whole logos only resided in Jesus Christ and accordingly those who partook of a part of the logos often contradicted themselves.[3]

In developing the biblical teaching of the Incarnation of the logos in Christ Justin conceived of him as the Father's intelligence or rational thought. Yet Justin realised that such a belief did not do justice to the fundamental Christian idea of Jesus as a separate being. So he argued that the logos was not only in name distinct from the Father, as the light is from the sun, but was also numerically distinct (ἕτερος ἀριθμῷ),[4] which meant for Justin 'different in person'.[5] The sharp personality ascribed to the logos distinguishes Justin's use from the prologue of the Fourth Gospel and also from Philo's usage.

It was in conflict with Jewish monotheism that Justin particularly developed his view as to the duality in the heart of the Godhead. Thus the otherness of the logos is evident (a) by the divine theophanies recorded in the Old Testament (e.g. that to Abraham by the oaks of Mamre, to Jacob, to Moses, etc.),[6] which point to another than God who appeared to these

---

[1] *I Apol.* v.　　　　　　[2] *I Apol.* xlvi.　　　　　　[3] *II Apol.* x.
[4] *Dial.* lxi, lxii, cxxviii, cxxix.
[5] Noted by Goodenough, *The Theology of Justin Martyr*, p. 146.
[6] *Dial.* lvi–lx.

patriarchs. This proof, based on Justin's peculiar exegesis of the Old Testament, is given at great length. This 'other' is called Angel, and God, and Lord, and Man.[1]

(*b*) By the Old Testament passages which represent God as conversing to another who is a rational being like himself. The stock passage used by Justin was Gen. i. 26, 'Let *us* make man after our image and likeness.' Cf. *Dial.* lxii.

(*c*) By the great texts found in the Wisdom literature which imply either a poetic or a real personification of Wisdom (e.g. Prov. viii. 22 f.), which Justin quotes with the interpretation: 'You perceive, my hearers, if you bestow attention, that the Scripture has declared that this offspring was begotten by the Father before all things were created; and that that which is begotten is numerically distinct from that which begets, anyone will admit.'[2]

Justin perceived that his biblical proofs for the numerical distinction of the logos from God could easily be turned against him and land him in ditheism. Hence he emphasises the unity of the Father and the logos anterior to the creation. The logos, according to Justin, was begotten by the Will and Power of God, as a preparatory step before the creation of the universe. The logos is 'a beginning before all created things'[3] (ἀρχὴ πρὸ πάντων τῶν ποιημάτων). As the Incarnate logos marked the beginning of the Christian race so the logos, though himself not created, marked the beginning of created things. This certainly seems to imply that Justin held that the logos was begotten not long before the creation although he does not speculate on the eternal nature of the Godhead. Yet he is clear that the logos is essentially a unity with the Father—indeed he was begotten by the Father's Will out of the Father himself. He is the Offspring who was really brought forth from the Father, and who was with the Father, and with whom the Father communed. He was not a creature, in the later Arian sense, neither was he an emanation from God like the rays from the sun; nor did he proceed from God by abscission such that the being of the Father was diminished. Justin illustrates the generation of the logos by the analogy of the spoken word and by the kindling of fire by fire which does not diminish the original fire.[4] The logos, for Justin, was not eternal in the later Nicene sense—yet he was the

---

[1] *Dial.* lix.   [2] *Dial.* cxxix.   [3] *Dial.* lxii.
[4] Justin does not use the terms λόγος ἐνδιάθετος, λόγος προφορικός.

product of the Father's Will. He was no emanation, no mode of appearance, no temporary effulgence of divine glory—but in essence a unity with the Father although distinct in personality. Hence the logos is called God and divine although depending on the exercise of the Father's Will.

Justin has one further point. The logos is for him essentially generated for the purpose of creation and revelation, as the agent and servant of the Father. On the one hand the Father communes with the logos and on the other the logos is the organ of creation which God conceived and made by him.[1] He is also the Father's messenger[2] (ἄγγελος, ἀπόστολος) and minister (ὑπηρέτης)[3] capable of immediate self-revelation to his creatures. As with the concept of Wisdom in the Jewish Wisdom literature the logos is the medium between the Transcendent God and the finite universe. He is thus subordinate to the Father, both as to his person which was begotten at some point anterior to the creation, and as to his office. Justin says that he is worshipped by Christians in the second place after God the Father of all.[4]

Such is the nature and function of the logos according to Justin Martyr. Where did he obtain his conception of the logos? What influences determined and shaped his attempt to explain the relationship between Christ and the Father and between Christianity and other knowledge? It would be fair to say that there is a wide divergence of opinion among scholars on this question—wider than that concerning the origin and use of the logos by St John. This is because Justin is more influenced by prevailing philosophical speculation than the writer of the Fourth Gospel—and it is precisely this philosophic element which is difficult to assess accurately.

We have already noted that Justin Martyr takes over the earlier Christian use of the logos. It must be emphasised that he is a biblical thinker and, whatever the philosophical influences to which he was exposed, this remained a primary influence. For Justin the logos was first and foremost Jesus Christ. He was the 'whole Word'.[5] Creation proceeded through him. Re-

---

[1] *I Apol.* lxiv; *II Apol.* vi; *Dial.* lxxxiv.   [2] *I Apol.* lxiii.
[3] *Dial.* lvi, lvii, lx, cxiii, cxxv, cxxvi.   [4] *I Apol.* vi, xiii, lxi.
[5] *II Apol.* viii, x, ἐπειδὴ δὲ οὐ πάντα τὰ τοῦ λόγου ἐγνώρισαν, ὅς ἐστι Χριστός.

demption flowed from his Incarnation, death and resurrection. 'He is the power of the ineffable Father, and not the mere instrument of human reason.'[1] This equation of the logos with Jesus Christ at once differentiates Justin from Stoicism and Philo, for whom history in the last resort had no meaning.

Whether Justin took over the idea of the logos direct from the Fourth Gospel or from the tradition of the Church as he knew it cannot be answered with certainty. We know that the logos doctrine was known in different Christian centres in the second century—particularly in places influenced by the Johannine theology such as Rome, Ephesus, Antioch and Alexandria. The very fact that Justin attempted to explain this belief philosophically testifies, with the whole philosophic movement in the early Church, to the previous existence of a non-philosophic belief. The Johannine logos is ultimately non-philosophical, for it is based on the Old Testament Word of the Lord active in creation and revelation.[2]

It was in his philosophical development of the logos idea that Justin admitted a larger element of non-biblical interpretation and we shall now consider this:

(a) Since the important work of Goodenough[3] it has often been assumed that *Philo's* doctrine of the logos and divine powers is the key which will unlock the secrets of Justin's thought. It is of course true, and full weight must be given to it, that there was a widespread Hellenistic-Jewish tradition which was regarded with favour by the Church—the more so after the period A.D. 70–135 when this tradition had fallen into disfavour with the Jews under the influence of the more rigid Pharisaic Rabbinism of Jamnia. But to assert an affinity with Hellenistic Judaism is something different from asserting *direct* influence of one particular Hellenistic-Jewish thinker on one particular Christian philosopher. It is this that Goodenough tries to do with reference to Philo and Justin Martyr. He be-

---

[1] *II Apol.* x, ἐπειδὴ δύναμίς ἐστι τοῦ ἀρρήτου πατρὸς καὶ οὐκ ἀνθρωπείου λόγου τὰ σκεύη.

[2] The best statement of this view is to be found in Manson, *On Paul and John*, pp. 136–59. It is however possible that there existed, in the early Church, a logos theology independent of the Fourth Gospel.

[3] *The Theology of Justin Martyr*, pp. 139–75.

lieves that *the titles* which Justin applies to the logos conclusively prove this dependence.[1] Let us look at his argument in detail:

(i) Justin four times states of the logos that 'the dayspring (or East) is his name' (ἀνατολὴ ὄνομα αὐτῷ)[2] with reference to Zech. vi. 12. These references occur amidst other titles based directly on Old Testament passages such as Num. xxiv. 17; Ps. lxxii. 17. Philo, on the other hand, says that ἀνατολή in Zech. vi. 12 could not refer to a man of body and soul but only to that incorporeal one who differs in no respect from the divine image of God.[3] It is difficult to trace any direct dependence here, for Philo is using his customary allegory while Justin is simply using the familiar Messianic interpretation of the Old Testament.

(ii) Goodenough believes that the title Stone or Rock which Justin derives from several Old Testament passages[4] is dependent on Philo. He particularly instances Philo's comment on the rock from which water flowed in the wilderness as 'the Wisdom of God which as the highest and first rock he cut off from his own powers, from which he gave drink to God-loving souls'.[5] Such a passage as Justin *Dial.* lxxvi. 1 is directly dependent on Philo: 'And his saying a stone cut without hands proclaims the same thing in a mystery. For saying that it has been cut out without hands means that it is not a human work, but of the will of God, the Father of the universe, who brought it forward.' Such an argument is however precarious as both passages depend on Dan. ii. 34, 45 (LXX). Moreover, the title stone or rock applied to Jesus was one of the primary *testimonia* in use in the early Church and is found in the New Testament.[6] Justin is developing earlier Christian exegesis rather than taking over Hellenistic-Jewish exegesis. It is not without significance that the stone cut out of the mountain mentioned in Daniel had been equated by Christian writers with the stone of Ps. cxviii. 22 and Isa. viii. 14 *before* the time of Justin; cf. Luke xx. 18 and Barn. vi. 2–4. There is therefore no need

---

[1] *Ibid.* pp. 168–73.   [2] *Dial.* c, cvi, cxxi, cxxvi.
[3] *De Conf. Ling.* lxii.
[4] *Dial.* xxxiv, xxxvi, lxx, lxxvi, xc, xciii, c, cxiv, cxxvi.
[5] *Leg. Al.* ii. 86.
[6] Mark xii. 10–11; Matt. xxi. 42; Luke xx. 7 based on Ps. cxviii. 22–3; cf. I Pet. ii. 6–8; Rom. ix. 33. See pp. 70–3.

to bring Philo into the discussion. Justin is primarily dependent on earlier Christian Messianic exegesis. It is, however, just possible that both Justin and Philo were acquainted with a rabbinic Haggadah on these Old Testament passages where various Stone texts are linked together.[1]

(iii) Justin, in one passage,[2] states that the logos *was* the beginning (ἀρχή) before all created works and did not simply exist ἐν ἀρχῇ. Philo twice uses the term ἀρχή in lists of titles of the logos.[3] But both writers appear to be using Prov. viii. 22—Justin explicitly says so—and it is unnecessary to postulate direct dependence. Indeed, as Goodenough admits, in the only passage in which Philo *quotes* Prov. viii. 22 he has πρωτίστην for the LXX ἀρχήν.

(iv) Justin uses the word ἡμέρα as a title for the logos in one passage: 'He also is termed both Wisdom and *Day* and Dayspring and Sword and Stone etc.'[4] He is the first Christian writer to do this although the word had later a varied use in Christian controversy.[5] Goodenough believes that Philo used the word for the logos and thus provided the antecedent for Justin's use. He is, however, involved in a tortuous exegesis of *De Opif. Mundi* xxxv to prove this. All that can be shown is that Philo uses φῶς of the logos as in *De Opif. Mundi* xxxi, τὸ δὲ ἀόρατον καὶ νοητὸν φῶς ἐκεῖνο θείου λόγου, which is quite a different thing from equating ἡμέρα with the logos. In view of the context of Justin's use in a catena of titles drawn from the Old Testament it seems more probable that he has derived this from Ps. cxviii. 24, 'This is the day which the Lord hath made.' It is not without significance that the author of the Epistle of Barnabas uses this text in a passage where Christ is equated with the Stone,[6] as in Justin, which may suggest that earlier Christian exegesis lies behind Justin's use.

(v) Justin says that the logos is called ἀνήρ and ἄνθρωπος because he appears in the likeness of such form as the Father wills.[7] He appeared to Abraham ἐν ἰδέᾳ ἀνδρός and to Jacob ἐν ἰδέᾳ ἀνθρώπου.[8] Philo also says that the logos is ὁ κατ' εἰκόνα

---

[1] See J. Daniélou, *Sacramentum Futuri*, p. 187; R. P. C. Hanson, *Allegory and Event*, pp. 22–3.　　[2] *Dial.* lxii.

[3] *De Conf. Ling.* 146; *Leg. Al.* I. 43.　　[4] *Dial.* c.

[5] See Clem. Alex. *Strom.* vi. 16, 145. See J. R. Harris, *Expositor*, 8th series, xiv (1917), 145–51.　　[6] *Barn.* vi. 4.　　[7] *Dial.* cxxviii.

[8] *Dial.* lviii.

ἄνθρωπος.[1] But in these passages Justin is interpreting Old Testament passages in the light of his belief that it was the logos who appeared to the patriarchs and it seems quite unnecessary to bring in Philo.

(vi) Justin calls the logos or Christ 'Israel' and 'Jacob' and is fond of using the two titles together.[2] He expounds the names as signifying a parallelism between Jacob, who was surnamed Israel, and who gave his name to the Israelites, and Christ, from whom the Christians have received their name. Philo, on the other hand, uses Israel as a title for the logos but explains it to mean 'Him who sees God'.[3] The 'house of Israel' signifies the human soul in which dwells the νοῦς which can see God. Philo does not use 'Jacob' as a logos title. It would appear that Justin and Philo are moving in different worlds of thought. The former is simply giving a typical Christian explanation of the Old Testament while Philo is allegorising biblical texts along psychological lines.

(vii) One of Justin's favourite titles for the logos is 'first begotten' (πρωτότοκος). Goodenough makes the extraordinary assertion that this is a verbal variant of Philo's πρεσβύτατος θεοῦ υἱὸς πρωτόγονος κτλ. which occurs in several passages in that writer.[4] It is, however, far more likely that Justin took this from the Christian tradition as he knew it or even directly from St Paul[5] where it already has a Christological connotation.

(viii) Two last titles which Justin uses of the logos are 'Priest' and 'King'.[6] Justin derives the former from Ps. cx. 4, 'Thou art a Priest forever after the order of Melchizedek' which is also used in the Epistle to the Hebrews. Philo finds in Melchizedek a figure both of the Kingly and Priestly character of the logos,[7] but he does not use this verse from the Psalms.

On the basis of the above Goodenough concludes that Justin is dependent on Philo for his titles of the logos—even in drawing up lists of titles. But, as we have seen, some of the points of similarity are due to both Justin and Philo being dependent on

---

[1] *De Conf. Ling.* 146. [2] *Dial.* cxxiii, cxxvi.
[3] *De Conf. Ling.* 146; *De Mut. Nom.* 81.
[4] *De Agr. Noe* 51; *De Conf. Ling.* 63, 146; *De Somn.* i. 215; *Leg. Al.* iii. 175.
[5] Col. i. 15, 18; Rom. viii. 29; cf. Heb. i. 6; Rev. i. 5, ii. 8.
[6] *Dial.* cxviii. [7] *Leg. Al.* iii. 79 f.

the Old Testament. Philo is an eclectic thinker and his system, if such it can be called, is based on a mixture of material inherited or acquired from his predecessors and Greek teachers. But he also has antecedents in non-philosophical Judaism such as when he calls angels λόγοι θεοῦ, when he calls the Old Testament ὁ ἱερὸς λόγος, and when he compares the High Priest to the divine Word. Philo is here using λόγος not in the Stoic sense of the immanent universal Reason but as the 'Word' or Speech of God. Both Philo and Justin have used the same source, the Old Testament, although Justin also draws on early Christian exegesis of the Old Testament. Philo's λόγος is ultimately Stoicism or Middle Platonism blended with the Old Testament 'Word of God'.[1] Justin's λόγος is Jesus Christ understood in the light of the same Old Testament 'Word of God' and Greek philosophy. But to postulate Philo as Justin's immediate source is to go beyond the evidence. At the most he was a peripheral influence on Justin. In fact it may well be the case that Philo's influence on early Christian thought has been exaggerated and was confined at the most to Christian literature emanating from Alexandria, such as the Epistle of Barnabas and the writings of Clement of Alexandria. It is a fact often forgotten that Justin never mentions Philo, while he does mention his philosophic environment in Middle Platonism from which he passed into Christianity. This must now concern us in connection with Justin's logos doctrine.

(b) A characteristic of Justin is his use of the term λόγος σπερματικός of the universal activity of the logos. For Justin each thinker, inasmuch as he conformed to the truth and spoke well, partook of a portion of this Seminal or Spermatic logos which in its entirety was Jesus Christ.[2] The seeds of truth sown in the hearts of men were the formative principle of right knowledge and right living.[3] Thus there were Christians before Christ,[4] and Christianity was brought into relationship with wider truth.

It has often been assumed that Justin is dependent on Stoicism

[1] See the excellent discussion in T. W. Manson, *On Paul and John*, pp. 140–1, 149.

[2] *II Apol.* viii, xiii. J. H. Waszink, *Festschrift Theodor Klauser* (1964), p. 387, has however queried the usual English translation 'share or portion of the Spermatic Logos' and would prefer 'part of the sowing logos' which is identical with Christ.

[3] *I Apol.* xliv.   [4] *I Apol.* xlvi.

for this idea of the λόγος σπερματικός.[1] For the Stoics the primal principle of fire was designated σπερματικὸς λόγος τοῦ κόσμου. In their cosmological pantheism the souls of men partook of the world substance of fire. The λόγος σπερματικός could be conceived in Stoic physiology as a fine gas which flowed into the bodily senses and functions and even into the sexual excretion. When this gaseous element from the male united with a similar gaseous element in the female conception took place. It is clear that in Stoicism we are dealing with a material conception which equated the λόγος σπερματικός with the pantheistic World Pneuma. It is in no way a spiritual or ethical principle which the λόγος σπερματικός certainly is for Justin, as may be seen from *I Apol.* xliv. Here everything that philosophers and poets have said about the immortality of the soul, punishments after death, and the contemplation of heavenly things, and all such theories, indicates that in all of them 'seeds of truth' are present. When Justin attributes the contradictions among the poets and philosophers to the fact that they failed to think exactly enough, it is clear that we are dealing with a spiritual principle of reason whose scope is connected with the faculty of knowledge possessed by poets and philosophers. Justin's usage is far removed from the pantheistic Stoic idea.

Where then did Justin obtain his idea of the λόγος σπερματικός? What influences played on him as he used it to explain the diffusion of truth and righteousness among men? Philo had adopted the term to designate the copies of the archetypal ideas which exist in the world and which, for him, constitute reality. This does not however help in the elucidation of Justin's background. More to the point is the Middle Platonist view of the λόγος σπερματικός. As was the case with Justin's doctrine of God the brilliant researches of Carl Andresen[2] have illuminated his philosophic environment in a new way and have provided an intelligible account of Justin's adoption of the term.

Andresen begins by tracing the antecedents of the λόγος · σπερματικός idea. He shows how Cicero, who depends on Antiochus of Askalon, speaks of the *semina justitiae* which have been present since the earliest generations of man. It was these which

---

[1] P. Pfättisch, *Der Einfluss Platos auf die Theologie Justins des Märtyrers* (Paderborn, 1910), p. 104.   [2] *Z.N.T.W.* xliv (1952–3), 157–95.

made possible the love of knowledge in the mind of man and an honourable and proper community life. Cicero links the seed forces of the Stoa with the seeds of justice, i.e. he gives them an ethico-moral, rather than a metaphysical, interpretation. The same development is found in Arius Didymus in his exposition of the Peripatetic ethics. He reads the idea of 'seed forces' into Aristotle in an exclusively ethical interpretation. Men, for Arius, possess by nature the 'beginnings' and 'seeds' of the virtues which are perfectible by 'morals and right habits of intercourse'. Arius attempted to bring together the Academy, the Stoa and the Peripatos by adopting a certain indifference to metaphysics. He is the first to give an exclusively ethical interpretation to the λόγοι σπερματικοί. In Andresen's view Arius Didymus is the link between the philosophy of Antiochus of Askalon and Cicero and Middle Platonism (as exemplified by Albinus) in which the idea of 'seed forces' is connected with that of the 'general ideas'.

Andresen instances the account of Apuleius of Madaura of man who is from birth neither good nor evil but bears within himself certain seeds of both qualities, which are connected with his birth. It is the task of education to make these seeds 'shine forth' for good.[1] In both Albinus and Apuleius the λόγοι σπερματικοί have escaped from the Stoic view of the logos spermatikos as the World principle and have been restricted to a purely ethical meaning.[2]

It would seem that Justin's references to the seeds of truth present in the intellectual, spiritual and moral strivings of men (which for him are but parts of the whole Word which is Christ) are best explained by reference to the School Platonist tradition.[3] For in both Justin and Middle Platonism the idea of the

[1] De Pl. II. 3.

[2] Note also Plutarch's speculations about the World Soul of the *Timaeus*, where he endeavours to give to the logos of the Platonic World Soul the role of the Stoic logos spermatikos and in the process eliminates all the material aspects of the Stoic idea. Andresen, *Z.N.T.W.* XLIV (1952–3), 176.

[3] J. H. Waszink, *Festschrift Theodor Klauser*, p. 390, believes that Justin's choice of the term logos spermatikos is due to the conjunction of these factors: (a) that it was a well-known Stoic term; (b) the influence of the parable of the Sower, Matt. xiii. 3; (c) the frequency of the picture of sowing and planting in the works of Philo. Professor Waszink however admits a considerable element of Middle Platonist influence elsewhere in Justin

'seed forces' is given a moral and ethical interpretation and is not connected with the Stoic World Reason. It was after all from this School Platonism that Justin passed into Christianity.

It is also interesting that Justin alludes to the Stoic idea of 'general concepts' (*communes notitiae*; *koinai* or *physikai ennoiai*). By these he understands the concepts given to man *a priori* which are predominantly of a religious and moral character. Thus the term 'God' is an intuition implanted in the nature of man;[1] so there is embedded in him the faculty of knowing good and evil.[2] This is similar to the Middle Platonist use of the Stoic 'naturally formed concepts'.[3] But in Justin the 'naturally formed concepts' and the 'seed forces' referred to above are closely connected. This is shown by his terminology. So he speaks of the 'seed of the logos implanted in the whole human race'[4] in one context and in another of the 'intuition of God implanted in the nature of man'.[5] It would seem that in both Justin is indebted to Middle Platonism, rather than to Stoicism direct, and this in spite of the wealth of Stoic ideas in his writings.

In describing the function of the logos Justin Martyr was a pioneer Christian thinker. He was dependent on the earlier Christian use of the term and assumes that his readers will understand his ideas. This Christian element was fundamental to Justin, for he firmly equates the logos with Jesus Christ whom he describes as the whole or entire Word.[6] This logos was essentially a unity with God the Father although distinct in personality. This equation of the logos with Jesus differentiates Justin's thought at once from the speculations of Philo, Stoicism and Middle Platonism. However, Justin admitted into his idea of the logos a larger philosophic element, mainly derived from Middle Platonism, than did earlier Christian thinkers and this element did not entirely harmonise with the Christian and biblical tradition.

(p.384) and it would seem best to find it here. R. Holte, *Stud. Theol.* XII (1958), 109–68, believes that the immediate source of Justin's theory was Philo. See further H. Chadwick in *B.J.R.L.* XLVII (1965), 294 n. 11, who follows Holte and Waszink in finding an echo of the parable of the Sower.

[1] *II Apol.* vi.   [2] *II Apol.* xiv.
[3] So Albinus. Andresen, *Z.N.T.W.* XLIV (1952–3), 177.
[4] *II Apol.* viii.   [5] *II Apol.* vi.   [6] *II Apol.* viii.

CHAPTER VIII

THE HOLY SPIRIT AND THE TRINITY:
THE ANGELIC POWERS

THE primary object of the second-century Greek Apologists was to demonstrate that the philosophic conception of a θεὸς λόγος was realised in the Person of the historical Christ. They were conscious, as a fact of Christian experience, of the presence and power of the Holy Spirit, but they paid comparatively little attention to the working out of any doctrine of the Third Person of the Trinity. Some of the apologists ascribed to the Son operations and offices which the Church was later to refer to the Holy Spirit. Thus, in the Epistle *ad Diognetum*, it is the Word who 'holds converse with men, by whom He chooses, and when He wills';[1] it is by the Word that 'the Church is perpetually enriched'.[2] Theophilus of Antioch attributes the inspiration of the Old Testament prophets to the second person; 'the Word, being God's Spirit, came down upon the prophets and spake by them.'[3] Even the miraculous conception is said by Justin to have been wrought by the Word himself[4]—a view which lingered on in the Church until the middle of the fourth century.[5] On the other hand it is Theophilus who first uses the word τριάς with reference to the Godhead.[6] There was undoubtedly a tendency to subordinate the Spirit to the Word. Tatian, Justin's pupil, even speaks of the Holy Spirit as the minister of the Son.[7] His view of the Spirit's operation is worthy of note:

The Spirit of God is not with all men, but with some, namely with those who live righteously; descending to the soul's level, and linking itself with it, whilst to other souls it announces its secret by means of prophecies. Souls which give heed to wisdom attract to themselves this kindred Spirit.[8]

---

[1] xi. 2.   [2] xi. 5.   [3] *Autol.* ii. 23.
[4] *I Apol.* xxxiii.
[5] Iren. v. 1; Tert. *Prax.* 26; Cypr. *de Idol. Van.*; Hil. *Trin.* ii. 24, 26.
[6] *Autol.* ii. 15; cf. Justin, *I Apol.* xiii.
[7] *Adv. Graec.* 13.   [8] *Ibid.*

It is only Athenagoras, among the Apologists, who approaches more nearly the later Church doctrine of the Holy Trinity. He visualises the Holy Spirit as the Bond of the Divine Unity[1] and even describes the Spirit as an 'effluence (ἀπόρροιαν) from God, from whom it emanates and to whom it returns like a ray of the sun' or as 'light from fire'.[2]

There was considerable fluidity in doctrinal matters in the second-century Church and it should cause no surprise that the doctrines of the Holy Spirit and the Trinity receive so little theological formulation. This is, in fact, the case with Justin Martyr.

THE SPIRIT IN JUSTIN

Justin's doctrine of the Holy Spirit is difficult to understand. There is no facet of his teaching which has been more variously interpreted than this. It has even been asserted that ultimately, for Justin, logos and Spirit were but two names for the same conception.[3] Such theories must be tested against what he actually says about the Spirit.

Justin mentions the Holy Spirit mainly in connection with prophetic inspiration. When he wishes to explain the traditional baptismal formula used in his day he links the mention of the Spirit with prophetic inspiration: 'This washing is called illumination, since those who learn these things are illumined within. The illuminand is also washed in the name of Jesus Christ, who was crucified under Pontius Pilate, and in the name of the Holy Spirit, who through the prophets foretold everything about Jesus.'[4] It is, however, significant that only in *one* passage[5] does Justin suggest that the prophet was in ecstasy when he had his prophetic vision, i.e. his natural powers were quiescent. As he nowhere else uses the word ecstasy it seems unlikely that he regarded this as the normal prophetic state. More to the point is Justin's view that the words of the prophet are Divine utterances and not just an expression of the prophet's own opinion.[6] The Psalms were spoken or dictated to David by the Holy Spirit.[7]

[1] *Suppl.* 10. [2] *Suppl.* 10, 24.
[3] See Goodenough, *Theology of Justin Martyr*, p. 176.
[4] *I Apol.* lxi. [5] *Dial.* cxv. 3.
[6] *I Apol.* xxxvi. 1. [7] *Dial.* xxxiv. 1.

Goodenough has pointed out[1] that in the second century the theory of inspiration of prophets and seers was widely accepted and required no defence *per se*—no more, we may add, than the authority of the 'holy man' in India today. What did need defence was the ascription of prophecy to the *whole* of the Old Testament, much of which was not prophetic utterance. Justin and other early Christian writers used the entire biblical record —narratives, discourses, statements about the past, and intimations of the future—as a foreshadowing of Christianity. Justin gives this explanation:

When you hear the words of the prophets spoken as in a particular character, do not think of them as spoken by the inspired men themselves, but by the divine Word that moved them. For sometimes he speaks as predicting the things that are to happen, sometimes he speaks as in the character of God the Master and Father of all, sometimes in the character of Christ, sometimes in the character of the people answering the Lord or his Father. You can see the same thing in your own writers, where one man is the author of the whole work but introduces different characters in dialogue. Not understanding this, the Jews, who are in possession of the books of the prophets, did not recognise Christ even when he came, and they hate us who declare that he has come and show that he was crucified by them as had been predicted.[2]

In other words whatever the literary or historical form of the utterance it is always the same Spirit or logos who inspires it. The Spirit adopts different roles according to his purpose—in the character[3] of the Father,[4] of Christ,[5] of the children of Abraham,[6] or of the apostles.[7]

What of the person and nature of this prophetic Spirit? Justin's ideas are fluid, as with much second-century thought, and it would be a mistake to press individual phrases or use them as a yardstick to judge other conceptions appearing in his writings. Justin believed the prophets were inspired by the Spirit, but he calls this Spirit by various names—sometimes *the* Spirit, Holy Spirit, Prophetic Spirit, logos, or even God. Of these 'Holy Spirit' and 'Prophetic Spirit' are most frequently used and occur throughout his writings. The difficult problem

---

[1] *Theology of Justin Martyr*, p. 178. [2] *I Apol.* xxxvi.
[3] ἀπὸ προσώπου. [4] *I Apol.* xxxvii. 1. [5] *I Apol.* xxxviii. 1.
[6] *Dial.* xxv. 1. [7] *Dial.* xlii. 2.

is whether the Spirit was, for Justin, a person distinct from the logos or whether this was simply an aspect of the activity of the logos. We have already seen that Justin can speak of the logos inspiring the prophets.[1] In one remarkable passage he speaks of the annunciation:

We believe them, since the prophetic Spirit through the above-mentioned Isaiah said that this would happen, as we noted before. The Spirit and the Power from God (τὴν δύναμιν παρὰ τοῦ θεοῦ) cannot rightly be thought of as anything else than the Word, who is also the First-born of God, as Moses the above-mentioned prophet testified.[2]

This seems decisive proof, at least on the surface, that for Justin Spirit and logos were two names for the same person. However, in Justin's theory of the Incarnation the coming down of the logos and entry into the womb of Mary was central. As however the traditional account spoke of the Spirit and Power Justin was forced to identify them as regards function. This however does not exclude the possibility of his believing in *the* Spirit distinct from the Father and the Son. Justin confused the function of the logos and the Spirit. There is however some evidence that he did believe in a personal Holy Spirit. After referring to Plato's discussion of the nature of the Son of God in the *Timaeus* Justin says:

He placed him like an X in the universe...Plato, reading this and not clearly understanding, nor realising that it was in the form of a cross, but thinking it was *Chi*, said that the Power next to the first God was placed X-wise in the universe. And he spoke of a third, since he read what I have quoted from Moses, that the Spirit of God was borne over the waters. For he gives the second place to the Word who is with God, who, he says, was placed X-wise in the universe, and the third to the Spirit which was said to be borne over the water, saying, 'The third (order of) beings around the third'.[3]

Justin is clearly distinguishing between the logos and the Spirit who, although similar in nature, are unequal in rank. Elsewhere he says that the Christians honour Jesus Christ in the second place after God and the prophetic Spirit in the third rank.[4] Four times he quotes the formula, 'In the name of the

---

[1] *I Apol.* xxxiii. 9, xxxvi. 1.   [2] *I Apol.* xxxiii. 6.
[3] *I Apol.* lx. 6–7; cf. Plato 2 Epist. 312 E—a very obscure passage.
[4] *I Apol.* xiii. 3, ἐν τρίτῃ τάξει.

Father and of the Son and of the Holy Spirit'.[1] In one remarkable passage Justin states that Christians worship the Spirit, but he introduces good angels before the mention of the Spirit:

So then, we are called godless. We certainly confess that we are godless with reference to beings like these who are commonly thought of as gods, but not with reference to the most true God, the Father of righteousness and temperance and the other virtues, who is untouched by evil. But him, and the Son who came from him, and taught us these things, and the army of the other good angels who follow him and are made like him, and the prophetic Spirit, we worship and adore (σεβόμεθα καὶ προσκυνοῦμεν).[2]

Attempts have been made to avoid the sudden introduction of the angels[3] in this passage, but it is hardly possible to read the passage otherwise than as it stands in the existing text. The construction of the sentence is against interpreting the angels as recipients of Christ's teaching. They are introduced to point the contrast with the evil daemons who oppose Jesus. As the Son is the captain of the angelic host (ἀρχιστράτηγος) the good angels who follow him are to be reverenced.[4] The fact that the Spirit is mentioned last implies that the Spirit is regarded as a distinct person.

As to the origin of the Holy Spirit Justin is silent. But we infer from his writings that he regarded the Spirit as a power (δύναμις) of God.

Justin had no real doctrine of the Trinity. He worshipped the Father as supreme in the Universe; he worshipped the logos or Son as divine but in the second place; he worshipped the Holy Spirit in the third place. This is the language of Christian experience rather than theological reflection. The Holy Spirit was, for Justin, the inspirer of the prophets, the guide of spiritual endeavour, the source of the spiritual gifts found in the Church. Justin's experience of Christian worship and the Christian life took precedence over his logic. His philosophic idea of God, deriving from Middle Platonism, was too abstract for any real

---

[1] *I Apol.* lxi. 3, 13, lxv. 2, lxvii. 2. [2] *I Apol.* vi. 1–2.

[3] See Otto's note on the passage: *S. Justini Philosophi et Martyris Opera* (Greek text and Latin translation) (3rd ed., Jena, 1876–9), I. 1. 21.

[4] Athenagoras *Suppl.* 10 mentions angels immediately *after* the Trinity as belonging to the θεολογία, whereas all that concerned the Incarnation belonged to the οἰκονομία.

distinction within the Godhead such as would equate the Love between the Father and the Son with the Spirit. In strict logic there is no place in Justin's thought for the person of the Holy Spirit because the logos carries out his functions. Nevertheless, the fact that he has so much to say about the Spirit and refers to the traditional formulas shows that Justin is strongly influenced by Christian experience and worship as he knew it in the life of the Church. Moreover it should not be forgotten that the conception of a divine Spirit was everywhere known in both Judaism and the Greek world in the time of Justin, and he was not therefore required to explain or justify his mention of the Prophetic Spirit.

THE ANGELIC POWERS

Justin held, in company with most of his compatriots in the second century, a belief in good and evil angels or powers. The good angels were closely associated with Jesus as messengers of God who would accompany him in his glory at the last day. The evil angels occupied a larger position in Justin's thought than the good angels. These angels had been given freedom of choice[1] and some had chosen the way of evil—Justin is here following Jewish tradition[2]—so that they need repentance and salvation.[3] Some of the evil angels had overstepped the limit in having illicit intercourse with women, which resulted in the birth of children called daemons. Justin here seems to be following an earlier Jewish or Jewish-Christian interpretation of Gen. vi. 2–5 which is also found in the Ebionite Pseudo-Clementine writings.[4] The Hebrew of Gen. vi. 2–5 says that the children of God, having been attracted by women, united with them and produced *giants*. In the LXX υἱοὶ θεοῦ and ἄγγελοι θεοῦ are synonymous and sometimes alternatives[5] and a tradition grew up in Greek Judaism that it was the union of angels

---

[1] *Dial.* cxli. 1, cxl. 4, lxxxviii. 5; *II Apol.* vii. 5.

[2] Pappos interpreted 'Man has become as one of us' as meaning 'Man has become as one of the angels' (quoted by Goodenough, *Theology of Justin Martyr*, p. 197). Akiba added that to be as one of the angels meant to have a free power of choice, to follow the way of life or of death.

[3] *Dial.* cxli. 1.   [4] *Clem. Hom.* vi. 18.

[5] See J. S. Sibinga, *The Old Testament Text of Justin Martyr.* I. *The Pentateuch* (Leiden, 1963), p. 146.

and women which produced giants.[1] Justin in substituting
daemons for giants is following another line of interpretation
which may be reflected in Papias' references to 'the angels who
had formerly been holy'.[2] Later Jewish tradition vacillated
in its interpretation of Gen. vi. In Bresh. R. on Gen. vi. 2
R. Simeon ben Jochai (c. A.D. 130–60) pronounces a curse on
those who say that 'the sons of God' are angels, but the Zohar
on Gen. vi. 4 agrees with Justin as do R. Judah (c. A.D. 200)
and another, according to Pirqe de R. Elizer xxii.

After the fall of the angels the daemonic children multiplied
to form a whole army of evil powers. These daemons lurked
everywhere seeking to bring the human race into subjection.
The consciousness of the daemonic element in the universe was
central to Justin's world view, as to so many of his contempor-
aries, and we do him an injustice if we minimise it. These
daemons were more real to Justin than the good angels associated with Our Lord.

Justin says little about the origin of the angels or daemons
apart from this one passage:

But (they assert) that this power can never be cut off or separated
from the Father, in the same way that, as they say, the light of the
sun on earth cannot be cut off or separated, though the sun is in
heaven. And when the sun sets the light is borne away with it. So
the Father, they affirm, makes, when he will, his power to spring
forward, and, when he will, he draws it back again into himself.
They teach that in this way he also made the angels. But that therefore angels are, and ever remain, without being resolved again into
that out of which they came into existence, has been demonstrated.[3]

The purport of this passage is clear. As the logos has a separate,
permanent existence from the Father so there are angels which
have a permanent existence. In addition there are angels which
have a temporary existence, coming forth from God and being
reabsorbed by him. Justin, in this latter belief, is following a
good Tannaitic tradition, commenting on Dan. vii. 9–10:
'Every single day angels that minister (to him) are created from

[1] This was later challenged by Philastrius *Haer.* 107 and Chryst. on
Gen. vi, *Hom.* 22.   [2] *Fr.* 4.

[3] *Dial.* cxxviii. 3–4. But Justin has not demonstrated this in the existing
text of the *Dialogue*.

the stream of fire,[1] and they utter a song, and cease to be';
'from every single utterance that goes forth from the mouth of
the Holy One, blessed be he, is created one angel, for it is said,
By the word of the Lord were the heavens made, and by the
breath of his mouth all their host'.[2] However, there are no
references in rabbinic tradition to a belief in the permanent existence of some angels[3] such as was held by Justin. His reason for
asserting this is made plain by the context of this passage. Justin
has just stated[4] that the God who appeared to Moses in the
burning bush was the second God, the logos. Some Jews dis-
puted this and claimed that the appearance was of an angel, so
ruling out the existence of a second divine Power in the universe.
Justin agrees with this to a point, but asserts that there are angels
which are permanently sustained and not reabsorbed into their
source. So Jesus, the logos, is a unique Power who is separate
from the Father, the source of all Being. It is Justin's Christology
which is at the root of his theory of the origin of angels. He
follows good Jewish tradition but supplements it to provide a
parallel for the generation of the logos–Christ, but he does not
bring his theory into relationship with his other belief in the
fall of the angels to which we must now return.

The leader of the host of daemons or evil angels was Satan
who had fallen as a result of his deception of Adam and Eve.[5]
Justin, in a remarkable passage,[6] says that his name really
means apostate–serpent, an interpretation also found in
Irenaeus.[7] The activity of this evil host of daemons was everywhere to be found in the universe. By deceitful magic and by
terror they had reduced the human race to servitude. War,
adultery, crime—all were due to their influence. Pagan poets

---

[1] A stream of fire was regarded as a ray of light in Jewish thought and by
Justin.

[2] T.B. Chagiga 14A. Cf. also Gen. Rab. 78; Echa. to 3.23 quoted by
Goodenough, *Theology of Justin Martyr*, pp. 190–1.

[3] This would in any case undermine Jewish monotheism.

[4] *Dial.* cxxviii. 1.   [5] *Dial.* cxxiv. 3.

[6] *Dial.* ciii. 5. *Sata*, in the language of Jews and Syrians, is 'decline from
religion' or 'apostate', while *nas* is serpent. *Nachash* is the usual Hebrew
word for serpent. It is interesting that the Samaritans, among whom Justin
lived, omitted the guttural between two homogeneous vowels in their
pronunciation. See A. L. Williams, *Dialogue with Trypho* (London, 1930),
p. 216.   [7] *Adv. Haer.* v. 21. 2; *Preaching* 16.

and mythologists were equally led astray by their mistaking them for gods[1] and singing their evil deeds.[2] When the mythologists spoke of the sons of God, born of women, of Bacchus, riding on his ass, and of his violent death and ascent into heaven; of Perseus Virgin-born, of Hercules 'strong as a giant', of Aesculapius raising the dead—the daemons were multiplying false fulfilments of scripture prophecies. The poets, ignorantly, were tools of the Devil as Plato had said.[3] So again the daemons confused human instincts with law, and framed laws to suit their own wickedness. Since the Christian dispensation the daemons had renewed their activity. They had caricatured Christian ordinances, such as the Eucharist, in the services of Mithraism,[4] and baptism, in the rites of pagan temple purifications.[5] They had attempted to produce confusion by prompting heretics to pervert the knowledge of the true way as revealed in Christ.[6] Indeed all along they had inspired persecution of those who were moved by the Spermatic Word, such as Heraclitus, Musonius and Socrates. Now these daemons were urging the persecution of Christians, not being able to stop the knowledge of Christ's advent, or of the last judgement, but by prompting wicked livers to hate and kill them.[7] The judges who persecute Christians are, in fact, inspired by the devil.[8]

Although, in Justin's view, the activity of the daemonic host was terrible in the extreme yet it was not beyond limitation and control. Before the Christian era the power of the daemons was broken by exorcism in the name of the God of Abraham, Isaac and Jacob.[9] Since then their power had been broken by the coming of Christ as was symbolised by the coming of the Magi to the infant Christ.[10] The dominion which Christians now exercise over the daemons is an omen of their utter overthrow at the second coming of Christ when they will be cast into eternal fire. This present dominion is seen in the rite of exorcism in the name of Christ by which the power of the daemons is broken.[11] It is this foreknowledge of his coming final overthrow

---

[1] *I Apol.* v. 4.   [2] *II Apol.* v.   [3] *II Apol.* x.
[4] *I Apol.* lxvi. 4; *Dial.* lxxviii. 6, lxx. 1.   [5] *I Apol.* lxii. 1.
[6] *Dial.* lxxxii. 3; *I Apol.* lvi. 1, lviii. 1.   [7] *I Apol.* lvii.
[8] *II Apol.* i.   [9] *Dial.* lxxxv. 3.   [10] *Dial.* lxxviii. 9.
[11] *Dial.* lxxxv. 1, 2, lxxvi. 6, cxi. 2; *II Apol.* vi. 6. The rite of exorcism culminated in the recital of an embryonic creed: *II Apol.* vi. 6: *Dial.* lxxxv. 2.

which makes Satan desperate and unrestrained in his present assaults against men.[1]

Justin's account of the good and evil angels (or daemons) is remarkably similar to that found in the Synoptic Gospels although he deals in greater detail with the activity of the evil host. It might be thought that he is merely expounding what he found in the 'Memoirs'. This however would be to misunderstand Justin's own background. He has no doubt as to the intense reality of the good, and especially the evil, angels. Their existence was a fact and their activities everywhere to be seen. His own experience confirmed what he had read in the 'Memoirs' and what he knew of Jewish and early Jewish Christian speculation about the angelic powers.[2] In delineating the picture of Justin as an apologist to the Greek world it should not be forgotten that his main practical concern, as with his fellow Christians, lay in winning the increasing fight against evil spirits which were seeking to win control of the universe and the souls of men.

[1] According to Justin the daemons never discovered in prophecy the sign of the Cross although the symbol is everywhere to be found.

[2] Justin, however, nowhere *names* the angels as did Jewish and later Christian tradition.

CHAPTER IX

CREATION, INCARNATION AND REDEMPTION

CREATION

(1) *The universe*

Justin's account of the process by which the universe came into existence is meagre in the extreme. This may be thought surprising when we consider his interest in the logos doctrine and his theory of the spermatic logoi at work in the universe. Justin, as might be expected, connects the creative Word of God of the Genesis account of the creation with the spermatic logos of the Middle Platonist tradition. But once this was done he was content to take the rest of the Genesis account quite literally. The fact that the origin and nature of matter was widely discussed by the eclecticism of his day does not appear to have worried Justin. He is content, as a biblical and Christian thinker, to take his stand on the Genesis account.

There are however a very few passages in his writings in which Justin states that God created the world out of unformed matter. Thus *I Apol.* x. 2: 'We have also been taught that in the beginning he in his goodness formed all things that are for the sake of men out of unformed matter' (καὶ πάντα τὴν ἀρχὴν ἀγαθὸν ὄντα δημιουργῆσαι αὐτὸν ἐξ ἀμόρφου ὕλης δι' ἀνθρώπους δεδιδάγμεθα). Who taught this to Justin? The Church tradition or his pre-Christian philosophic teachers? The latter seems more likely as in the previous sentence (*I Apol.* x. 1) Justin explicitly refers to a tradition received from the Church by using the phrase regularly used for the acceptance of a sacred tradition (παρειλήφαμεν).[1] A similar passage occurs in *I Apol.* lxvii. 7 in which Justin states, in a reference to Sunday worship, that this is held on the first day 'on which God transforming darkness and matter made the universe'. However, in neither of these passages does Justin state whether matter had an eternal existence antithetical to God (as Plato taught) or whether it was

---

[1] As in I Cor. xi. 23, xv. 1.

itself a creation of God in an unformed state which he *then* used
to create the material world.

There is one other passage in which Justin deals with this
question:

So that you may learn that Plato borrowed from our teachers, I
mean from the Word (speaking) through the prophets, when he said
that God made the universe by changing formless matter (ἄμορφον
οὖσαν), hear the precise words of Moses, who as declared above was
the first of the prophets and older than the Greek writers. The
prophetic Spirit testified through him how in the beginning God
fashioned the universe, and out of what, saying: 'In the beginning
God made the heaven and the earth. And the earth was invisible
and unfurnished, and darkness (was) over the abyss; and the Spirit
of God was borne over the waters. And God said, Let there be light.
And it was so.' So by God's Word the whole universe was made out
of this substratum (ἐκ τῶν ὑποκειμένων), as expounded by Moses,
and Plato and those who agree with him, as well as we, have learned
it (from him), and you can be sure of it too. We also know that
Moses had already spoken of what the poets call Erebus.[1]

There is no suggestion in this passage that Justin is criticising
the Platonic doctrine although several commentators have
maintained this.[2] Justin, in fact, only mentions formless matter
in order to emphasise that this was accepted by Moses in Gen. i.
1–3; and that, for both Moses and Plato, God had brought the
universe into existence by working on, and changing, formless
matter. It is idle to speculate how Justin interpreted Gen. i. 1,
'In the beginning God made the heaven and the earth'. It is
equally uncertain whether Justin believed in the eternity of
matter in the Platonic sense as an antithesis to God. We must
be content to state that Justin had no particular theory of the
origin and nature of matter. He is content to accept Gen. i. 1
as it stands and to see in it no conflict with the teaching he had
received from Middle Platonism. His rather illogical and non-
speculative approach may have been due, as Goodenough
suggests,[3] to the fact that he did not connect the origin of evil
with that of matter. In this he is at one with certain circles in

---

[1] *I Apol.* lix. It is possible that Erebus is based on the 'evening' ('*erev*)
of the days of creation. Cf. also *I Apol.* xx. 4.
[2] P. Pfättisch, *Der Einfluss Platos auf die Theologie Justins des Märtyrers*,
pp. 96 f. [3] *Theology of Justin Martyr*, p. 211.

Palestinian Judaism[1] rather than with the Hellenistic Judaism of the diaspora and Gnosticism where this question was eagerly discussed.

Justin believed that the purpose of the creation was good and for the benefit of the human race.[2] It is not without significance that he adds to the *verbum Christi* 'no one is good but God' the phrase 'the one who made all things'.[3] He states that all earthly things were made subject to man while the heavenly elements and the seasons were ordained for man's advantage.[4] God revealed his goodness in creating the world—beyond that Justin does not speculate. A creation *ex nihilo* does not come within his purview.

(2) *Anthropology*

Justin's doctrine of man is strongly influenced by his philosophic presuppositions, as might be expected in view of his emphasis on human reason. Man, Justin held, was created from the material elements.[5] He was endowed with a soul which included his non-physical constitution with the exception of the reason—and this soul was the seat of his personality. Life and reason were however imparted to the soul by a divine element (ζωτικὸν πνεῦμα). It is the soul which is the focus of personal existence—rather than the body or the spirit. Justin nowhere gives an account of the origin of the soul although, from the fact that he rejects the Platonic belief in reincarnation,[6] it would seem he regarded the soul as begotten, although not necessarily begotten in connection with the body.[7] Justin, in company with orthodox Middle Platonism, here rejects the Aristotelian belief[8] that the soul was an attribute of the body and could not exist without it. The fact that Justin believed in the immortality of the soul was, no doubt, the reason for this.

What of the divine element in man? Justin, as Goodenough shows,[9] uses two terms for this. It is a part of the logos or of the spermatic logos,[10] and it is the πνεῦμα in man.[11] However, this

---

[1] R. Josh. b. Chananja. See Weber, *Jüdische Theologie*, pp. 200 f.
[2] *II Apol.* iv. 2.   [3] *I Apol.* xvi. 6–7; cf. *Dial.* xciii. 2.
[4] *II Apol.* v. 2; cf. *Dial.* xli. 1.   [5] *Dial.* lxii. 2.
[6] *Dial.* iv. 5.   [7] *Dial.* v. 2.
[8] σώματός τι. See *De Anima* 417 a.
[9] *Theology of Justin Martyr*, p. 214. This section of his book is of great value.
[10] *II Apol.* x. 8, xiii. 3.   [11] *Dial.* vi. 2.

fragment of the logos in man is not an emanation from the logos and so, in some way, inferior to the totality of the logos. It *is* the whole logos. This is made clear in a remarkable passage. After stating that Socrates had been accused of the same crimes as Christians Justin says:

For no one trusted in Socrates so as to die for this doctrine, but in Christ, who was partially known even by Socrates (for he was and is the logos who is in every man, and who foretold the things that were to come to pass both through the prophets and in his own person when he was made of like passions, and taught these things), not only philosophers and scholars believed, but also artisans and people entirely uneducated, despising both glory, and fear, and death; since he is a power of the ineffable Father, and not the mere instrument of human reason.[1]

The universal logos is present in all men and brings inspiration and perception of spiritual truth. As each man, even before the coming of Christ, suppressed his lower nature and lived according to the direction of the logos he was a follower of Christ and knew him in a partial sense (ἀπὸ μέρους). The totality of the logos is however the Personal Christ.

It would therefore seem that Justin believed in the traditional threefold division of human nature—body, soul and πνεῦμα or μέρος τοῦ σπερματικοῦ λόγου—such at least we may infer from *Dial.* vi. In this he was at one with early Christian teaching[2] and with Middle Platonism.[3]

Justin held firmly to a belief in man's moral freedom. He declares that man was created intelligent and with the power to choose the true and do the good[4] and that he still retains the same ability.[5] Each man by his own free choice does right or wrong.[6] Man's responsibility lies in his power of choice—and in this alone. Justin gives scriptural proof of human liberty and even states that the famous Platonic dictum, 'the blame is his who chooses, but God is blameless', was taken by Plato directly from Moses.[7] If this human freedom did not exist then men could be neither rewarded nor punished and the moral structure of the universe would collapse. The fact that men change

---

[1] *II Apol.* x. 8.   [2] I Thess. v. 23.
[3] See the discussion on pp. 96–9.
[4] *I Apol.* xxviii; *Dial.* lxxxviii, cxli.
[5] *I Apol.* x.   [6] *II Apol.* vii, xiv.   [7] *I Apol.* xliv; cf. *Republic* x. 617.

from evil to good and from good to evil is the proof that moral freedom is a reality and not imagination.[1] Justin did not believe in inherited guilt or original sin. Adam's transgression is mentioned as marking the origin of human sin and death but not the cause of it during history. 'Since Adam, the race has fallen under death and the deceit of the serpent, each man having done evil through his own fault.'[2] Being made like unto Adam men work out death for themselves through their power of moral choice. Justin's view is very close to that of rabbinic Judaism which held that although Adam's fall put men under the influence of Satan, yet nevertheless free-will remained.[3] There is no inherited sinfulness separate from *actual* acts of sin. For Justin man sins because he allows the daemons to lead him into rebellion against the law of God which every man has within him as part of his equipment for life.

With such an uncompromising semi-pelagianism Justin inveighs particularly against the Stoic idea of fate (*heimarmene*). Indeed he devotes a whole chapter to this subject:[4]

So that none may infer from what we have said that the events we speak of, because they were foreknown and predicted, took place according to inevitable fate (καθ᾽ εἱμαρμένης ἀνάγκην)—I can explain this too. We have learned from the prophets, and declare as the truth, that penalties and punishments and good rewards are given according to the quality of each man's actions. If this were not so, but all things happened in accordance with fate (καθ᾽ εἱμαρμένην), nothing at all would be left to us. For if it is destined that one man should be good and another wicked, then neither is the one acceptable nor the other blameworthy.[5]

Andresen[6] has pointed out that Justin's arguments against Stoic fatalism are markedly similar to those of the Middle Platonists Albinus and Apuleius. Albinus in fact devotes a special chapter to this question although he carries through his argument against the Stoic view of *heimarmene* as an eternal, valid law

[1] *I Apol.* xliii; *II Apol.* vii. Justin held that all souls survive death—the good souls live eternally but the bad only so long as God wishes them to exist and be punished (*Dial.* v. 3).   [2] *Dial.* lxxxviii.
[3] See Weber, *Jüdische Theologie*, pp. 224, 239 f., quoted in Goodenough, *Theology of Justin Martyr*, p. 229.   [4] *I Apol.* xliii; cf. *II Apol.* vii.
[5] *I Apol.* xliii. 1–2.
[6] *Z.N.T.W.* XLIV (1952–3), 184–8, who gives full references.

from a metaphysical, rather than an ethical, point of view. It was Plutarch however who showed the logical fallacy of the Stoic position by demonstrating that the concept of individual responsibility was incompatible with a belief in *heimarmene*.

Justin's argument in *I Apol.* xliii for man's moral freedom and the objective nature of virtue and wickedness is also found in Middle Platonism. Earlier in his *Apology* Justin states that if one denies that God has even a partial care for man then either one denies that God exists or one asserts that he has pleasure in evil:

In the beginning he made the race of men endowed with intelligence, able to choose the truth and do right, so that all men are without excuse before God, for they were made with the powers of reason and observation. Anyone who does not believe that God cares for these things either manages to profess that he does not exist, or makes out that he exists but approves evil or remains (unaffected) like a stone, and that virtue and vice are not realities, but that men consider things good or bad by opinion alone; this is the height of impiety and injustice.[1]

The final sentence of this passage appears word for word in *I Apol.* xliii. 6. Andresen[2] believes that Justin is confuting the Epicurean teaching which held that ethical concepts have only a hypothetical character. Even the ancient Stoa had attacked the belief that virtue only acquires significance when connected with pleasure. Middle Platonism took over this anti-Epicurean argument. Thus Atticus fights, like Justin, for the idea of a personal providence of God against the Peripatetics: 'the denial of providence is the furtherance of injustice'.[3] Plutarch affirms that the *heimarmene* theory of the Stoics leads to a denial of the divine *pronoia* and he places the Stoics alongside Epicurus, the despiser of God.[4] Justin seems to be influenced by this when he points to the dangerous consequences for ethics of the Stoic belief in *heimarmene*. Justin interprets the biblical emphasis on man's moral freedom from a Middle Platonist standpoint. It is this which explains his use of two Old Testament texts, Deut. xxx. 15, 19 and Isa. l. 16–20, in *I Apol.* xliv. 17. Justin deliberately alters the context of the Deuteronomy passage by stating that God, through Moses, said to the *first-formed* man,

---

[1] *I Apol.* xxviii. 3–4.   [2] *Z.N.T.W.* xliv (1952–3), 186.
[3] Eus. *Praep. Ev.* xv. 5. 5.   [4] Andresen, *Z.N.T.W.* xliv (1952–3), 187.

'Behold I have set before thee good and evil, choose the good', although in fact these words were addressed to the Jewish people. Similarly when Justin affirms[1] that Plato's words from the *Republic*, 'the blame is his who chooses, but God is blameless', were taken by the Greek philosopher from Moses then such a statement is in no way justified by the context. Justin's view is however explained by the fact that this passage from Plato played a significant role in Middle Platonism in connection with the theory of *heimarmene*.[2]

Justin's anthropology diverges from that of the New Testament. He has no conception of the solidarity of the human race as falling short of the Glory of God. The seventh chapter of St Paul's Epistle to the Romans finds no echo in his writings. Sin, for Justin, is purely an individual thing and it is to be noted that, in the account of his own conversion, a conviction of sin, or a sharing in its effects, does not appear. Justin is very close to both popular Judaism and Middle Platonism in his conviction that man's responsibility lies solely in his power of choice and that all men are endowed with the ability to choose the good if they so wish. However much we should like to accept this optimistic theory of man's moral freedom Christian experience throughout the ages is a witness to its lack of depth. Sin goes far deeper than Justin would allow.[3] His philosophic presuppositions so modified his biblical inheritance that he had no clear perception of the delicate interaction between Divine Grace and human free-will. But he was not the first, and certainly will not be the last, to fail in this.

INCARNATION

We have had occasion to note, several times in this book, how Justin's philosophical presuppositions have affected his presentation of Christianity and, in some respects, have seriously modified it. However, in his doctrine of the Incarnation, which must now concern us, Justin treads on more traditional ground. Although using the logos doctrine to explain the relationship

---

[1] *I Apol.* xliv. 8; *Republic* x. 617.

[2] Andresen, *Z.N.T.W.* XLIV (1952–3), 188.

[3] Although he places great emphasis on the activity of daemons in causing men to choose the wrong, his emphasis is on sinners rather than sin.

between God and Christ Justin, throughout his writings, pre-supposes the earlier faith of the Church in the person of Christ. This is made certain by the congruity of his doctrine of the Incarnation with the teaching of the New Testament and by his confessed reliance on apostolic doctrine.

For Justin Jesus Christ was both divine and human. In Mary's womb the cosmic Reason had become available to men as a human being of flesh and blood. Justin nowhere argues why this has happened—he accepts it as a fact. The Virgin Birth looms large in Justin's account. He defends it as a common belief and follows closely St Luke's account. His only variation is his introduction of the Holy Spirit into the account of the annunciation, 'Behold thou shalt conceive of the Holy Spirit, and shalt bear a Son'. However, Justin was rather vague on the doctrine of the Spirit and he seems to have identified the δύναμις θεοῦ or πνεῦμα ἅγιον with the logos,[1] or at least re-garded them as only names for the logos.

Justin does not explain how the logos acted upon Mary. He is content with the biblical account of how she was overwhelmed (ἐπεσκίασεν) or overpowered by his divine brilliance. This account was more credible than the stories of the births of Perseus, Dionysius or Hercules[2] because these myths repre-sented the deity as having intercourse with human women. And, in any case, it had been foretold by the prophets—especially Isa. vii. 14—in spite of Trypho's determined objections.[3] The divine nature of Christ's birth was also indicated by the prophecy of the 'Stone cut without hands',[4] and his blood, made by God, typified by the blood of the grape.[5]

Justin insists on the fact that Christ was both divine and human. Although a crucified man Christ was the first-born of the unbegotten God who will be appointed Judge of all men.

[1] *I Apol.* xxxiii. 6. In two other passages (*I Apol.* xlvi. 5 and *Dial.* cxxxix. 4) Justin states that through the agency of a δύναμις τοῦ λόγου (or the power of the omnipotent Father) Jesus was born of the Virgin as man. The power of the logos was thus given by the Father to the logos. It seems improbable that this δύναμις is a personal power, the Holy Spirit, but rather that God has endowed the logos with power to become incarnate. Goodenough, *Theology of Justin Martyr*, pp. 236–7.

[2] *I Apol.* xxii. 5; *Dial.* lxx. 5; *Dial.* lxix. 2–3.

[3] *I Apol.* xxxiii. 1; *Dial.* lxvii. 1, lxx. 1, 3, lxxxiv. 1.

[4] *Dial.* lxxvi. 1.   [5] *Dial.* lxxvi. 2.

We have already discussed the titles which Justin applies to the logos.[1] What is significant is that, for Justin, these apply as fully to the incarnate Christ as to the pre-incarnate logos. Justin is insistent that the incarnate Christ is the whole logos.[2] In the Incarnation the logos did not assume a body but became entirely a man of body, logos or spirit, and soul.[3] In the section on Justin's anthropology we have seen that Justin held the traditional threefold division of human nature, but it is significant that he nowhere implies that Christ was divine in the higher part of his nature and only man in body or body and soul. Christ was man inasmuch as he was, like all men, compounded of body, spirit, and soul, but he was the whole logos inasmuch as his body, soul, and spirit were what the logos, in his entirety, had become.[4] This is quite different from the later Apollinarian teaching and it is an error to suggest that Justin anticipates the later heresy. Apollinaris was concerned with the relation of the human and divine natures in the person of Christ and ultimately he came to hold the belief that in the Incarnation the logos was substituted for the human mind of Christ. It is likely that he came to this belief because he could not find a place for a human mind in his psychology. Dr G. L. Prestige, in his brilliant study of Apollinaris, has reminded us that, in ancient times, psychology was ever the parent of heresy.[5] Justin however belonged to an earlier period before psychology had begun to torture the minds of Christian thinkers. Justin was not worried, as was Apollinaris, by the question how two separate minds, wills, and principles of action could co-exist in a single living being. For him Christ was the one, whole logos— whether in his pre-incarnate or incarnate state—and he does not work out the logical implications of this belief. Thus: 'But these words (i.e. the accounts of divine manifestations to the patriarchs) were uttered to demonstrate that Jesus Christ is the

[1] Pp. 93–6.   [2] *II Apol.* x. 8.
[3] *II Apol.* x. 1: διὰ τοῦ τὸ λογικὸν τὸ ὅλον τὸν φανέντα δι' ἡμᾶς Χριστὸν γεγονέναι καὶ σῶμα καὶ λόγον καὶ ψυχήν.
[4] Goodenough, *Theology of Justin Martyr*, p. 241, gives an admirable statement of this.
[5] *Fathers and Heretics* (London, 1940), p. 110. This essay (pp. 94–119) goes far to rehabilitate Apollinaris as a Christian thinker of the first magnitude: 'It is the supreme merit of Apollinaris that he plotted the right course by insisting on the unity of Christ's Person' (p. 116).

Son of God and Apostle, who was first the logos, and appeared, now in the form of fire, now in the likeness of bodiless creatures. Now, however, having become man by the will of God for the sake of the human race he has endured...'[1] In other words the logos, who once appeared in theophanies, has now become man in Jesus Christ. That is the sum and substance of Justin's doctrine of the Incarnation.

Justin does not consider how the humanity is related to the divinity in Christ beyond affirming that Jesus Christ was divine and human. On occasions he gives the impression that Jesus, in his incarnate life, had no real blood relationship with the human race. He was ἄνθρωπος ἐν ἀνθρώποις[2] rather than ἄνθρωπος ἐξ ἀνθρώπων.[3] Jesus was not of human seed and humanity had no more to do with the making of his blood than with the making of the blood of a grape.[4] The Virgin was the instrument of the Incarnation, but his flesh was not her flesh, his blood not her blood. Justin insists that the title Son of Man should be rendered *like* the Son of Man so as to deny his human affiliations.[5]

Nevertheless, Justin asserts that the humanity of Jesus was a true humanity. He was a man capable of suffering (ὁμοιοπαθής).[6] He grew from infancy to manhood and ate human food like the rest of humanity.[7] He was really afraid during the Agony in the Garden and his sweat fell like drops of blood.[8] Yet although human in his bodily life and growth Jesus possessed, throughout his incarnate life, the full powers of the logos. Justin proves this from the traditional account of Jesus' life. Even as a babe, he says, the daemons recognised his supremacy when the magi, who had previously been under their control, revolted and visited Christ as their new master.[9] Justin tells the story of the birth of Christ, his growth to manhood,[10] and his work as a carpenter[11] until the age of about thirty. Justin's account of Jesus' baptism is interesting. As is well known he was acquainted with the utterance of the Divine Voice in the

---

[1] *I Apol.* lxiii. 10.
[2] *I Apol.* xxiii. 3.
[3] *Dial.* lxxvi. 2, liv. 2. Goodenough, *Theology of Justin Martyr*, p. 242.
[4] *Dial.* liv. 2.
[5] *Dial.* lxxvi. 1.
[6] *II Apol.* x. 8; *Dial.* xlviii. 3.
[7] *Dial.* lxxxiv. 2, lxxxviii. 2.
[8] *Dial.* ciii. 8.
[9] *Dial.* lxxviii.
[10] *Dial.* lxxxviii. 2.
[11] *Dial.* lxxxviii. 8.

reading of the Western text: 'Thou art my Son: this day have I begotten thee',[1] which was clearly open to an adoptionist interpretation. Justin counters this by stating that the Spirit had inspired the Hebrew prophets, but when it descended upon Christ at the baptism it ceased from such activity, rested on him and was from then on given only to the followers of Christ. The Voice is a proof of Christ's divinity and an invitation to salvation.[2] In other words Christ did not, at his baptism, receive his powers—because he was born with them. To have interpreted the baptism from the point of view of adoptionism would have undermined Justin's belief that the whole logos was incarnate in Christ.

The temptation following the baptism, according to Justin, typified the whole career of the logos.[3] Christ's miracles he accepts as having been prophesied in the Old Testament[4] although he does not use them as evidence for Jesus' divine sonship. He affirms that in his earthly life Jesus was sinless.[5]

Justin gives copious extracts from Jesus' teaching which he takes, in the main, from the Synoptic Gospels. This teaching is a power which strikes home to the mind and heart: 'For his word of truth and wisdom is more blazing and more brilliant than the sun's might, and enters into the very depths of the heart and of the understanding.'[6] This is similar to the New Testament idea of the Christian Gospel as a word or power.

Justin pays much attention to the Passion narratives. The crucifixion, for him, was the supreme incident in Jesus' life. He finds references to the Cross in almost every part of the Old Testament,[7] in nature,[8] and in Plato's *Timaeus*.[9] It is the Cross which above all delivers men from idolatry and turns them to the worship of God. Justin adds only a few small details to the synoptic account of the crucifixion such as the mockery of the bystanders[10] and the soldiers' cry, 'Judge us', at the actual crucifixion.[11]

Justin's theory of the Incarnation is not systematised and, to

---

[1] *Dial.* lxxxviii. 8 quoting Ps. ii. 7 and in *Dial.* ciii. 6, Luke iii. 23 (D); Old Latin, Clem. Alex., Aug. and other 'Western' authorities.

[2] See the whole of *Dial.* lxxxviii.   [3] *Dial.* cxxv. 3–4.

[4] *I Apol.* xlviii. 1; *Dial.* lxix. 4.   [5] *Dial.* xvii. 1, cii. 7 *inter alia.*

[6] *Dial.* cxxi. 2.   [7] *Dial.* lxxiii. 1, lxxxvi, xcvii.

[8] *I Apol.* lv.   [9] *I Apol.* lx. 5.

[10] *Dial.* ci. 3.   [11] *I Apol.* xxxv. 6.

later ages, must have appeared somewhat naïve and ill-balanced. Yet we must never forget that Justin was a pioneer Apologist and, considering the pitfalls into which he might have fallen, it is all to his credit that he maintained so strongly that Jesus Christ was both divine and human. His logos doctrine could easily have led him to underestimate Jesus' humanity, like the later Alexandrian theologians, and the fact that, on the whole, he avoids this is significant. Docetism, Ebionite Adoptionism and Marcionism had no attraction for him and his own Middle Platonist presuppositions did not have the influence that they had on other aspects of his thought. Justin is a witness to what the main stream of the Church believed in the mid-second century although he acknowledges that some Christians, as in our own day, denied the Virgin Birth of Our Lord.[1]

REDEMPTION

For Justin Christianity was supremely the full revelation of truth because Christ himself was the incarnation of the whole, divine logos. In accordance with his emphasis on logos he tended to attribute the evil of life to the subjection of men's rational powers by the daemons who were everywhere active in the universe. Justin believed that if men are shown the truth they have the power to recognise it and can then choose to obey it. The purpose of Christ's coming is to save men from evil deeds and powers and to teach assured truth.[2] He brings to a race diseased and deceived by the action of daemons the full divine energy. He is the medicine to cure[3] which he becomes by sharing our humanity. He is therefore called the Saviour[4] in whom we receive remission of sins and regeneration. How then are men saved?

(a) Justin emphasises that Christ saves as *Teacher*. He cannot conceive of anyone accepting the Christian doctrine of the future state without a determination to choose the good rather than the evil. The daemons however have darkened the light within men and deceived and led astray the human race,[5] making slaves and servants of men. What understanding men

---

[1] *Dial.* xlviii. 4 where ἀπὸ τοῦ ὑμετέρου seems to refer to Ebionite Christians. [2] *I Apol.* xxiii; *II Apol.* ix.
[3] *II Apol.* xiii. [4] *I Apol.* lxi. [5] *I Apol.* liv. 1.

had of the truth was dim and weak until the coming of the whole logos in Christ. Now the apprehension of truth was strong through the illumination given by the teaching of Jesus. It is by his teaching that men rightly know and worship the one Father and God.[1] It is by his teaching of a second advent and of the dread Judgement Day that men know how to prepare themselves for the great assize and division of humanity. It is this truth which enables men to sift the true and the false in human speculations since the logos alone distinguishes, amid the confusion of philosophies, what is his own.

On the surface Justin appears to rationalise a doctrine of redemption and to teach an exemplarist theory by which Christ comes to destroy the daemons, reveal light and knowledge and so enable men to overcome their faults, purify themselves and choose the higher life. Certainly texts can be found in Justin very similar to the later teaching of Abelard which is expressed with admirable conciseness in one of his propositions condemned by the Council of Sens in 1141 and by Innocent II: 'I think, therefore, that the purpose and cause of the incarnation was that he might illuminate the world by his wisdom and excite it to the love of himself.'[2] However, we do Justin an injustice if we seize on one aspect of his thought to the exclusion of others. It is true that, for him, Christ saves men as Teacher and Example. But his teaching is an active power or force—a δύναμις from God—which pierces the depths of the heart and mind[3]—a burning fire which inflames man's whole being. Justin's own conversion had left him with an inner fire of love for the prophets and for Christ.[4] Redemption is not therefore for Justin an ethical or metaphysical theory which men can either choose or reject but the imparting to men of illumination and power which enables them to conquer the power of the daemons. The whole logos is a factor in the inner life of every Christian. Christ is not simply an external Teacher but an active power.

(b) This theory of redemption has strictly no place for the Cross as it is in the Incarnation that men come to know the

---

[1] *I Apol.* xiii.

[2] *Epist. ad Rom., Opera* ed. Cousin, II, p. 207, quoted in Rashdall, *The Idea of the Atonement in Christian Theology*, p. 358.

[3] *Dial.* cxxi. 2.   [4] *Dial.* viii. 1.

whole logos. However, Justin, more than any other second-century Apologist, states repeatedly that Christ saves us by his death on the Cross and by his resurrection. Christ brought us healing by becoming a partaker of our sufferings.[1] By his blood he cleanses believers.[2] He endured all for our sakes and on account of our sins.[3] By dying and rising again he conquered death.[4] 'He became the beginning of another race, who have been born again by him through water and faith and wood, which contains the mystery of the Cross.'[5] In baptism believers receive remission of sins by the blood of Christ.[6] 'His Father', says Justin, 'caused him to suffer on behalf of the human race.'[7] The Jews knew not, when they inflicted the suffering upon him, that he was 'the eternal Priest and King and Christ'.[8] Justin repeatedly applies Isa. liii to Christ and refers to almost every clause of that chapter. Christ is the Paschal Lamb whose blood will deliver from death those who have believed.[9] Christ served men even unto the Cross and acquired them through its blood and mystery.[10] He saved men by submitting to all that men deserved for sin, that is, the curse pronounced on all who did not keep the Law; therefore he was crucified, because the curse lay on crucifixion; but he was no more under God's curse when he endured our curse than was the brazen serpent, which was ordered by God although he had condemned all images. God saved of old by an image without violating the second commandment. He saves now by a Crucified those who are worthy of the curse without however laying his curse on the Crucified. It is the Jews, and not God, who now fulfil the text by 'cursing him that hung on the tree'.[11] This Cross and suffering the Father willed for man's sake that on his Christ might fall the curse of all men. He willed it, knowing that he would raise him again from this death, as Christ testified on the Cross by his appeal to the Father.

Justin justifies the coming of Christ to be despised, to suffer and to die by many appeals to prophecy, especially to Ps. xxii,[12] and to Jacob's blessing in Gen. xlix. 8, 12 f. It is, he says, 'the hidden power of God which is exhibited in the crucified Christ'.[13]

[1] *II Apol.* xiii; *Dial.* lxxxvi, cxxxvii.   [2] *I Apol.* xxxii; *Dial.* xiii, xl, liv.
[3] *I Apol.* lvi, lxiii; *Dial.* ciii.   [4] *I Apol.* lxiii.
[5] *Dial.* cxxxviii.   [6] *Dial.* liv, cxv.   [7] *Dial.* xcv.
[8] *Dial.* xcvi.   [9] *Dial.* cxi.   [10] *Dial.* cxxxiv.
[11] *Dial.* xciv–xcvi.   [12] *Dial.* xcviii.   [13] *Dial.* xlix.

With great emphasis Justin represents Christ's death and resurrection as a triumph over the daemons.[1] Death has come to the Serpent through him who has been crucified, by coming to whom men also may be saved.[2] The daemons are now subject to his name and to the dispensation of his suffering.[3] They are frequently exorcised in his name, so that his power over them is proved.[4]

The significance of Justin's statements about the Cross should not be underestimated. In strict logic his philosophical presuppositions, which controlled his intellectual apprehension of Christianity, had no place for any objective theory of the Atonement. The fact that he has so much to say about the Cross and what it had effected is a strong proof that the Church of his day held this belief. Its faith rested not only on the Word of truth which Christ had spoken but also on the redemption which he had wrought by his death and resurrection. Christ's power lay not only in his character and example; not only in his power to inflame and illuminate the hearts of men; but in what he was believed to have done for men on the Cross. Justin accepted this faith as fundamental although it did not easily fit into the philosophy which he had imbibed. Justin is thus revealed as one who accepted, in this connection without question, the traditional faith of the Church.

[1] *I Apol.* xlvi; *II Apol.* vi; *Dial.* xci, cxxxi.
[2] *Dial.* xci.   [3] *Dial.* xxx.
[4] *Dial.* lxxvi. The Cross played a conspicuous part in exorcisms.

CHAPTER X

CHURCH AND SACRAMENTS

THE CHURCH

THE New Testament writings and the early post-apostolic literature bear witness to the expansion of the Christian Gospel during the first two centuries A.D. From its early beginnings in Jerusalem the Church rapidly made converts and gained a footing in many prominent cities of the Graeco-Roman world. However, the actual intensity of the spread of the Gospel is largely undocumented and we have to rely, in the main, on general statements and the consciousness of growing strength which is found in early Christian literature. The only exceptions to this before the time of Justin are: (a) Acts xxi. 20, which states that at the time of St Paul's last visit to Jerusalem[1] Christians were to be found, in their many thousands, among the Palestinian Jews. (b) Pliny *Ep. ad Traj.* xcvi–xcvii which testify to the spread of the Church throughout Bithynia and Pontus even into villages and country areas so that 'many of all ages and ranks, and even of both sexes, are in risk of their lives, or will be'.[2] The Church had clearly found, in this area, congenial soil for its expansion.[3]

Justin speaks of the diffusion of Christianity in strong though general terms. Christians were 'men of every race'[4] and comprised both educated and ignorant people.[5] There were more Christians from among pagans than from the Jews or Samaritans.[6] 'All the earth has been filled with the glory and grace of God and his Christ.'[7] In the Eucharist the sacrifice of thanksgiving was offered 'in all places throughout the world'...'For there is not a single race of human beings, barbarians, Greeks,

---

[1] Or, if one adopts the arguments of *Formgeschichte*, at the time when Acts was written.

[2] *multi enim omnis aetatis, omnis ordinis, utriusque sexus etiam, vocantur in periculum et vocabuntur.*

[3] See Harnack, *The Expansion of Christianity in the First Three Centuries* (Edinburgh, 1908), II, 148–9, 172–3. Cf. also Clem. *Rom.* vi and Tacit. *Annals* xv. 44.   [4] *I Apol.* i, xxv, xxxii, xl, liii, lvi *inter alia*.

[5] *II Apol.* x.   [6] *I Apol.* liii.   [7] *Dial.* xlii.

or whatever name you please to call them, nomads or vagrants or herdsmen living in tents, where prayers through the name of Jesus the crucified are not offered up to the Father and Maker of the universe.'[1] Justin's language tells us little of the actual numerical strength of the Christians although his reference to the herdsmen living in tents seems to refer to nomadic Arabs. Clearly some of his statements are the product of a belief that the Gospel must already have spread over the whole earth and his language is not to be taken too literally. What is significant is his statement that Gentile Christians already outnumbered Jewish Christians, for this accords with a similar statement in II Clement ii. 3 which comes perhaps from the same period as Justin.[2] Justin was conscious of the growing strength of the Church in his day, for he believed that the Gospel had already spread through the different classes of society and had representatives among many nations. His language, idealised though it is, would have sounded hollow unless Christianity had already adapted itself to the races within and beyond the confines of the Empire. Justin, like most other early Christian writers, gives no figures, but the fact of the Church's considerable expansion from its Jewish cradle is presupposed by his writings.

What information does Justin give concerning the internal constitution and doctrinal beliefs of the Church as he knew it? The writings of Ignatius of Antioch witness to an early rise of the monarchical episcopate, at least in Syria, and notices from the last decades of the second century show, not only the near universal spread of episcopacy, but the emergence of more developed doctrinal beliefs. What light does Justin throw on the character of the Church in the mid-second century?

It is, I believe, important to note that Justin openly claimed that he was a representative of the great body of Christians and that he had received his Christianity from the Church of the preceding age. It is necessary to stress this, as a cursory study of his writings—and especially the *Apology*—might suggest that he was fundamentally a Middle Platonist philosopher who incorporated into his philosophic presuppositions a smattering of Christianity. Nothing could be further from the truth. We have

---

[1] *Dial.* cxvii. Nomads = Scythians; cf. Horace, *Odes* III. xxiv. 9 f.

[2] ἔρημος ἐδόκει εἶναι ἀπὸ τοῦ θεοῦ ὁ λαὸς ἡμῶν, νυνὶ δὲ πιστεύσαντες πλείονες ἐγενόμεθα τῶν δοκούντων ἔχειν θεόν.

already seen[1] how his philosophy did, in fact, modify the biblical basis of his faith, *but Justin himself was unaware of this*. He presented his *Apology* in the name of all true Christians and he makes the point that they should not be confounded with Christians falsely so called.[2] The doctrine which Justin represented was, he believed, the traditional belief of the Church: 'We have learned from tradition that God has no need of material offerings from men...we have been taught and firmly believe that he accepts only those who imitate the good things which are his...'[3] So likewise the rite of baptism and the reason for its observance had been received from the Apostles;[4] and the evident desire of Justin to adhere to the apostolic commands is revealed when he says of the Eucharist that the Apostles, in the 'Memoirs', delivered what was enjoined on them.[5] In opposition to heretical Christians he classes himself with those 'who are disciples of the true and pure doctrine of Jesus Christ'.[6] He admits however that 'many who are of the pure and pious faith' reject chiliasm.[7] Justin, however, chooses not to follow men's doctrines but God and the doctrines which come from him, and states that he and those who agree with him are 'in all respects right-minded Christians'.[8]

It is evident from these statements that, for Justin, Christianity was a body of beliefs which he had received from the Church, to which the main stream of Christians in his own day subscribed. This body of beliefs had been handed down from the Apostles. Justin's philosophy, important though it was to him, had not made his Christianity. Rather he understood and interpreted the Christianity which he professed by the aid of Middle Platonism. And this Christianity had been delivered to the Church at the beginning of its existence by Our Lord's Apostles.

The above interpretation is confirmed by Justin's attitude towards the heresies. Justin was aware, no doubt from his sojourn in Rome, that heretical and semi-heretical beliefs were being propagated by teachers who claimed the name of Christian. He regarded these as novelties introduced by daemons to destroy the work of Christ. Thus he states that Simon

---

[1] See chapters VI and VII.
[2] *I Apol.* iv.
[3] *I Apol.* x.
[4] *I Apol.* lxi.
[5] *I Apol.* lxvi.
[6] *Dial.* xxxv.
[7] *Dial.* lxxx.
[8] *Ibid.*

Magus, Menander and Marcion had been put forward by the daemons to deceive men.[1] The former two were magicians while Marcion was a real heretic who was alive in his day and sought to cause many in every nation to blaspheme the Creator of the universe. Justin, usually the apotheosis of reason, even states that the slanderous tales circulated about the Christians might be true of the Marcionites.[2] Justin shrewdly points out that the heretical groups bear the names of their founders, such as the Marcionites or Valentinians or Basilidaeans or Saturnilians,[3] while the Church, he implies, bears the name of no human founder: 'With none of them do we hold communion, who know that they are godless and impious and unrighteous and lawless, and instead of worshipping Jesus acknowledge him only in name.'[4] Justin, in no uncertain terms, repudiates these heretics as recent perverters of Christianity who stand outside the pale of the Church. He is conscious that the Church, as he knew it, held to the apostolic teaching and was separate from the heretical groups. It had not come into being from a fusion of pagan philosophy with earlier Christian teaching but was the bearer of the doctrines handed down from the Apostles. This Church knew Gnosticism to be a novelty and considered Jewish Christianity to be, at the best, a pardonable weakness.

Justin has no developed doctrine of the Church such as we find worked out in St Paul's Epistles to the Colossians and the Ephesians. He accepts, with most second-century Christian writers, that the Church is a supernatural society founded by the apostles in Christ's name.[5] This did not require argument. Moreover, since his writings were directed, in the main, to non-Christians there was no need to state a doctrine of the Church. However, incidental references in Justin's writings give a clear idea of his belief in the spiritual unity of Christians belonging to different Christian communities. Expounding Psalm xlv Justin

---

[1] *I Apol.* xxvi, lvi, lviii.   [2] *I Apol.* xxvi.
[3] *Dial.* xxxv.   [4] *Dial.* xxxv. 5.
[5] See the important remarks of M. Goguel, *The Primitive Church* (London, 1963), p. 78: '...the idea of the Church, as a supernatural society founded by the apostles..., is now no more open to question than the conception of the Church as a depository of a doctrine of salvation. By the end of the first century and the beginning of the second, there seems to have been fairly wide agreement as to the conception of the Church and the character of the ministries exercised within it.'

writes: 'And they likewise proclaim that them that believe on him, as men of one soul and one synagogue and one Church, the ‑Word of God addressed as *Daughter*, namely the Church which came into being from his name and shares his name, for we are all called Christians.'[1] Again Christ 'hath made us a house of prayer and worship'.[2] Christians are 'the vine planted by God and Christ the Saviour',[3] and are 'the robe of Christ' because in them the seed of God, the logos, dwells.[4] They have believed 'as one man' in God, and 'being inflamed by the word of his calling, are the true high-priestly race'.[5] They are the true Israel.[6] The prophet Isaiah had predicted[7] that the wicked shall become subject to Christ 'and that all shall become as one child'. 'Such a thing', Justin adds, 'as you may witness in the body; although the members are enumerated as many, all together are called one, and are a body. For a populace too and an assembly,[8] though they are many men in number, yet as forming but one thing are called and addressed by one appellation.'

It is evident that behind Justin's language is the earlier belief that Christians form a spiritual temple or body united to Christ as the Head. The unity of Christendom in Christ is, for him, a fact and follows from his belief that the Church held to the apostolic teaching.

As to the organisation of the Church in his day Justin gives but little information. It was no part of his apologetic purpose to expound the nature or function of the Christian Ministry. He throws light on the subject only when describing the public worship of the Church and the celebration of baptism and the eucharist. And even then, as a result of his evident desire to emphasise the simplicity of the Christian sacraments, Justin does not give an accurate description of the officers of the Church or their relations to one another and the whole body of Christ. The sum of Justin's information is this:

After describing the rite of baptism[9] Justin says that the adult candidate is led to those called brethren where they are

---

[1] *Dial.* lxiii. 5.   [2] *Dial.* lxxxvi.   [3] *Dial.* cx.
[4] *I Apol.* xxxii; cf. *Dial.* liv, lxxxvii.   [5] *Dial.* cxvi.
[6] *Dial.* cxix, cxxv, cxxx, cxxxv.
[7] *Dial.* xlii. This chapter is fundamental to Justin's belief in the Church.
[8] ἐκκλησία. Justin uses the analogy of a legally-summoned gathering of Greek citizens.   [9] *I Apol.* lxi.

assembled,[1] that is, in the house-church or meeting place. After common prayers and the greeting of one another with a kiss the eucharistic elements are brought *to the ruler of the brethren* (τῷ προεστῶτι τῶν ἀδελφῶν). After the prayers and thanksgiving, offered by the ruler, those called deacons (διάκονοι) give to each of those present a portion of the consecrated bread, wine and water, and later take this to the absent. In *I Apol.* lxvii Justin describes the ordinary Sunday worship of the Church at which the ruler instructs the assembled Christians. This is followed by the eucharist which the ruler celebrates. A voluntary alms collection is taken and deposited with the ruler who is responsible for charitable distribution to orphans, widows, the sick and other needy persons.

What is the exact meaning of the term ὁ προεστώς or ὁ προεστώς τῶν ἀδελφῶν which is found five times in *I Apol.* lxv and lxvii? T. G. Jalland, in an important article,[2] has argued forcibly in support of the translation 'ruler' or 'ruler of the brethren' instead of the usual English translation 'president',[3] or the Latin *is qui fratribus praeest*.[4] He points out that προεστώς, the 2nd aorist participle active, with intransitive sense, of προΐστημι, used as a substantive, is found in Herodotus, Thucydides and Plato in the singular with a meaning analogous to ὁ ἄρχων.[5] In the LXX the verb προΐστημι is used with reference to an official appointment. Jalland shows that the sense 'be at the head (of), rule, direct' has a continuous tradition behind it from classical usage onwards and by way of the LXX and New Testament itself.[6] He suggests that the term ὁ προεστώς τῶν ἀδελφῶν in Justin means not merely 'he who presides over the brethren' but 'he who is at the head of the brethren' or 'the ruler of the brethren', i.e. most probably the bishop.

Why then did Justin describe the chief officer of the Church in this way and not as ὁ ἐπίσκοπος? Jalland believes that

---

[1] *I Apol.* lxv.　　　　[2] *Studia Patristica*, v (1962), 83–5.

[3] Rendered 'President' by M. Dods (A.N.C.L.), C. C. Richardson (Library of Christian Classics), Bettenson (Documents of the Christian Church), Stevenson (A New Eusebius), Gwatkin (Selections from Early Christian Writers).

[4] J. C. Otto, *Opera*, 3rd ed., p. 179.

[5] Jalland, *Studia Patristica*, v (1962), 83–4.

[6] Rom. xii. 8; I Thess. v. 12; I Tim. v. 17. The N.E.B. translates 'leaders' in each context.

Justin deliberately avoided the technical term ἐπίσκοπος out of deference to pagan susceptibilities to whom the expression might have been obscure or misleading. Hence his choice of a word capable of a non-technical interpretation. Jalland's linguistic arguments as to the correct translation of ὁ προεστώς may be accepted, but his further view that Justin was deliberately using a non-technical term is open to the serious objection that Justin, *in this same account*,[1] mentions the order of *deacons* who have the definite function of distributing the consecrated elements at the eucharist. Moreover in his account of the rite of baptism he uses the technical term 'regeneration' with marked emphasis[2] and he also defines the bread, wine and water as 'this food we call eucharist'.[3] We should not assume that the technical terms 'bishop', 'presbyter' would have been unfamiliar to pagans. Hadrian, in his letter to Servianus, which is to be dated *c*. A.D. 134, knew of the existence of both bishops and presbyters[4] although he had no high regard for the office.

What then is the explanation of Justin's use of ὁ προεστώς? It may be significant that the same term is found in Hermas, but it is there applied, expressly in one instance, and probably in others, to the presbyters.[5] It is also an interesting fact that the term ὁ ἐπίσκοπος is not applied to the chief officer of the Roman Church until a period later than that of Justin although in Syria and Asia Minor it had been used some forty years earlier.[6] Hegesippus however applied the term to Symeon of Jerusalem[7] as Polycrates did to Polycarp, Thraseas and other Church leaders in Asia Minor.[8] But not only does Clement of Rome use 'bishop' and 'presbyter' interchangeably,[9] but Ignatius himself is silent, in his Epistle to the Romans, as to any 'bishop' in Rome, as is also Polycarp, in his Letter to the Philippians, as to a 'bishop' at Philippi. On the other hand, at a time a little later than that of Justin, Dionysius of Corinth wrote

---

[1] *I Apol.* lxv.   [2] *I Apol.* lxi.

[3] *I Apol.* lxvi.

[4] Vopiscus, *Vita Saturni* 8. See L. W. Barnard, *C.Q.R.* CLXIV (1964), 286–8.

[5] Vis. ii. 4, μετὰ τῶν πρεσβυτέρων τῶν προϊσταμένων τῆς ἐκκλησίας. Cf. Vis. ii. 2 and iii. 9.

[6] See Ign. *ad Polyc.*, *ad Eph.*, *ad Magn.*, *ad Trall.*

[7] Eus. *H.E.* IV. 22.   [8] Eus. *H.E.* V. 24.

[9] *Ad Cor.* xxi, xlii, xliv.

to the Roman Church and spoke of 'your blessed bishop Soter';[1] but Irenaeus, who was familiar with Church organisation in Asia Minor and Rome, calls Polycarp in one place a 'bishop'[2] and in another a 'presbyter'[3] and, in his Letter to Victor of Rome, speaks of 'the *presbyters* preceding Soter in the government of the Church which thou dost now rule'.[4] Moreover, none of the extant epitaphs of the Roman bishops gives the title *Episcopus* during the second century.

It would therefore seem that Justin's ὁ προεστώς was a permanent officer of the Church—the 'ruler of the brethren'— whose function included leading public worship, the celebration of the eucharist and the administration of Church finances. But because *the title* applied to this officer (although not necessarily his functions) varied in Justin's time in different localities (and perhaps even in the same locality) he deliberately refrained from specifying this further.[5] In an *Apology* primarily intended for the non-Christian world[6] Justin did not wish to give more particulars than were necessary and he accordingly uses a term, which implies rulership and a permanent status, without going further into the matter. We are therefore not strictly justified in stating categorically that Justin's ὁ προεστώς was the bishop, although this may have been the case.[7]

There are reasons for doubting whether the Church in Rome was an organisational entity in Justin's day. There were in Rome numerous groups of resident aliens, some of whom became Christians, and a number of congregations of a semi-heretical tinge. Some of these heretical teachers were anxious to capture 'the Church' for their views. There is also the fact that no trace of an indigenous Latin Christianity is found in Justin's time. Converts came mainly from orientals and until the end of the second century the Roman Church was pre-

---

[1] Eus. *H.E.* IV. 23.   [2] *Adv. Haer.* III. 3. 4.
[3] Eus. *H.E.* v. 20.   [4] Eus. *H.E.* v. 24.

[5] Note that Justin nowhere refers to 'elders' or 'presbyters'.

[6] Many pagans knew quite a lot about the Church. They would have soon queried Justin's information if incorrect. Moreover if the *Apology* was also intended for circulation as a manual for inquirers Justin's strict devotion to the truth would have prevented his portraying the Ministry other than it was.

[7] Eusebius uses προεστώς as a synonym for ἐπίσκοπος with reference to Publius, bishop of Athens; *H.E.* IV. 23.

dominantly Greek-speaking and oriental in character. L. E. Elliott-Binns suggests that there may have been a number of bishops or presbyter-bishops ruling different congregations in the city until well on into the second century.[1] Be that as it may it is likely that the residences of prominent Christian teachers might be the only 'publicly' known Christian places of worship.[2] In *I Apol.* lxv–lxvi Justin may therefore be describing a Christian baptismal-eucharist *as he knew it in Rome* while in *I Apol.* lxvii he is describing regular Sunday worship as he had known it in several different places. That is why he states: 'And on the day called Sunday there is a meeting in one place of those who live in cities or the country, and the memoirs of the apostles or the writings of the prophets are read as long as time permits.'[3] This is a reference to a general gathering of the church of a city or of the surrounding countryside—which certainly Justin did not know in Rome. The wonder is that he was so conscious of the Church's being the Body of Christ and a spiritual unity—the bearer of the apostolic doctrine and faith. He believed that he was a fair representative of the great body of Christians and that he taught only the apostolic doctrine which he had received. Such is the faith which moves mountains.

THE SACRAMENTS

Justin's account of the Christian sacraments of baptism and the eucharist, in his *First Apology*,[4] is of great importance and is the fullest description we possess of the second-century rites. Indeed apart from the *Apostolic Tradition* of Hippolytus of Rome his is the most detailed account to come down from pre-Nicene times. This is all the more remarkable in view of the fact that the *Apology* was primarily intended for a non-Christian public. Justin clearly wished to emphasise the harmlessness of the Christian rites and to assure his readers that no horrors were perpetrated at Christian gatherings. This is why he introduces

[1] *The Beginnings of Western Christendom* (London, 1948), p. 102.
[2] Justin, according to *Acts of Martyrdom* 3, states that Christians meet in a number of places 'where each one wishes to and is able'. He then adds (significantly) that during the whole of his second visit to Rome he has known of only one place of meeting—'above a certain Martinus at the baths of Timotinus'.
[3] *I Apol.* lxvii.   [4] *I Apol.* lxi–lxvi.

his account almost incidentally and without warning. It is however significant that he uses the technical terminology of the Church in his description of both dominical sacraments and assumes that, with a suitable exposition, this terminology will be intelligible. Of a doctrine of reserve, such as was later to come into prominence, Justin knew nothing and even if he had it is unlikely he would have agreed with it.

Recent study has shown[1] that it is a mistake, at least in regard to the early centuries, to treat the rite of baptism in isolation. It was part of a complex of ideas comprising instruction, repentance, forgiveness of sins, the gift of the Spirit, laying-on-of-hands, death and resurrection, salvation, conversion and the first partaking of the eucharist. What to us are separate rites, namely baptism, confirmation and first communion, were, in the earliest age of the Church, regarded as one whole—one baptism for the remission of sins. The usage varied in different centres—sometimes only two elements in the complex appearing —and the order varied as between Syria, Africa and Rome. Yet there was no divorce between the rites as is the case with us. This is illustrated by the long debate over the interpretation of the symbols used in early Christian paintings in the catacombs. Most of these have some clear reference to baptism or eucharist or to both and they are usually signs of salvation. But all attempts to gain a consensus of scholarly opinion have failed, for to some they mean baptism, to others the eucharist and to others simply the Gospel.[2]

The fullest account of the baptismal ceremonies to come down from the early period is that found in the *Apostolic Tradition* of Hippolytus *c.* A.D. 215 which may represent earlier Roman usage. Other traditions are found in the *Didascalia Apostolorum*, which represents Syrian usage *c.* A.D. 250, and in Tertullian's *De Baptismo*, which is to be dated *c.* A.D. 206. Justin's account contains fewer elements of the complex than appear in the later documents. This is possibly to be accounted for by his desire to stress the simplicity of the Christian rites. What is

[1] F. L. Cross, *I Peter: A Paschal Liturgy* (London, 1954); G. Every, *The Baptismal Sacrifice* (London, 1959). One of the first to investigate this question was F. E. Brightman, *J.T.S.* xxv (1923–4), 254–70.

[2] I owe this observation to G. Every, *The Baptismal Sacrifice*, p. 32, quoting W. Weidle, *The Baptism of Art* (1949), pp. 16–17.

significant is that Justin describes fully the baptismal-eucharist *before* he speaks of the weekly Sunday eucharist. The way in which he compares and contrasts this baptismal-eucharist with initiation into the pagan mysteries suggests that it is, for him, the greater mystery. We must now look at Justin's account in detail. In *I Apol.* lxi Justin says:[1]

Those who are persuaded and believe that the things we teach and say are true, and promise that they can live accordingly, are instructed to pray and beseech God with fasting for the remission of their past sins, while we pray and fast along with them. Then they are brought by us where there is water, and are reborn (ἀναγεννήσεως) by the same kind of rebirth by which we ourselves were reborn; for they are then washed in the water (τὸ ἐν τῷ ὕδατι τότε λουτρὸν ποιοῦνται) in the name of God the Father and Master of all, and of our Saviour Jesus Christ, and of the Holy Spirit.

After quoting John iii. 3, 4 and Isa. i. 16–20 Justin goes on:

And we learned from the apostles this reason for this (rite)...So that we should not remain children of necessity and ignorance, but (become sons) of free choice and knowledge, and obtain remission of the sins we have already committed, there is named at the water, over him who has chosen to be born again and has repented of his sinful acts, the name of God the Father and Master of all. Those who lead to the washing the one who is to be washed call on (God by) this term only. For no one may give a proper name to the ineffable God, and if anyone should dare to say that there is one, he is hopelessly insane.[2] This washing is called illumination (φωτισμός), since those who learn these things are illumined within. The illuminand is also washed in the name of Jesus Christ, who was crucified under Pontius Pilate, and in the name of the Holy Spirit, who through the prophets foretold everything about Jesus.

In *I Apol.* lxii Justin states the parallels and contrasts with pagan worship which, he holds, was a pale imitation of the Christian rites. And in *I Apol.* lxiii Justin digresses on the fact that the Word of God, who is God's Son, is also called 'Angel' and 'Apostle'. It is perhaps significant that this section contains a

---

[1] I have used C. C. Richardson's translation.

[2] Justin is aware that the Old Testament Divine name had been used for magical purposes in Gnostic circles.

credal statement embracing the Incarnation, death and resurrection of Christ.[1] In *I Apol*. lxv Justin continues his description of the baptismal-eucharist:

We, however, after thus washing the one who has been convinced and signified his assent, lead him to those who are called brethren, where they are assembled. They then earnestly offer common prayers for themselves and the one who has been illuminated and all others everywhere, that we may be made worthy, having learned the truth, to be found in deed good citizens and keepers of what is commanded, so that we may be saved with eternal salvation. On finishing the prayers we greet each other with a kiss.

There follows a description of the baptismal-eucharist which is celebrated by the 'ruler of the brethren'—this we shall consider later.

There are several interesting features in Justin's account. A period of pre-baptismal instruction is presupposed, as in the *Didache*.[2] The prayer and fasting, in which members of the Church join as witnesses, seem to be the immediate prelude to baptism although no period for this is specified.[3] It is significant that Justin speaks in the plural of both witnesses and baptised...*we* teach...*they* are instructed...*we* pray and fast along with them...*they* are brought by us...*they* are then washed in the water. This suggests a collective baptism on a certain day of the year with possibly a number of officiants. This may possibly be the Pascha which commemorated, in the pre-Nicene period, the whole complex of Christ's birth, incarnation, death and resurrection, and the gift of the Spirit. In the time of Tertullian baptism was administered only at the Pascha or at

---

[1] In *I Apol*. lix–lx (immediately before Justin's description of baptism) and in *I Apol*. lxii–lxiv (between the baptism and the baptismal-eucharist) the figure of Moses is very prominent. The position of these chapters is probably not fortuitous as the mysteries of Genesis and Exodus formed part of the baptismal ritual from the beginning. In baptism Egypt is left behind and the land of promise entered.

[2] vii. 1. The catechumenate received definite form *c*. A.D. 200. On its introduction in Rome see the important article of B. Capelle in *Recherches de Théologie Ancienne et Médiévale*, v (1933), 129–54. Recent scholarship has traced baptismal forms of instruction behind the New Testament Epistles. See especially P. Carrington, *The Primitive Christian Catechism*, and E. G. Selwyn, *The First Epistle of St Peter* (1946), pp. 363–466.

[3] *Did*. vii. 4 limits this to one or two days before baptism.

Pentecost.[1] However, later in *I Apol.* lxi and in *I Apol.* lxv Justin uses the singular in speaking of the candidate (although not of the witnesses) who is brought to the baptismal-eucharist, but this may have been due to a desire to write from the point of view of the individual convert.

The actual baptism, according to Justin's account, is in the threefold name of the Trinity[2] and is accompanied by a confession of faith[3] which may have been in answer to questions, although this is not specifically stated. Unfortunately Justin does not tell us what this confession embraced although it appears to have included assent to the three persons of the Trinity and the phrases 'who was crucified under Pontius Pilate' and 'who through the prophets foretold everything about Jesus'.[4] Perhaps we have here a trace of a baptismal creed? Oscar Cullman's investigations have shown that in the New Testament period candidates for baptism were asked if there was anything which hindered their being baptised, that is, whether they had fulfilled the conditions demanded.[5] We are not told, in the sources, who put this question. But it is clear from the *Didache*'s account,[6] as from Justin's, that members of the Church took some part in the baptism. This included prayer and fasting with the candidates, presence as witnesses during the actual baptisms, and the subsequent leading of the candidates back to the place where the Christian brethren were assembled.[7] It is not unreasonable to assume that these witnesses put questions to the baptised, heard their confession of faith, and baptised them. Their function, in Justin's time, was similar to that of the disciples of the rabbis in Judaism who,

---

[1] *De Baptismo* xix.

[2] Justin does not appeal to Matt. xxviii. 19.

[3] *I Apol.* lxi. 2: ὅσοι ἂν πεισθῶσι καὶ πιστεύωσιν ἀληθῆ ταῦτα τὰ ὑφ' ἡμῶν διδασκόμενα καὶ λεγόμενα εἶναι, καὶ βιοῦν οὕτως δύνασθαι ὑπισχνῶνται; cf. *I Apol.* lxv. 1: ἡμεῖς δὲ μετὰ τὸ οὕτως λοῦσαι τὸν πεπεισμένον καὶ συγκατατεθειμένον ἐπὶ τοὺς λεγομένους κτλ.

[4] *I Apol.* lxi. 13. It is not clear, from Justin, whether exorcism was connected with the baptismal rite. According to *Dial.* xx. 3, lxxvi. 6, lxxv. 2, *II Apol.* vi. 6 the ritual of exorcism culminated in the recital of a creed.

[5] 'Les traces d'une vieille formule baptismale dans le Nouveau Testament', *R.H.P.R.* XVII (1927), 424–34; *Baptism in the New Testament* (London, 1950), pp. 71–80.

[6] *Did.* vii. 1–4.   [7] Justin, *I Apol.* lxv. 1.

when a proselyte received baptism, reminded him of the commandments of the *torah*.[1]

Where was baptism administered? Justin implies that the group of candidates were baptised at a distance from the regular Christian meeting place: 'Then they are brought by us where there is water'...'We, however, after thus washing the one who has been convinced and signified his assent, lead him to those who are called brethren, where they are assembled.'[2] According to the *Didache* baptism was preferably to be in living, that is running, water, by immersion although, if running water was not at hand, other water could be used; if however neither was available then affusion could be used as second best.[3] Justin does not specify where or how baptism takes place. This may have been in a stream or river or in a primitive baptistery although, if the latter, we should have expected it to have been situated in or near to the regular Christian meeting place. Justin merely states that the candidate is washed three times in water and the name of each person of the Trinity pronounced over him at each washing.[4] There is no mention of a laying-on-of-hands preceding or following baptism before the candidates receive the eucharist for the first time, neither is the bishop specifically associated with baptism, as in the Ignatian Epistles, although the 'ruler of the brethren' celebrates the baptismal-eucharist immediately following the actual baptism. The agreement of Justin's account with that of the *Didache* is

---

[1] See J. Leipoldt, *Urchr. Taufe*, p. 16, quoted in M. Goguel, *The Primitive Church*, p. 323. Inscriptions in the Jewish catacomb of Monteverde in Rome (third century A.D.) mention *patroni* and *patronae*, evidently sponsors of proselytes. J. N. D. Kelly, *Early Christian Creeds* (London, 1950), pp. 73–4, points out that in Justin there are no instances of a *declaratory* creed but only baptismal interrogations. But side by side with this baptismal Trinitarian confession (in answer to questions) Justin knew a simple Christological *kerygma* of the type found in the apostolic age.

[2] *I Apol.* lxi and lxv.

[3] *Did.* vii. 2–3. It should be noted that the writer does not contrast baptism in running water, i.e. in a stream or river, with baptism by affusion, i.e. sprinkling, but baptism in running water *or static water* with sprinkling. Perhaps he has in view the use of a pond or water in a tank in certain circumstances. The latter is suggested by the qualification 'if thou canst not in cold, then in warm'. Have we here a trace of a rudimentary baptistery?

[4] *I Apol.* lxi.

remarkable.[1] Both seem to reflect a more primitive stage of development than that found in Tertullian and Hippolytus.

How did Justin regard baptism? His main thought is that baptism is a new birth (ἀναγέννησις). This is in line with the earliest baptismal tradition of the Church—indeed he explicitly states that the reason for the rite had been learnt from the apostles and quotes John iii. 3–4, 'Unless you are born again you will not enter into the Kingdom of heaven'. It is in the rite of baptism that the new birth literally takes place and candidates receive forgiveness of their past sins of which they have repented. In the *Dialogue* Justin says that the old rites of Judaism were broken cisterns, for they were performed without a turning from evil doings: 'Baptise your soul (free) from anger and from covetousness, from envy, from hatred—and behold your body is clean.'[2] The spiritual circumcision which alone is of any value Christians receive in baptism which is a laver of repentance and of the knowledge of God.[3] Baptism, for Justin, is the normal way of becoming a Christian and the new birth or spiritual circumcision occurs in the rite. It would, however, be pressing his words too hard to say, with Kirsopp Lake, that Justin connected forgiveness explicitly with the water, and the new life with 'the name'.[4] Repentance, forgiveness and the new birth are part of a single complex of ideas and cannot be partitioned. It is also significant that in *Dial.* xxix. 1 Justin connects Christian baptism with the Holy Spirit: 'What account should I, to whom God has borne testimony, then take of circumcision? What need of that other baptism[5] to one who has been baptised by the Holy Spirit?' This connection does not occur in *I Apol.* lxi–lxv although it was part of the received tradition of the Church. Instead, in *I Apol.* lxi. 12–13 Justin describes baptism as illumination (φωτισμός) and states that the candidates who have faithfully received baptismal instruc-

---

[1] The *Didache* however does not give any description of the introduction of the newly baptised into the public worship of the Church. See P. Carrington, *The Early Christian Church*, II, 118–19, who points out that Justin was not giving instructions for carrying out *the rite* but giving a short account of it to show there was nothing unseemly going on. Carrington says Justin's omission of any mention of laying-on-of-hands or anointing does not prove they were not in use in his day (p. 118). Neither does it prove it!

[2] *Dial.* xiv. 1–2.　　　　　　　[3] *Dial.* xiv. 1.
[4] *E.R.E.* II, 386.　　　　　　　[5] I.e. Jewish proselyte baptism.

tion are illumined within. Although this term had a long usage behind it Justin appears to have been the first to have associated the noun specifically with baptism,[1] although the association of light with baptism is very old.[2]

What did this φωτισμός imply? Justin believed that in baptism men were empowered with a divine force which will enable them to live a truly moral life. The whole logos had now come into a man's life with which he must co-operate for the attainment of salvation: 'They then earnestly offer common prayers for themselves and the one who has been illuminated and all others everywhere, that we may be made worthy, having learned the truth, to be found in deed good citizens and keepers of what is commanded, so that we may be saved with eternal salvation.'[3] It may justly be claimed that Justin has succeeded, perhaps better than any other second-century writer, in disassociating the rite of baptism from a 'magical' view of regeneration by emphasising that it is the beginning of a new life during which a man must strive to make his soul a habitation for the Spirit. His chances of doing so are immeasurably strengthened by the illumination, the presence of the whole logos, which came to him in his baptism. The test of the tree is

[1] See J. Ysebaert, *Greek Baptismal Terminology: Its Origin and Early Development* (Nijmegen, 1952), pp. 157–78, who shows that it is by no means certain that φωτίζειν, φωτισμός ever formed part of the technical vocabulary of the Mystery Religions. In the LXX φωτίζειν gained popularity as it translated 'wr (to be light, to shine) in almost all its meanings. The noun φωτισμός is used in the poetical writings of the LXX both literally and metaphorically. In the New Testament both verb and noun are used metaphorically of Christian belief as enlightenment; cf. II Cor. iv. 4, Eph. i. 18, II Tim. i. 10. In Heb. vi. 4, cf. x. 32, the verb is used in the passive of the enlightenment received at baptism. φωτίζειν however only became a technical term for baptism from the second century onwards, cf. Ign. *ad Rom. Inscript.* Justin clearly uses φωτίζειν in this technical way, cf. *I Apol.* lxi. 13, lxv. 1, *Dial.* xxxix. 2, cxxii. 1, 3 (cf. also Clem. Alex. *Paed.* i. 26. 1, *Strom.* v. 15. 3), but he is the first to use the noun φωτισμός specifically of baptism, *I Apol.* lxi. 12. By the time of Clem. Alex. it is used of baptism without further explanation, cf. *Protr.* xciv. 2.

[2] Selwyn, *The First Epistle of St Peter*, pp. 375–82, on the New Testament evidence.

[3] *I Apol.* lxv. 1; cf. *I Apol.* lxi. 10: 'So that we should not remain children of necessity and ignorance, but (become sons) of free choice and knowledge and obtain remission of the sins we have already committed...'

in the quality of the fruit and not only in the quality of a man's faith. In stating this so forcibly Justin is in line with the best Catholic tradition of the Church.[1]

Justin, in his *Apology*, gives a short account of what the Eucharist was in the mid-second century. In the *Dialogue* he supplements this account by stating that the Eucharist is a sacrifice and a commemoration of Christ's sufferings. How far Justin's account of the rite, in the *Apology*, represents the liturgical usage of the Roman Church in his day is not certain although the information which he gives, although rudimentary, fits in with that found in the more developed rite of Hippolytus' *Apostolic Tradition c.* A.D. 215. It is possible that Justin attended, in Rome, the liturgy of the Asian community and that there were local variations in the liturgy which may not have been of any great importance.[2] In his second account of the Eucharist, which he sets in the context of the regular Sunday worship of the Church, Justin may simply be presenting a picture of the rite as he had known it in several Christian centres and which, he believed, was offered everywhere.

We now turn to Justin's text. He describes two celebrations of the Eucharist: The first, in *I Apol.* lxv, is a baptismal-eucharist celebrated by 'the ruler of the brethren' in the presence of the assembled Christian community, the newly baptised and their witnesses. After common prayers for the new members of the Church and Christians everywhere, and the exchanging of a kiss,[3] bread and a cup of water and of wine mixed with water[4] are brought to the celebrant, who takes them and offers a prayer of praise and glory to the Father of the universe through the name of the Son and the Holy Spirit and offers further thanksgiving at some length. The people assent by saying *Amen* which, Justin explains, means 'so be it'. The deacons then give to each of those present a portion of the eucharistised bread and wine and water and later take these to the absent. It is significant that there is no mention, in

---

[1] Goodenough, *Theology of Justin Martyr*, p. 269, has some good remarks on this.

[2] P. Carrington, *The Early Christian Church*, II, 120.

[3] This is the kiss of peace. It is found in the same place in *Apost. Trad.* xxii. 6.

[4] On Harnack's theory that, in Justin's time, the Eucharist was celebrated with bread and water only and not water mixed with wine, see Appendix 4.

Justin's account, of presbyters or elders taking part in the service.[1]

In *I Apol.* lxvii Justin gives another and similar account of the Eucharist celebrated at the regular Sunday worship of the Christian community. Christians, he says, hold a common gathering every 'day of the sun'—'this first day on which God transforming darkness and matter made the universe, and Jesus Christ our Saviour rose from the dead on the same day'. At this gathering the 'Memoirs' of the Apostles or the writings of the prophets are read as long as time permits. Then the ruler gives an exposition of the reading which is followed by prayers said in a standing position. Then the bread, wine and water are brought and the ruler offers prayers and thanksgivings 'to the best of his ability'. Then follows the distribution to, and reception of, the eucharistic elements by those present and the sending to the absent by the deacons. This description is the same as that in *I Apol.* lxv, save that Justin mentions a voluntary collection of alms which is deposited with the ruler who is responsible for the care of orphans, widows, the sick, visitors and other needy persons.

In *I Apol.* lxvi, between his two descriptions of the rite, Justin explains its meaning:

This food we call Eucharist (εὐχαριστία), of which no one is allowed to partake except one who believes that the things we teach are true, and has received the washing for forgiveness of sins and for rebirth, and who lives as Christ handed down to us. For we do not receive these things as common bread or common drink; but as Jesus Christ our Saviour being incarnate by God's Word took flesh and blood for our salvation, so also we have been taught that the food consecrated by the Word of prayer which comes from him, from which our flesh and blood are nourished by transformation, is the flesh and blood of that incarnate Jesus. (Οὐ γὰρ ὡς κοινὸν ἄρτον οὐδὲ κοινὸν πόμα ταῦτα λαμβάνομεν· ἀλλ' ὃν τρόπον διὰ λόγου θεοῦ σαρκοποιηθεὶς 'Ιησοῦς Χριστὸς ὁ σωτὴρ ἡμῶν καὶ σάρκα καὶ αἷμα ὑπὲρ σωτηρίας ἡμῶν ἔσχεν, οὕτως καὶ τὴν δι' εὐχῆς λόγου τοῦ παρ' αὐτοῦ εὐχαριστηθεῖσαν τροφήν, ἐξ ἧς αἷμα καὶ σάρκες κατὰ μεταβολὴν τρέφονται ἡμῶν, ἐκείνου τοῦ σαρκοποιηθέντος 'Ιησοῦ καὶ σάρκα καὶ αἷμα ἐδιδάχθημεν εἶναι.) For the apostles in the memoirs composed by them, which are called Gospels, thus handed down what was com-

---

[1] The contrast with *Apost. Trad.* is marked.

manded them: that Jesus, taking bread and having given thanks, said, 'Do this for my memorial, this is my body'; and likewise taking the cup and giving thanks he said, 'This is my blood'; and gave it to them alone. This also the wicked daemons in imitation handed down as something to be done in the mysteries of Mithra; for bread and a cup of water are brought out in their secret rites of initiation, with certain invocations which you either know or can learn.

There are three passages in the *Dialogue* which supplement the accounts in the *First Apology*. In *Dial.* xli. 1–3 Justin describes the Eucharist as the antitype of the offering of fine flour for the purification of lepers:

For Jesus Christ our Lord ordered us to do this in remembrance of the suffering which he suffered on behalf of those who are being purged in soul from all iniquity, in order that we should at the same time give thanks to God for having created the world with all that is in it for man's sake, and also for having set us free from the evil in which we had (hitherto) been, and for having destroyed the powers and the authorities with a complete destruction by means of him who became liable to suffering according to his will.

This Eucharist is the pure sacrifice of which Malachi speaks (Mal. i. 10–11). In *Dial.* lxx. 3–4 Justin quotes Isa. xxxiii. 16:

'Bread shall be given him and his water is sure.' This, he says, refers to 'the bread which our Christ taught us to do in remembrance of his incarnation for those that believe on him, for whom he became even liable to suffering; and also of the cup which he taught us as we give thanks to do in remembrance of his blood'.

Lastly, in *Dial.* cxvii. 1, Justin says that the Eucharist is a sacrifice offered by Christians in every place on earth. In v. 3 he says, 'for these alone were Christians taught to make, even at the remembrance of their food, both dry and liquid,[1] in which also the suffering which the Son of God has suffered for their sake is brought to mind'. Although God accepts prayers and thanksgivings offered by worthy men at any time the Christian Eucharist, according to Justin, is the only one which has been worthy to be truly called a sacrifice.

There are several points in Justin's references to the Eucharist which deserve comment:

[1] The Jews distinguished the form of their 'grace' according to the type of food partaken. Mishna, *Berakoth* vi. 1–4.

(*a*) The Eucharist is for him, as for the writer of the *Didache*
and Ignatius, the central act of Christian Sunday worship. Only
the baptised are allowed to partake of it[1] and they must be living
in accordance with the precepts of Christ. Justin strongly emphasises the corporate[2] and ethical nature of the Eucharist
which is offered by Christians throughout the world. Such is the
bond of charity engendered that Christians gladly contribute
to a voluntary collection[3] on behalf of the needy which the
leader of the community administers.

How far does Justin's 'liturgical' language imply the use of a
fixed liturgy in his day? Lietzmann,[4] as is well known, derived
all extant eucharistic liturgies from two types—the Roman and
the Egyptian—both of which date from the beginning of the
third century. The first is found in the *Apostolic Tradition* of
Hippolytus of Rome and the second in the offertory prayer of
Serapion, bishop of Thmuis in Egypt. Lietzmann, from his
study of these two liturgical traditions, inferred that, prior to the
beginning of the third century, there existed two types of
liturgy. The first, the Roman, found in Hippolytus, is ultimately derived from St Paul's liturgical material; the second,
found in Serapion's anaphora, had its origin in that of the
Didache. Lietzmann's theory has received strong criticism, particularly at the hands of Dom Gregory Dix,[5] which need not
concern us here. What is significant is that Lietzmann discovered it was impossible to recede further into the period
before the beginning of the third century and was forced to rely
on inference or conjecture when interpreting the scattered
liturgical material from that period.

[1] This was a universal Christian tradition; cf. *Apost. Trad.* xxxii. 2.
[2]   And with them every spirit blest,
From realms of triumph or of rest,
From him who saw creation's morn,
Of all the angels eldest-born,
To the poor babe who died today,
Takes part in our thanksgiving lay.
              J. Keble, *Christian Year*, '*Holy Communion*'.
[3] It is interesting to note the *voluntary* collection at the Eucharist—'each
one as much as he chooses to'. The assessment of people's ability to contribute according to their income had not yet cast its shadow. There is no
suggestion however, in Justin, that Christian Stewardship was any less real
for this omission.   [4] *Messe und Herrenmahl* (Bonn, 1926).
[5] *The Shape of the Liturgy* (London, 1945).

Gregory Dix has however sought to prove that *the structure* of the eucharistic prayer in Hippolytus' *Apostolic Tradition* c. A.D. 215, and some of its wording, were traditional in Rome and were indeed an inheritance from the days of the Jewish apostles 'which the Roman Church with its usual conservatism had maintained more rigidly in the second century than some other Churches'.[1] Justin knew, he believes, this traditional eucharistic prayer. Dix[2] cites Justin's reference to the ruler sending up praise and glory to the Father of the universe through the name of the Son and of the Holy Spirit (*I Apol.* lxv) and the association, in *Dial.* xli, with the creation of the world. He also cites the *anamnesis* passages in *I Apol.* lxvi and *Dial.* xli. However, it is significant that, later in his book, Dix wrote these words:

It is quite true that we have already established that there is nothing in the contents of the second half of Hippolytus' prayer which would not have been accepted by Justin sixty years before him. But this is not necessarily quite the same thing as saying that it was all in the prayer in Justin's day...The expansion of the prayer may quite well have taken place in the generation between Justin and Hippolytus, a period about which we know very little...all that we can safely say is that Justin's language is quite consistent with the idea that the Roman prayer in his day consisted only of an Address and 'Naming' of God followed by a series of 'Thanksgivings' for creation, redemption etc., and nothing more. If his prayer contained other elements, he has not mentioned them.[3]

This is a clear admission that there was no fixed liturgy with a 'structure' known to Justin. The address and 'naming' of God followed by a series of thanksgivings is not a fixed liturgy *per se* but an example of how the original thanksgiving of the Last Supper had been expanded by Justin's time through the use of liturgical material deriving from Judaism. It is surely significant (and Dix fails to note this in his desire to systematise Justin's evidence) that Justin states that the Ruler at the Eucharist sends up prayers and thanksgivings 'to the best of his ability' (ὅση δύναμις αὐτῷ),[4] i.e. extempore. This reflects a

---

[1] *The Shape of the Liturgy*, p. 160.   [2] *Ibid.* p. 159.   [3] *Ibid.* p. 224.
[4] *I Apol.* lxvii. 5; cf. also *Did.* x. 7: 'suffer the prophets to hold Eucharist as they will' (τοῖς δὲ προφήταις ἐπιτρέπετε εὐχαριστεῖν ὅσα θέλουσιν). An element of extempore prayer however remained in the liturgy; cf. *Apost. Trad.* x. 4.

fluidity appropriate to a time before the eucharistic prayer had become fixed or of a definite structure.[1] In this connection M. Goguel's remark cannot be bettered: 'It must be added that while the principle of the permanent nature of the liturgy is indisputable, it is not certain that it was a factor at the time when the liturgy was in process of being formed as at a later date.'[2] But Justin does show how the original thanksgiving at the Last Supper had been expanded in his day. We are on the way to the first liturgies.

(b) The theology of the Eucharist: Justin's language marks an advance on that of the *Didache* and Ignatius. He describes the eucharistic gift with greater precision and applies the word εὐχαριστία to the consecrated elements which he identifies with the body and blood of Christ. It is no longer 'common food' after the thanksgiving has been pronounced over it, but has acquired a sacred character. The passage which has caused most difficulty is that quoted above: 'But as Jesus Christ our Saviour being incarnate by God's word took flesh and blood for our salvation, so also we have been taught that the food consecrated by the Word of prayer which comes from him, from which our flesh and blood are nourished by transformation, is the flesh and blood of that incarnate Jesus.'[3] The interpretation of this passage has been bedevilled by denominational considerations. It would seem an error to interpret it apart from Justin's theory of the logos. Justin refers explicitly in this passage to the incarnation of the divine logos in the flesh and blood of Jesus for our salvation. So in the Eucharist there is a further action of the logos such that the elements of bread and wine become united with the logos and so become the flesh and blood of the incarnate Jesus. How this occurs Justin does not state apart from saying that the food is consecrated 'by the Word of prayer which comes from him', which could refer to a thanksgiving deriving from the εὐχαριστήσας of the institution

---

[1] Is it significant that Justin makes no reference to the singing of Psalms although he was much interested in the Psalms as texts for his exegesis and is said to have written a book called *Psaltes*? *Apost. Trad.* xxvi. 28–32 mentions the singing of Psalms at a Private Agape.

[2] *The Primitive Church*, p. 329 n. 5. Note also the remark of R. P. C. Hanson: 'The search for the early liturgy of the Church may well, therefore, be a search for a mare's nest' (*Tradition in the Early Church*, p. 172).

[3] *I Apol.* lxvi.

narratives. To go beyond Justin's words into an explanation as to *how* the elements become the flesh and blood of Christ is to go beyond the evidence. And to state that the mere recital of Christ's words effects transubstantiation of the elements is to read later theories into Justin.[1]

Justin says nothing in the *Apology* about the sacrificial aspect of the Eucharist although he quotes the words 'Do this for my memorial' from the institution narratives in the Gospels. However, in the passages cited above from the *Dialogue* he dwells at greater length on these words and interprets 'do' and 'remembrance' as having a sacrificial meaning. This conception of the Eucharist as a sacrifice and a memorial of the Passion, which is based on the Pauline words of institution, is peculiar to Justin among second-century writers[2] although, as in the *Apology*, he gives no real explanation or theory of the Eucharist. He was content to accept its spiritual blessings without questioning how the elements had become the flesh and blood of Christ.

(*c*) The reference in the *Apology* to the sending of a portion of the consecrated elements to absent members of the Church is the earliest reference to a practice which received considerable extension in later ages. There is however nothing in Justin's account to suggest more than the spiritual sustenance of the sick, aged, and those unable, for one reason or another, to attend the Christian assembly for worship. By the time of Tertullian[3] Christians were allowed to carry away and keep the

[1] It is interesting to compare Justin's theory of the Eucharist with that of Irenaeus. Irenaeus emphasises, more clearly than Justin, the composite character of the Eucharist. While retaining Justin's realism he introduces an invocation of the elements (ἐπίκλησις) and states that a heavenly element (πρᾶγμα οὐράνιον) is added to them and operates through them (*Adv. Haer.* IV. 18. 4). He also stresses, more than Justin, the effects of the Eucharist as a means of imparting life to the body and soul of man (cf. Ignatius' 'medicine of immortality').

[2] The idea of the Eucharist as a sacrifice is, of course, found; e.g. in I Clement and Ep. Barnabas. But it is not explicitly connected with the *anamnesis*. This conception came from the assimilation of Christian Worship to that of Israel and from the offerings which, from an early time, accompanied the celebration of the Eucharist (Goguel, *The Primitive Church*, p. 356).

[3] *Ad Uxorem* ii. 5; *Apost. Trad.* xxxii. 2 seems also to refer to this practice. Dix, *The Apostolic Tradition of St. Hippolytus* (London, 1937), p. 84.

sacrament in private for their own use. This custom, which was open to abuse, became widespread but is not now allowed anywhere. The ancient practice of reserving a portion of the consecrated elements for those unable to receive them in Church is however practised today throughout Eastern and Western Christendom although the administration is restricted to those in authorised orders.[1] The practice of using the reserved sacrament as a centre of devotion and worship did not begin until the eleventh century[2] and has no support in the earliest Christian writers.

Justin's doctrine of the Church and sacraments is not systematised. He belonged to a period when considerable fluidity of doctrine and practice still prevailed. What is significant is that he accepted that the Church was a supernatural society founded by the Apostles in the name of Christ which held to the apostolic teaching. Justin was not conscious of being an innovator in doctrinal or practical matters. His Christianity he believed, rightly or wrongly, he had received from the Church of the preceding age. Justin's descriptions of the sacraments of baptism and the Eucharist are of high value—the more so since they were introduced into his writings almost incidentally. These two sacraments, he believed, were essential to the fullest Christian life although he did not deny that the fruits of the Spirit were sometimes seen outside the Church. Christian Sunday Worship, without the Eucharist, was unknown to him although the celebrant in each community had a certain amount of freedom in the form of prayer used at this service. Although he faithfully reproduces the Church's technical terminology Justin stresses strongly the ethical and religious aspect of the sacraments and disassociates them from a magical view of their operation and efficacy. The sacraments are, for him, life-giving and the spiritual life and illumination which Christians receive must issue in good Christian lives. He manages to avoid many of the pitfalls to which later Christian thinkers succumbed. It is unlikely that any fixed or structural form of the liturgy existed in his day, although his liturgical material represents a stage further advanced than that of the

---

[1] C. B. Moss, *The Christian Faith: An Introduction to Dogmatic Theology*, pp. 375–81, has some interesting remarks on the practice of Reservation.

[2] It is still unknown in the Eastern Churches.

CHAPTER XI

THE CHRISTIAN LIFE

THE Christian life has always to be lived out in concrete historical situations and the virtues which Christians show forth in their lives, while not ultimately determined by the particularities of history, are nevertheless shaped and influenced by 'the changes and chances of this fleeting world'. Different circumstances call forth different facets of a man's character and faith. Before then considering Justin's view of the Christian life it would be wise to look at the particular problems which the Christian communities faced in his day.

Justin, as we have already seen,[1] represents Christianity as widely diffused throughout the Roman world of his day. The Church, he believed, was growing in strength and adapting itself to the needs of the various races within the Empire and even beyond its borders. Yet the very success of the Church had caused a bitter enmity to arise and the principal causes of this enmity are given by Justin with remarkable clarity. He complains that the Christians were 'unjustly hated and abused'[2] and that report charged them with the utmost 'impiety and wickedness'.[3] It was said that in their secret assemblies hideous crimes were committed—human victims were sacrificed and their blood drunk by the worshippers, and these impious banquets were followed by indulgence in hideous and lustful orgies.[4] These charges show the suspicion and hatred with which the Christians were regarded. Justin complains that the charge of being a Christian was often used as a pretext for wreaking personal revenge.[5]

He mentions three charges in particular which were frequently made against the Christians. The first was that of atheism[6]—a charge made as long as the traditional deities and beliefs were the nominal ruling power of the State. Yet in Justin's day the gods were denied by philosophers, ridiculed by popular writers and largely neglected by the people. The

---

[1] Pp. 126–7 above.
[2] *I Apol.* i.
[3] *II Apol.* xii; *I Apol.* xxvi; *Dial.* x.
[4] *I Apol.* vi–xii.
[5] *II Apol.* i–ii.
[6] *I Apol.* vi.

charge of 'atheism' was simply a suitable battle cry to use against any association of people which denied the gods of the State. It was more a charge of unpatriotic behaviour than of religion as such. But the cry of 'atheism' could be used to kindle mob fury as occasion demanded when the Christians were at the mercy of unbridled passions. They could only logically meet the charge of atheism by patiently showing the folly of worshipping man-made gods in which few people really believed and by declaring boldly that they were, in the true sense, not atheists.[1]

The second charge was one of wickedness and evil behaviour.[2] Justin, in reply, admits that as there are philosophers whose teachings are contradictory so there are nominal Christians; but nevertheless all should not be condemned because of the wrongs committed by some who bear the name. He demands that every accused person be examined, not as to the name he bears, but as to the life he has led. Justin is confident that no orthodox Christian will be found guilty of wrong-doing.[3]

The third charge was that of disloyalty to the Roman state.[4] This was more difficult to refute in view of the Christian claim as to the kingship of Christ and the kingdom of God. Moreover the populace was quick to note that Christians refused to offer worship to the *genius* of the Emperor, that they denied the efficacy of the State deities and so cut themselves off from the political and social duties of the Roman citizen. The Church appeared to them as a diffused secret society whose existence threatened the security of the State. In vain did the Christians reply that they obeyed the laws, prayed for the Emperor, paid taxes and often fought in the army.[5] In vain did Justin argue that the acceptance of Christianity would make good citizens of all men.[6] The suspicion remained and when charges of atheism and moral wickedness were added it is evident that popular prejudice could easily explode into acts of violence.

In addition to these formal charges there was a popular impatience with Christians and what they stood for. One cause

[1] *I Apol.* vi, ix, x.
[2] Justin says: 'But someone will say, "some (Christians) have been arrested and convicted as criminals".' *I Apol.* vii.
[3] *I Apol.* vii.   [4] *I Apol.* xi.
[5] *I Apol.* xvii.   [6] *I Apol.* xi.

of this was their moral purity which acted as a rebuke to contemporary society;[1] another was the willingness of the Christian confessors to die rather than deny Jesus Christ which was regarded as hopeless obstinacy.[2] Another was the apparent failure of the Christian God to protect his worshippers.[3] With such people society had little patience—and when to this was added the alleged danger of the Christian communities to public welfare, fuel was added to the flames of hatred. The Jews in particular led the Gentiles in ridicule and misrepresentation of the Christians and their beliefs.[4]

Justin's allusions to the pagan attitude towards Christians are confirmed by other notices coming from the second century. Clement of Rome, writing just before the turn of the century, testifies that he and his fellow Christians were 'hated wrongly' while in his great prayer for rulers he proves how law-abiding and loyal they really are.[5] Pliny, in his celebrated letter to Trajan, betrays the temper of the age—and this in spite of his fair-mindedness—when he states that Christians deserve punishment on account of their obstinacy whatever their character.[6] It is also surely significant that Plutarch and Dio Chrysostom, who, in many ways, had much in common with Christianity, preferred to ignore it rather than show any sympathy with it. And Christian writers subsequent to Justin refer to the same hatred and charges against Christians that he himself had referred to. Such is the witness of Athenagoras' *Supplicatio*, of Tertullian's *Apology* and the *Octavius* of Minucius Felix. Justin's testimony of popular enmity towards the Christians is thus the common testimony of the century to which he belonged. Individual hatred of goodness, the opposition of the Jews, the love of the rabble for witch-hunting, the ill-will of some local magistrates and other causes combined to impute infamous deeds to the Christians and to make them objects of unreasonable hatred. Justin believed that an era of persecution was just beginning and he expected persecution to wax worse and worse until the time of Christ's return.[7]

Justin's *Apology* was, in essence, an appeal against a policy which classed Christianity among the number of illegal societies.

[1] *II Apol.* ii. [2] *II Apol.* iv. [3] *II Apol.* v.
[4] *Dial.* vi, xvii, cxvii. [5] *I Clem.* lx–lxi. [6] *Ep.* x. 96.
[7] *Dial.* xxxix, cx.

This is never stated formally but is implied in the defence he makes. He complained—and complained bitterly—against the injustice of condemning men merely for a name. He insisted that every man should be tried on the grounds of moral character and conduct. He appealed for liberty of opinion and worship; that Christianity should be tolerated and protected from attacks of violence. Justin based his demand for toleration on the grounds that Christianity was a philosophy and he joined to this a description of the moral purity of Christians and the innocence and simplicity of their worship which is one of the most valuable testimonies to the Christian life which has come down from the second century.

Justin, in his desire to show the harmlessness of Christianity, represents the two great Christian sacraments as entirely innocent. Baptism was a washing in water 'in the name of God the Father and Master of all, and of our Saviour Jesus Christ, and of the Holy Spirit'.[1] At the weekly Eucharist[2] the memoirs of the apostles or the writings of the prophets were alone read, an exhortation was given by the ruler of the brethren, prayers, celebration of the Eucharist and offerings for the needy followed. Nothing more. Yet it is Justin's witness to the moral elevation of Christians in their daily lives which illustrates how this sacramental grace bore fruit. He shows us men and women who were without fear of death,[3] who loved truth more than life,[4] yet who thought it a duty to preserve life so long as God delayed to take it.[5] These people desired fellowship with God,[6] rested their hope for the future on God's promises and felt the duty of faithful obedience to him. Justin, in a famous passage, describes the change wrought by Christianity:

Those who once rejoiced in fornication now delight in continence alone; those who made use of magic arts have dedicated themselves to the good and unbegotten God; we who once took most pleasure in the means of increasing our wealth and property now bring what we have into a common fund and share with everyone in need; we who hated and killed one another and would not associate with men of different tribes because of (their different) customs, now, after the manifestation of Christ, live together and pray for our enemies and

---

[1] *I Apol.* lxi.
[2] *I Apol.* lxvii.
[3] *I Apol.* ii, xi, xlv.
[4] *I Apol.* ii; *II Apol.* iv.
[5] *II Apol.* iv.
[6] *I Apol.* viii, xiv, xxv, xlix.

try to persuade those who unjustly hate us, so that they, living according to the fair commands of Christ, may share with us the good hope of receiving the same things from God the Master of all.[1]

Justin then cites examples of Christ's teaching, mainly drawn from the Sermon on the Mount, especially emphasising the directions to be pure in heart, temperate and generous.[2] He boldly contrasts Christian morality with the vices of pagan society[3] and speaks of the care of Christians for children,[4] their solemn estimate of the value of human life,[5] their peaceableness,[6] their compassion for their enemies,[7] their patience and prayers even when persecuted,[8] and their philanthropy.[9] Justin states the inherent difference between right and wrong[10] and man's responsibility for his moral choice.[11] Yet shining through the virtues described by Justin, there is the Christian hope of personal immortality, of divine reward and the final destruction of the devil and the powers of evil. Christianity is no abstract code of conduct but a real change of life, begun in baptism, which issues in a universal brotherhood.

Justin, in common with later Apologists, assails fiercely the immoralities of paganism. He declares paganism to be the work of daemons;[12] he ridicules its idolatry[13] and contradictions;[14] he denounces its impure stories[15] and shameless rites.[16] He even denounces the recent deification of Antinous by Hadrian[17]—a bold action—in order to show in contrast the lofty ideal of purity which Christians sought and displayed. Justin was an intense moralist and Christianity for him issued in morality *par excellence*. Christians were therefore wholly different people from the picture given by the slanderous accusations levelled at them. They had totally repudiated pagan vices and were seeking holiness. Universal love was their motif. Truth, purity, generosity, humility with fearlessness, patience with courage, were their characteristic traits. They had broken down racial

[1] *I Apol.* xiv. [2] *I Apol.* xv. [3] *I Apol.* xxvii.
[4] *I Apol.* xxvii. [5] *I Apol.* xxix. [6] *I Apol.* xxxix.
[7] *I Apol.* lvii; *Dial.* cxxxiii. [8] *Dial.* xviii.
[9] *Dial.* xciii, cx. [10] *II Apol.* vii.
[11] *I Apol.* x; *Dial.* cxxiv, cxl. [12] *I Apol.* v, xxiii, liv, lxiv; *II Apol.* v.
[13] *I Apol.* ix. [14] *I Apol.* xxiv. [15] *I Apol.* xxv.
[16] *II Apol.* xii. [17] *I Apol.* xxix.

barriers and had risen above the fear of death. They might be slain—but they could not be injured,[1] since they believed death for Christ's sake to be only a deliverance.

It may well be asked whether the picture presented by Justin is not too idealised. It is of course true that in any age there are many nominal Christians whose conduct and moral level is no different from that of the surrounding non-Christian population. Yet Justin could hardly have made such a bold claim—and this to the fount of Imperial power—unless the astounding moral change of which he writes was a fact. No amount of special pleading would have availed if the moral power of the new religion had not been slowly pervading society so that its effects could be seen. 'No one trusted in Socrates so as to die for this doctrine,' Justin says, 'but in Christ, who was partially known even by Socrates...not only philosophers and scholars believed, but also artisans and people entirely uneducated, despising both glory, and fear, and death.'[2]

Whence did this morality arise? Justin, in spite of his failure to grasp the corporate nature of sin, was no Pelagian blindly believing in man's innate power to elevate himself. All was due, he says, to the Incarnation of the Son of God. From this Christianity arose. This was the source of the specifically Christian life and morality. It was the teaching of the incarnate logos which had given men their new ideal. It was the life, words, death and resurrection of Christ which had created their hope and made them fearless and pure. The Christian life was one of communion with God and the logos. At the time of Justin's conversion the aged Christian had said to him, 'Pray that before all else the gates of light may be opened to thee. For things are not seen nor comprehended of all, save of him to whom God, and his Christ, shall have given understanding'.[3] Christians, Justin believed, possessed the fulness of the Spirit. This was the source of the moral elevation which had come, like a bright light, into the darkness of contemporary paganism. Is it possible to believe that all this was a figment of the imagination?

[1] *I Apol.* ii. [2] *II Apol.* x. [3] *Dial.* vii.

CHAPTER XII

ESCHATOLOGY

No consideration of Justin Martyr's life and thought would be complete without a consideration of his eschatology, for belief in a second advent of Christ was fundamental to his outlook. In considering Justin's eschatology a starting-off point is provided by a recent article of Professor C. F. D. Moule of Cambridge[1] which is, I believe, relevant to Justin. Briefly Professor Moule's thesis is that it is an error to seek for a sequence of development or evolution in eschatological formulations within the New Testament as the hope in the Parousia weakened:

My point is not only that these (i.e. New Testament statements about the last things) are incapable of being built into a single system, but also that they have, intrinsically, no logical sequence or successive order of evolution, but may arrive on the scene at any moment, and in almost any order, whether to 'peg' two opposite ends of a paradox or to defend different aspects of the truth as they chance to come under attack. They are produced (to use Papias' celebrated phrase) πρὸς τὰς χρείας, to meet each need as it arises.[2]

Professor Moule has no difficulty in showing that the language of realised eschatology is used more when the *individual* believer is in mind; futurist eschatology when *the group destiny* is being emphasised; the mythical and quasi-physical language of apocalyptic when *the future of the entire cosmos* is in view. So St Paul can use realised eschatology, apocalyptic and non-apocalyptic language according to his theme, not according to the stage of his theological development.[3] The question of the delay in the Parousia was hardly in view in the New Testament and did not affect the shaping of theological thought.[4]

Professor Moule's conclusions (and he is dealing only with the New Testament) would appear to be of importance for the understanding of Justin's eschatology. Justin had a vivid belief in the second advent of Christ, *yet it is remarkable how little the*

---

[1] 'The Influence of Circumstances on the Use of Eschatological Terms', *J.T.S.* xv (April 1964), 1–15.

[2] *Ibid.* p. 5.   [3] *Ibid.* p. 11.   [4] II Peter iii is unique in this respect.

delay in the Parousia seems to have worried him. The 'time scale' type of argument is hardly found in his writings. Goodenough's explanation of this is that Justin was a simple type of Christian 'to whom the written and oral traditions of early Christianity ...have meant more than the attempts of thoughtful men to reconcile them with the facts of life'.[1] This is, I believe, to underestimate Justin who after all was a philosopher who had come to Christianity from a mid-Platonist *milieu*.[2] We shall try to show in this chapter that Justin, writing in the mid-second century, was still dominated by the tension between the 'already' and the 'not yet'; by what had happened in the coming of Christ, the whole Word, rather than by problems of the delay of the Parousia. His eschatological language varies according to circumstance, as with the New Testament writers, and this is the cause of his apparent contradictions. Goodenough's judgement that Justin's is an inferior mind and that 'one of the chief values of a study of his eschatology is the testimony it bears to the completely uncritical character of his thinking'[3] could equally well be applied to St Paul or St John.

We must now pass to a consideration of Justin's eschatology.

THE TWO ADVENTS

Again and again in both the *Dialogue* and the *Apology* Justin states his belief in the two advents of Christ.[4] The first has already happened in the Incarnation when he came as a dishonoured and suffering man without glory—the second coming will reveal him in glory with the angelic host. Justin uses the word παρουσία no fewer than twenty-nine times while the only other occurrence of the word in the Greek Apologists is found in Tatian, *Oratio ad Graecos* xxxix. 3. The two comings—the first in lowliness, the second in exaltation—have been, for Justin, prophesied in the Old Testament and he adduces a succession of proof texts in support of his view, some not found in the New Testament. Thus Ps. cx. 7, 'Of a brook in the way shall he

---

[1] *Theology of Justin Martyr*, p. 279. Note his remark: 'It is one of the marvels of history that Christianity did not collapse when its eschatological hope had to be indefinitely postponed.'
[2] *Dial.* ii. 6.   [3] *Theology of Justin Martyr*, p. 291.
[4] *I Apol.* lii; *Dial.* xxxii, xxxiii, xl, xlv, xlix, cx, cxi *inter alia*.

drink, therefore shall he lift up his head', describes the humility and the glory of Christ.[1] In the first advent Christ was pierced, in the second they will recognise the one whom they have pierced and bitterly mourn.[2] Even the events associated with Moses and Joshua are brought in to support Justin's views:[3] Moses stretched out his hands as he sat on the hill and continued until evening while Joshua was the leader in battle enabling Israel to prevail—the former symbolising by his outstretched arms the first coming and the Cross while Joshua (Jesus) symbolises the second coming when the power of the name will prevail over the daemonic hosts. Likewise the two goats offered on the Day of Atonement represent the two advents—the scapegoat symbolising Christ's suffering and death and the other goat his second coming which Justin seems to imply will take place in Jerusalem.[4]

This belief in the two advents of Christ is found consistently in the New Testament and Justin's linking of it with the status of Christ as humiliated and glorified is also thoroughly biblical. The fact that he overlays and supports this belief with much fanciful exegesis and quotes proof texts which sometimes appear to have been picked at random should not blind us to his fundamentally biblical outlook. What is significant is that Justin preserves the tension found in the New Testament between the *already* and the *not yet*, that is, between realised and futurist eschatology. While many of his references to the second advent are, as might be expected, *collective*, that is, Christ comes as the arrival of a king to a community,[5] some are individualistic. Thus in *Dial.* xxviii. 2–3 Justin says to Trypho:

It is but a short time that is left you for coming over to us; if Christ come suddenly, you will repent in vain, you will lament in vain; for he will not hear you. 'Break up fallow ground for yourselves,' Jeremiah has cried to the people, 'and do not sow over thorns. Circumcise to the Lord, and be ye circumcised in the uncircumcision of your heart.' Do not therefore sow in thorns and unploughed land whence you have no fruit. Know Christ, and behold there is fair fallow, fair and rich in your heart.

---

[1] *Dial.* xxxiii. 2.   [2] *Dial.* xxxii. 2. Cf. Zech. xii. 10–14.
[3] *Dial.* cxi.   [4] *Dial.* xl. 4–5.
[5] Moule points out (*J.T.S.* xv (1964), 7) that παρουσία is mostly a collective word. So Chrysostom, *Hom. in Ascens.* (*P.G.* L. 450–1).

This is the language, not of apocalyptic, but of realised eschatology: 'Watch therefore, for ye know neither the day nor the
hour wherein the Son of Man cometh.'[1]

THE DELAY IN THE PAROUSIA

In Justin's day the Church had existed for more than a century.
Generations of Christians had lived on earth and had, no doubt,
believed in a second coming of Christ. The Church in Rome had
survived the fires of the Neronian persecution and the lesser
assault of Domitian. What is surprising is that anxiety over the
delay in the Parousia seems to have left but little trace in early
Christian literature. The following references comprise the
sum total of references to a 'delay' before the time of Justin:
II Peter iii. 4; I Clem. xxiii. 3; Barn. xix. 5; Hermas *Vis.* III.
4. 3; II Clem. xi. 2,[2] and most of these refer to the 'double-
minded' who are disputing 'whether these things are so or not'.[3]
In view of the paucity of references to the 'delay' in the Parousia
as constituting a difficulty it is all the more surprising that
scholars have surmised that the non-occurrence of the second
advent was the cause of a radical reformulation of Christian
doctrine and practice.[4] Justin, as a good representative of
second-century thought, was little troubled by the non-arrival
of the second advent. There are but three passages in his
writings which bear on this question. In *Dial.* xxxii. 3 he quotes
Dan. vii. 25 that the Man of Iniquity is to reign for a season,
seasons and half a season. Trypho and his friends, says Justin,
explain a season as a hundred years, in which case, if *and
seasons* refers to two seasons, the Man of Iniquity will reign for
at least 350 years before the end comes. Justin rejects this and
holds that, since the time of the Ascension, the Man of Iniquity
is at the door, that is, the last times are about to appear. What
is significant is that Justin nowhere suggests that *Christians* have
been querying the non-arrival of the end—it is only a question
of proving to Jews that *their* interpretation of Dan. vii is wrong.

[1] Matt. xxv. 13.
[2] Moule, *J.T.S.* xv (1964), 15, quoting Dr E. Bammel who did not intend
this as an exhaustive list. But I have been unable to find any further
references.   [3] Hermas *Vis.* III. 4. 3.
[4] The classic position of M. Werner, *The Formation of Christian Dogma.*

In two passages in his *Apologies* Justin explains to the non-Christian world why the destruction of the world has been postponed.[1] According to *II Apol.* vii. 1 God has delayed the destruction of the world (and of the daemons and men) 'because of the seed of the Christians, who know that they are the cause of preservation in nature' (διὰ τὸ σπέρμα τῶν Χριστιανῶν, ὃ γινώσκει ἐν τῇ φύσει ὅτι αἴτιόν ἐστιν). In *I Apol.* xxviii. 2 Justin says that 'God delays doing this (i.e. destroying the world) for the sake of the human race, for he foreknows that there are some yet to be saved by repentance, even perhaps some not yet born'.

The first passage seems to have in mind the Old Testament idea that the destruction of a city by God will be postponed if there is a seed or small remnant of righteous people in it.[2] Yet the context makes it clear that Justin has in mind the spermatic logos conception.[3] The researches of Andresen,[4] as we have seen, have recently shed new light on the antecedents of this idea. Andresen shows how Cicero, who depends on Antiochus of Askalon, speaks of the *semina justitiae* which have been present since the earliest generations of man. Cicero links the seed forces of the Stoa with the seeds of justice, that is, he gives an ethical rather than a metaphysical interpretation of them. The same development is found in Arius Didymus in his exposition of the Peripatetic ethics. He reads the idea of 'seed forces' into Aristotle in an exclusively ethical interpretation. Men, for Arius, possess by nature the 'beginnings' and 'seeds' of the virtues which are brought to perfection by morals and right behaviour. Arius is the first to give a purely ethical interpretation of the λόγοι σπερματικοί. In Andresen's view Arius is the link between the philosophy of Antiochus of Askalon and Cicero and Middle Platonism (as exemplified by Albinus).[5] He believes that Justin's ideas are best explained by reference to Middle Platonism where the 'seed forces' are given a moral and ethical interpretation and are not connected with the Stoic

---

[1] Professor H. Chadwick has kindly drawn my attention to *I Apol.* xlv. 1 where Ps. cx. 1–3 is used as a proof text.

[2] Gen. xviii. 16–33.

[3] See below and *II Apol.* viii and xiii.

[4] See pp. 96–9 above.

[5] Full references in Andresen, *Z.N.T.W.* xliv (1952–3), 171–6.

World Reason. It was after all from this type of Platonism that Justin passed into Christianity.[1]

The intricacies of Andresen's argument need not detain us as we have examined them in a previous chapter. What is significant is that Justin, in *II Apol*. vii, after giving his view that God delays the destruction of the world because the seed of Christians are the cause of preservation in nature, states that men have embedded in them the faculty of knowing good and evil: 'But neither do we affirm that it is by fate that men do what they do, or suffer what they suffer, but that each man by free choice acts rightly or sins'...'this is the nature of all that is made, to be capable of vice and virtue.' This is similar to the Middle Platonist use of the Stoic general concepts (*communes notitiae*; *koinai* or *physikai ennoiai*). Justin, however, closely connects these general concepts with the 'seed forces'. This is shown by his terminology when he speaks in this passage of the seed of the Christians who are the cause of preservation in nature and the seed of the logos implanted in the whole human race;[2] and in another context of 'the intuition of God implanted in the nature of man'.[3]

In the second passage from *I Apol*. xxviii. 2 Justin states that God delays the end in order that future generations (some perhaps unborn) may have the opportunity of repentance. This is the nearest we get in Justin to the 'time scale' type of argument.

There is no suggestion in these passages from the *Apologies* that Justin is troubled by the non-arrival of the second advent or that it has affected his innermost thought. His ideas vary according to a change of circumstance. He is no longer confronting a Jew who was familiar with the LXX but is seeking to demonstrate, to the educated world, the *rationality* of the Christian position. Accordingly he places the emphasis on individual choice, as did the prevailing Middle Platonist philosophy, and seeks to show that Christianity is in harmony with nature. In a sense this is a type of realised eschatology although transmuted into a philosophical key. Apocalypticism can thus be relegated into the background and the emphasis placed on individual responsibility in choosing good or evil. Elsewhere Justin represents Christians as looking forward to the end of the present order of things and the destruction of the

---

[1] *Dial*. ii. 6.   [2] *II Apol*. viii.   [3] *II Apol*. vi.

world. These two beliefs should not be considered mutually contradictory. Justin can use apocalyptic and non-apocalyptic language according to his theme, not according to the stages of his development as a Christian philosopher, much as St Paul did.

THE RESURRECTION AND THE MILLENNIUM

Justin, in common with traditional Christian eschatology, held that Christ and his angels will suddenly appear on the clouds of heaven.[1] Then will come the resurrection in which the souls of men will be reunited with the bodies discarded at death. Justin says that his opponents ought not to object to the idea of survival after death since they have much the same in their own traditions:[2] 'Treat us at least like these; we believe in God not less than they do, but rather more, since we look forward to receiving again our own bodies, though they be dead and buried in the earth, declaring that nothing is impossible to God.'[3]

In the *Dialogue* the collective nature of the Parousia is emphasised. The resurrection of the saints occurs at this time, a renewing of heaven and earth takes place and Christians inherit an eternal Jerusalem. Justin likens this to the entry into the promised land under Joshua:

And just as he (i.e. Joshua), not Moses, led the people into the Holy Land, and as he divided it by lot to them that entered with him, so also will Jesus the Christ turn the dispersion of the people, and will distribute the good land to each, though not again in the same manner. For the one (Joshua) gave them the inheritance for a time, for he was not Christ our God, nor Son of God, but the other (Jesus) will, after the holy resurrection, give us our possession forever... This is he who is to shine in Jerusalem as an everlasting light.[4]

Cf. *Dial.* cxxxix. 5: 'Wherefore men from every quarter, whether bond or free, believing on Christ, and knowing the truth that lies in his words and those of his prophets, are aware that they will be together with him in that land, and will inherit the incorruptible things of eternity.'

[1] *I Apol.* li. 8–9, lii. 3; *Dial.* xxxi. 1.
[2] Note the *argumentum ad hominem* in *I Apol.* xviii referring to *Odyssey* xi. 25 f.
[3] *I Apol.* xviii. 16.   [4] *Dial.* cxiii. 3–5. Cf. Tert. *Adv. Jud.* ix.

It is possible to infer from this that the general resurrection and judgement, the renewing of heaven and earth, and the establishment of an eternal kingdom with Jerusalem as its capital all occur together. Justin's language is certainly capable of a spiritual interpretation and is in line with much New Testament eschatology.

However, in the *Dialogue* another view is found. Justin introduces the idea of the millennium or a thousand-year reign of the saints in Jerusalem which is inaugurated by a resurrection of the righteous and closed by a resurrection of the righteous and wicked after which follows the final judgement. There is no doubt that Justin held that Jerusalem would be *physically* rebuilt. In answer to Trypho's question he replies:

I have acknowledged to you earlier that I and many others do hold this opinion, even as you also know well that this is to take place. But I also informed you[1] that even many Christians of pure and godly mind do not accept it[2]...But I, and all other entirely orthodox Christians, know that there will be a resurrection of the flesh, and also a thousand years in a Jerusalem built up and adorned and enlarged, as the prophets Ezekiel and Isaiah, and all the rest, acknowledge.[3]

In *Dial.* lxxxi Justin quotes Isa. lxv. 17–25 and Ps. xc. 4 ('a day of the Lord is as a thousand years') and then goes on:

And, further, a man among us named John, one of the apostles of Christ, prophesied in a Revelation made to him that they who have believed our Christ will spend a thousand years in Jerusalem, and that afterwards the universal, and, in one word, eternal resurrection of all at once, will take place, and also the judgement. And this too our Lord said: 'They shall neither marry, nor be given in marriage, but shall be equal to angels, being children of God, (that is) of the resurrection.'[4]

As Justin only applies the *verba Christi* to conditions *after* the general resurrection it is likely that he is referring the prophecy of Isa. lxv to *actual* conditions which would come to pass in Jerusalem, although, unlike Papias, he does not emphasise the sensuous element of the millennium.

---

[1] This is, however, nowhere to be found in the *Dialogue*.
[2] *Dial.* lxxx. 2.   [3] *Dial.* lxxx. 5.
[4] *Dial.* lxxxi. 4. The reference appears to be to Luke xx. 35 f.

It is a hopeless task to reconcile this belief in an earthly millennium in Jerusalem with Justin's other opinion that the new Jerusalem will be an immediate, spiritual, eternal land or inheritance. The argument that there is no mention of the millennium in the two *Apologies* and that therefore this belief was of no real significance to Justin will hardly bear examination, as to have stated boldly the collapse of all earthly power and the rule of Christians under Christ in a rebuilt Jerusalem would have been very untactful, to say the least, in an *apologia* intended primarily for the non-Christian world. Rather both views were held by Justin and it would seem that this is another example of how circumstance has affected his eschatology. In stating the doctrine of the eternal Jerusalem Justin is following good New Testament tradition about the spiritual destiny of mankind.

In holding to an earthly millennium in a rebuilt Jerusalem Justin may have been strongly influenced by the events of the great Jewish war of A.D. 132–5 and the Messianic pretensions of Bar-Chochba or Bar-Cosiba.[1] It is not without significance that in the *Dialogue* Justin refers to the war *as still in progress*. Thus in *Dial*. i. 3 Trypho says that he has recently fled from the war to Greece and Corinth; cf. ix. 3. *Dial*. xvi. 3 seems to refer to Hadrian's edict after the destruction of Jerusalem forbidding Jews from visiting the city, cf. xl. 2, xc. 2, *I Apol*. xlvii, liii. In *Dial*. cviii. 3 the city has been taken. This war set in motion large numbers of refugees fleeing from Palestine who came to many of the larger cities in the Roman world. Discussion, with a Jew, could hardly avoid the question 'What is to become of the ruined Jerusalem?' Justin claims the city for Christ by drawing on an earlier strand of millennial teaching found in Rev. xx. 4, 6 and in Jewish speculation.[2] Both views, the spiritual and millennial Jerusalem, are held by Justin, not because he was simple-minded and incapable of logical thought—the whole tenor of his philosophy is against this—but because circumstances affected his eschatology. He can use the

[1] Recent discoveries suggest this was his real name.

[2] Bohairic Death of Joseph (T.S. iv. 2. 142); cf. Apoc. Bar. xxix. 5 f., Enoch x. 19. In Christian teaching in Papias (Iren. *adv. Haer.* v. 33); Barn. xv; Tert. *adv. Marc.* III. 24; Lact. vii. 20 f. *inter alia*. Also found among the Ebionites and Montanists.

mythical and quasi-physical language of apocalyptic according to his theme—although he admits that many Christians do not subscribe to his quasi-physical views.[1]

THE JUDGEMENT AND WORLD CONFLAGRATION

Justin puts the judgement, when men will be judged before the throne of God according to their deeds, immediately after the second advent or at the close of the millennium. Every man—the living and the dead—reaching as far back as Adam—will appear before the great assize: 'We are in fact of all men your best helpers and allies in securing good order, convinced as we are that no wicked man, no covetous man or conspirator, or virtuous man either, can be hidden from God, and that everyone goes to eternal punishment or salvation in accordance with the character of his actions.'[2] As Isaiah was sawn asunder so will Christ divide the human race at the judgement, some being destined for his everlasting kingdom and some for unquenchable fire.[3] Justin associated the angels with men in the judgement as both have been given free-will.[4] The daemons will be finally and totally conquered and sent to the eternal fires[5] while Christ will reign as eternal king and priest.[6]

The general impression Justin gives is that men and angels who have done evil and misused their free-will will be condemned to eternal fire suffering forever. However, he also states that in the eternal fire every man will suffer in proportion to his deeds:

If you pay no attention to our prayers and our frank statements about everything, it will not injure us, since we believe, or rather are firmly convinced, that every man will suffer in eternal fire in accordance with the quality of his actions, and similarly will be required to give account for the abilities which he has received from God, as Christ told us when he said 'To whom God has given more, from him more will be required'.[7]

---

[1] *Dial.* lxxx. 2. If the above suggestion is correct then there is reason to believe that Justin preserves the tenor of an *actual* discussion with Trypho in the period A.D. 132–5. This, however, need not exclude the possibility that he has made additions at a later period.

[2] *I Apol.* xii. 1.
[3] *Dial.* cxx. 5.
[4] *Dial.* cxli. 1–2.
[5] *I Apol.* xxviii. 1, lii. 3.
[6] *Dial.* xxxvi. 1.
[7] *I Apol.* xviii. 4; Luke xii. 48.

The wicked are only punished so long as God wills them to exist and be punished.[1] Goodenough says that Justin is here retaining distinct traditions and it is idle to speculate as to which he regarded as the true one.[2] Would it not be more true to say that Justin's ideas vary with change of circumstance? The imagery of the great assize is taken over from the New Testament and is used when a personal decision—for or against —is at issue, while in his *apologia* to the non-Christian world Justin emphasises more the *rationality* of the Christian position. The quality of actions is thus all-important and punishment varies according to this quality.

Justin's views on the subject of a world conflagration after the judgement are again diverse. In a remarkable passage in *II Apol.* vii he criticises the Stoic identification of God with matter which is ever-changing and destructible. Christians believe, Justin says, that the end of the world will come when the fire of judgement descends and utterly dissolves everything as in the days of Noah. At this destruction evil angels, daemons and men will cease to exist. How this is to be reconciled with the doctrine of the eternal rule of Christ from the new Jerusalem, found in the *Dialogue*, is not stated. A significant clue lies in the fact, rarely noticed, that only the *Apologies* speak of a final conflagration while only the *Dialogue* knows of the eternal Jerusalem. It would seem that again Justin's views vary according to circumstance, for in the *Second Apology* he is concerned to refute the Stoic view (as understood by Middle Platonism) that the deity is periodically destroyed in changeable matter. In the *Dialogue* Justin is more concerned with refuting Jewish beliefs and asserting the fact of Christ as the light of an eternal kingdom the capital of which is Jerusalem.

Professor Moule, in his study of New Testament eschatology in the article already mentioned, says 'different formulations have to be enlisted in the service of different affirmations, all of which may prove to be simultaneous aspects of a single great conviction too large to be expressed coherently or singly'.[3] Our short investigation in this chapter has shown that this statement is an apt description of Justin Martyr's eschatology. The assertion that he is a simple-minded, uncritical, muddled

---

[1] *Dial.* v. 3. This is a philosophical context.
[2] *Theology of Justin Martyr*, p. 288.   [3] *J.T.S.* xv (1964), 9.

Christian is, I believe, wide of the mark. He is, in fact, no more confused than St Paul or St John. Justin's language varies according to his theme, not according to his stage of development as a Christian philosopher. There is little in his writings to suggest that the delay in the Parousia caused him concern or that time-scale calculations of the end of the world had any significant influence on his theology. His fundamental interest is the Whole Word[1] incarnate in Christ—in other words with what has happened—and he preserves the rich tension between this 'already' and the 'not yet' found in the New Testament. In Justin's extensive writings we can trace no evolutionary sequence of eschatological formulations. Rather affirmations of individual realised eschatology (leading to the call to repentance), futurist eschatology bound up with the destiny of the group, the language of Apocalyptic both mythical and quasi-physical are used according to the theme under discussion. We have seen that Justin in some instances unknowingly allowed the biblical basis of his theology to be modified to too great an extent by his philosophical presuppositions—this is perhaps particularly true of his logos doctrine.[2] But this is not a charge which it would seem can legitimately be brought against his eschatology.

[1] *II Apol.* viii.   [2] See Chapter VII.

CHAPTER XIII

CONCLUSION

WHEN we study objectively and dispassionately the first two centuries of our era we cannot but be struck by the way in which Christianity, originally a semitic faith, spread throughout the Graeco-Roman world and laid hold of the Greek tradition moulding it to its purpose. In this process, which was inevitable, Justin Martyr was a pioneer. He made an outstanding contribution to the intellectual tradition of Christian thought by his interpretation of the logos. He was moreover the first thinker after St Paul to grasp the universalistic element in Christianity and to sum up in one bold stroke the whole history of civilisation as finding its consummation in Christ. It cannot be said that the Church has as yet fully explored Justin's insights, although there are signs, in the contemporary encounter with the non-Christian faiths, that these are proving relevant again.[1]

Justin was no mere academic philosopher but a man with a mission. Christianity was, for him, not a theory but philosophic truth itself and this he served with unswerving devotion and courage. It is not without justice that he is revered as Justin the Martyr who gave his life for his faith.

Justin did not believe that he was an innovator drastically revising and reinterpreting the traditional faith. He believed exactly the opposite—that he was a traditionalist who was handing on the faith which had come down to him.[2] His approach is biblical, pastoral and evangelistic rather than radical. His own ideas were of less importance to him than his desire to demonstrate that God had revealed himself through the prophets and redeemed mankind in Jesus Christ the Son of God. It is not without significance that he is the first post-apostolic writer to describe openly what went on in the weekly worship of the Church.

[1] See the Christian Presence series published by the S.C.M. Press.

[2] This baffled Albert Schweitzer who said: 'there is something unformed about him [i.e. Justin], though, curiously enough, it is uncertain whether he is to be numbered among the pioneers or the epigoni' (*The Mysticism of Paul the Apostle*, p. 349).

Justin, the philosopher, was not conscious that he was grafting on to the biblical basis of Christianity a philosophical interpretation which was bound to modify it—even in essentials. Although his writings faithfully reflect the eclectic Middle Platonism of his day they are no neat amalgam of Plato (as he understood him) and the biblical faith. Platonism, for Justin, was as valid a preparation for the Gospel as Judaism had been. But the Gospel came first all the time. The heart of Christianity, for Justin, was God's care and love for man revealed in the Bible and supremely in Jesus Christ. Whatever Justin's shortcomings and however incomplete his theology this fact stands to his credit. It places him in the main stream of the Christian tradition and not on the outskirts as one who grievously distorted the Christian *kerygma* by his excursions into philosophy.

Many readers of Justin miss the immediacy of the Pauline conception of 'being in Christ'. Justin never says explicitly anything about the believer's inner life of communion with God and Jesus Christ. But in fairness we must remember that St Paul was sharing his deepest thoughts with fellow believers in the communities he had founded or visited. He was writing for Christians while Justin was writing primarily for the non-Christian world. How difficult it would be to know anything of St Paul's mysticism if we only had the reports of his speeches contained in the Acts of the Apostles! Justin's beliefs are not circumscribed by the special purpose of his writings. When he speaks to non-Christians of the whole logos as being in Christians he might well have spoken, in a Christian context, of the indwelling Christ. His conception of baptism as 'illumination' (a highly mystical idea) might well have become 'dying and rising with Christ' to another audience.

Justin's strong emphasis on the Christian life and his witness to the moral elevation found among Christians is one of the most convincing proofs of the difference Christianity had made by its coming to the Graeco-Roman world. The marvellous spectacle of a specifically Christian morality arising from within the depraved society of paganism, portrayed in his pages, cannot but encourage us in an age which is likewise facing 'the shaking of the foundations'.

Justin impresses us by his rugged simplicity, modesty, love of fair play, honesty and courage. He was no plaster saint tortured by his own inhibitions but an uncomplicated character who openly states what he believes—and he is courageous enough to assume that his message will be clearly understood and heeded. Loyal to the past and to the Church he was yet open and alive to the intellectual currents of his age and friendly to the stirrings of the human spirit.

Dean Inge was fond of saying: 'We cannot preserve Platonism without Christianity, nor Christianity without Platonism, nor civilisation without both.' Justin Martyr would have endorsed this. For him Christianity was philosophic truth itself. Christian philosophers may yet find that he was not mistaken.

WORKS ATTRIBUTED TO JUSTIN

JUSTIN MARTYR is one of the outstanding figures of the second-century Church and it is only to be expected that many later writings of unknown authorship and also forgeries would be ascribed to him. This *Pseudo-Justinian* corpus of writings includes the following:

(*a*) Address to the Greeks.
(*b*) Hortatory Address to the Greeks.
(*c*) On the Unity of God.
(*d*) A Fragment on the Resurrection.
(*e*) Exposition of the True Faith.
(*f*) Letter to Zenas and Serenus.
(*g*) Refutation of certain Aristotelian Doctrines.
(*h*) Questions and Answers to the Orthodox.
(*i*) Christian Questions asked to the Greeks.

The arguments against accepting any of the above works as genuine productions of Justin are overwhelming and have been conclusively stated by Harnack, *Geschichte der altchristlichen Literatur*, I, 99–114. The *Expositio Rectae Fidei* has now been proved to be the work of Theodoret. See J. Lebon, *R.H.E.* XXVI (1930), 536–50, and R. V. Sellers, *J.T.S.* XLVI (1945), 145–50.

Justin's own literary activity undoubtedly extended beyond the two *Apologies* and the *Dialogue* with Trypho. He refers in *I Apol.* xxvi to a treatise against all the heresies, and Irenaeus, *adv. Haer.* IV. 6, mentions a treatise of Justin against Marcion. Eusebius, *H.E.* IV. 18, says that Justin, in addition to the two *Apologies* and the *Dialogue*, wrote an Address to the Greeks, treatises on the Unity of God and on the Soul, a work called *Psaltes* (apparently a Psalter or Hymn Book) of which we know nothing. Photius, Bibl. cod. 125, 95, adds to these a work on Nature and a general Refutation of the arguments against Christianity. There are four small fragments, almost certainly genuine, preserved in later writers. See further R. M. Grant in *Biblical and Patristic Studies in memory of R. P. Casey* (Freiburg, 1963), pp. 182–8.

HADRIAN'S LETTER TO MINUCIUS FUNDANUS

JUSTIN appended this Rescript to the conclusion of his *First Apology*. It is the reply Hadrian sent to an inquiry from Minucius' predecessor, Silvanus Granianus, concerning the treatment of accusations made against Christians.

I have received the letter addressed to me by your predecessor Serenius[1] Granianus, a most illustrious man; and this communication I am unwilling to pass over in silence, lest innocent persons be disturbed and occasion be given to the informers to practise villainy. Accordingly, if the inhabitants of your province will so far sustain this petition of theirs as to accuse the Christians in some court of law, I do not prohibit them from doing so. But I will not suffer them to make use of mere entreaties and outcries. For it is far more just, if anyone desires to make an accusation, that you give judgement upon it. If, therefore, anyone makes the accusation, and furnishes proof that the said men do anything contrary to the laws, you shall punish them in proportion to the offences. And this, by Hercules, you shall give special heed to, that if any man, through mere calumny, bring an accusation against any of these persons, you shall award to him more severe punishments in proportion to his wickedness.

The genuineness of this Rescript was at one time challenged by a number of German scholars[2] although the external evidence in its favour is strong. It is true that Eusebius, *H.E.* iv. 8, states that Justin appended a copy to his *First Apology* in Latin and that he (Eusebius) translated it into Greek—while the present text of Justin has Eusebius' Greek version.[3] A later scribe has no doubt substituted this for the original Latin. Rufinus has preserved a Latin text of the Rescript and there seems to be no insuperable objection to regarding this as the original text rather than a re-translation of Eusebius' Greek

---

[1] This appears to be a mistake for Silvanus.

[2] See J. B. Lightfoot, *Apostolic Fathers*, pt II, vol. I, 477/8.

[3] See the important note of Dom B. Capelle in *R. Bén.* XXXIX (1927), 365–8, who shows that Justin himself added the Rescript.

version. Rufinus certainly knew Ulpian's collection of the Imperial Ordinances relating to the Christians and, as he lived in the West, he may well have been acquainted with Justin's *Apologies*. A further point is that the Latin text has a juristic tone which is unlike Rufinus' own hand.

The language of the Rescript is perfectly clear and its effect must have been wholly favourable to the Christians—that is why Justin appended it to his *First Apology*. No longer, at least in Asia Minor, could Christians be falsely accused by the hated *delator* or informer. Law, not prejudice or mob violence, was to be the Roman basis of dealing with them. Accusers must from now on bring a charge against Christians in a form which was to be the subject of a legal inquiry. Many would now shrink from the light accusation based on hearsay. Even to accuse Christians of the 'Name' would not be too easy as the burden of proof lay directly on the accuser. The Church had good reason to regard Hadrian with favour and later Apologists, such as Melito, made a cautious use of the Rescript.

JUSTIN'S OLD TESTAMENT TEXT

JUSTIN MARTYR's authentic works are contained in only one extant MS, *Parisinus* 450, dated 11 September 1363. Harnack[1] held that the text was in a hopeless condition and his estimate has been echoed by many subsequent investigators.[2] The discoveries by the Dead Sea since 1947 have however provided firm evidence that some of Justin's Old Testament quotations, in spite of the condition of the text, may be of high value.[3] Furthermore recent study of the Testimony tradition underlying the New Testament and early Patristic writings suggests that certain of Justin's erroneous attributions, in quotations from the LXX, may have had a previous history in the Church's *midrash pesher* rather than be mistakes on Justin's part.[4] A fresh, detailed study of Justin's Old Testament quotations was therefore a prime need and this is now in process of being carried out. J. Smit Sibinga published in 1963 the first part of his work, *The Old Testament Text of Justin Martyr. I. The Pentateuch*,[5] in which he deals with the evidence in two parts: the *Lists*, giving the external attestation of the variant readings, and the *Notes*, which as far as possible examine every single instance on its own merits, in order to determine its most probable explanation. As to internal attestation Sibinga applies a threefold classification:[6] (*a*) Readings uniformly attested in two or more passages, either as allusions or formal citations. These deserve confidence,

---

[1] *T. & U.* I, 1–2 (Leipzig, 1882), 77–9.

[2] W. Bousset, *Die Evangeliencitate Justins des Märtyrers in ihrem Wert für die Evangelienkritik von neuem Untersucht* (Göttingen, 1891), pp. 21–31 (on Isaiah and Amos). A. Rahlfs, *Der Text des Septuaginta-Psalters* (Göttingen, 1907), pp. 203–6 (on the Psalms). W. Schmid, *Z.N.T.W.* XL (1941), 87–137. P. Katz, *Studia Patristica* (Berlin, 1957), I, 343.

[3] D. Barthélémy, 'Redécouverte d'un chaînon manquant de l'histoire de la Septante', *R. Bibl.* LX (1953), 18–29, and *Les Devanciers d'Aquila*, Suppl. to *V.T.* vol. x.

[4] See especially B. Lindars, *New Testament Apologetic* (1961), p. 26 n. 2.

[5] E. J. Brill, Leiden. This book is produced to the highest standards of critical scholarship.

[6] *Old Testament Text of Justin Martyr. I. The Pentateuch*, p. 15.

although not all are genuine; (*b*) variants on which the evidence conflicts; and (*c*) variants of isolated attestation. (*b*) and (*c*) must be considered on their own merits.

Sibinga's important investigations are, as yet, in an early stage and he is not predisposed to attempt a synthesis of his results until he has analysed Justin's Old Testament quotations outside of the Pentateuch. He is however able to draw the following tentative conclusion,[1] namely that in Justin's quotations from the Pentateuch there is much material that is both ancient and valuable in spite of a certain amount of lemma and text alteration. He believes that a substantial part of Justin's quotations, including those variants which may be called archaic, belong to a stage in the LXX's history which ante-dates the data in our codices. There is the possibility that not only did Hebrew texts influence the Greek traditions before Origen's time but that this influence may have worked the other way round.

Sibinga's further investigations will be eagerly awaited by students of Justin. His results, so far, indicate that *ad hoc* judgements as to the relative worthlessness of Justin's Old Testament text may be misplaced. These results are also of considerable significance for the study of the Testimony tradition underlying Justin's *Dialogue with Trypho*.[2]

---

[1] *Old Testament Text of Justin Martyr. I. The Pentateuch*, pp. 149–50.

[2] The best critical review of Sibinga's work is that of R. A. Kraft in *Gnomon*, XXXVI (1964), 572 f. See also D. W. Gooding in *J.T.S.* XVI (1965), 187–92.

HARNACK ON THE ELEMENTS USED IN THE EUCHARIST

A. von Harnack, in his learned monograph *Brod und Wasser, die eucharistischen Elemente bei Justin, T. & U.* vii, ii (1891), 117–44, sought to show that in Justin's day the Eucharist was celebrated with bread and water only—no wine being used. Harnack placed great emphasis on Justin's references to the Blessing of Judah (Gen. xlix. 8–12) which he comments on five times without any allusions to the Eucharist (*Dial.* lii, liv, lxiii, lxxvi, *I Apol.* liv). Harnack thought that this was significant as, had wine been used, he would have drawn the parallel between the reference to wine in Gen. xlix. 11 and the Eucharist. This omission would however only be convincing if other early Christian writers *had* used this text as a type of the Christian rite. But Irenaeus, Clement of Alexandria, Hippolytus and Origen all quote the Blessing of Judah without connecting it with the Eucharist [see Zahn, *Brod und Wein im Abendmahl der alten Kirche* (1892), p. 74; Jülicher, *Zur Geschichte der Abendmahlsfeier in der ältesten Kirche* (1892), p. 218; Veil, *Justins des Philosphen und Märtyrers Rechtfertigung des Christentums* (1894), p. 99]. Harnack also made play with the parallel which Justin draws between the rites of initiation in Mithraism and the Christian Eucharist [*I Apol.* lxvi. 4: 'This also the wicked daemons in imitation handed down as something to be done in the mysteries of Mithra; for bread and a cup of water are brought out in their secret rites of initiation, with certain invocations which you either know or can learn']. It is however pressing Justin's language too far to argue that because bread and water were solely used in the Mithraic initiation *then* the Christian Eucharist likewise *only* used these elements. There is another explanation of Justin's reference to Mithraism as we shall see.

We are thus left with three passages in the *Apology* which specifically refer to wine at the Eucharist (*I Apol.* lxv. 3, 4, lxvii. 5). In his attempt to get round these Harnack fell back on textual emendations. In *I Apol.* lxv. 3 Justin says: ἔπειτα προσφέρεται τῷ προεστῶτι τῶν ἀδελφῶν <u>ἄρτος καὶ ποτήριον</u> <u>ὕδατος καὶ κράματος</u>. Harnack proposed to eliminate <u>καὶ</u> <u>κράματος</u> as a gloss (it is missing in C. Ottobianus)—the original reading then referring only to bread and a cup of water. This emendation was adopted by a number of German critics. Jülicher, however (p. 221), Zahn (p. 14) and Goguel (*The Primitive Church*, p. 360) have held that the omission of καὶ κράματος in C. Ottobianus was due to a copyist who was deceived by the similarity of the ending of the words <u>ὕδατος</u> <u>καὶ κράματος</u>. It must of course be recognised that Justin's language is rather unwieldy (in the other two references in *I Apol.* Justin has the easier ἄρτος–οἶνος–ὕδωρ). κρᾶμα is a mixture of water and wine (Liddell and Scott give Tim. Locr. 95E, Plut. 2. 1109E, Plut. 2. 140F, LXX). In modern Greek it has come to mean wine alone. Justin's words as they stand definitely imply that at the Eucharist the elements were bread, a cup of water, and (a cup of ?) water mixed with wine. This would certainly fit in with Justin's other two references to bread, wine and water as if they were three separate elements.

It is interesting, in this connection, to look at Hippolytus' *Apostolic Tradition* xxiii. 1–7 which is worth quoting in full:

And then let the oblation (at once) be brought by the deacons to the bishop, and he shall eucharistise (first) the bread into the representation of the Flesh of Christ; (and) the cup mixed with wine for the antitype of the Blood which was shed for all who have believed in him; and milk and honey mingled together in fulfilment of the promise which was (made) to the Fathers...water also for an oblation for a sign of the laver, that the inner man also, which is psychic, may receive the same (rites) as the body. And the bishop shall give an explanation (λόγος) concerning all these things to them who receive.

And when he breaks the bread in distributing to each a fragment he shall say: The Bread of Heaven in Christ Jesus. And he who receives shall answer: Amen.

And the presbyters—but if there are not enough (of them) the deacons also—shall hold the cups and stand by in good order and with reverence: first he that holdeth the water, second he who holds the milk, third he who holds the wine.[1]

---

[1] I have used Dix's translation.

In this account of the baptismal-eucharist there are three cups —water, milk and honey—and mixed wine. Justin does not mention the cup of milk and honey, but he does refer, in *I Apol.* lxv, to the two other cups—and in the same order as Hippolytus. It therefore seems not improbable that Justin's separate cup of water alluded to the baptismal washing which the catechumen had recently received. This is also the explanation of Justin's reference to the bread and cup of water found in Mithraism, which, he says, 'are brought out in their secret rites of initiation'. This was a pale daemonic imitation of the Christian baptismal-eucharist where bread and the cup of water (representing Christian initiation) were received by the communicant —although he also received the cup of mingled wine as the blood of Christ. This is a better explanation of Justin's account than the usual one[1] that, writing for non-Christians, he wished to show that calumnies against Christians, as to their sobriety at the Eucharist, were unfounded—hence the stress on water.

Harnack is thus right in stating that bread and a cup of water were used at the Eucharist in Justin's day—although wrong in excluding the cup of mingled wine which was Christ's blood. The use of the cup of wine is also demonstrated by Justin's quotation, in *I Apol.* lxvi. 3, of the dominical words of institution, which specifically mention the cup, and the words, 'This is my blood.' If the Christian rite had been celebrated *only* with bread and water (and nothing else) in Justin's day what sense would these words have made to Christians—let alone intelligent pagans?

Justin believed that the sacraments celebrated in his day had come down from the apostles. We have no evidence in the main stream of Christian literature prior to Justin, nor in that immediately following him, that bread and water *alone* were used as the eucharistic elements.[2] This fact, in view of Justin's adherence to tradition, is sufficient to throw the gravest suspicion on Harnack's theory quite apart from the doubts which his textual emendations raise.

[1] E.g. M. Goguel, *The Primitive Church*, p. 360.

[2] Irenaeus condemns the Ebionites for rejecting the mixed chalice and says that when the mixed cup and broken bread receive the Word of God they become the Eucharist of the body and blood of Christ (*Adv. Haer.* v. 1–2). Cf. also the mention of the mixed cup (κέρασμα) in the epitaph of Abercius *c.* A.D. 160 and by Cyprian Ep. lxiii.

SELECT BIBLIOGRAPHY

Altaner, B. *Patrology* (E.T. by H. C. Graef). Edinburgh–London, 1960.

Andresen, C. 'Justin und der mittlere Platonismus', *Z.N.T.W.* XLIV (1952–3), 157–95.

—— *Logos und Nomos*. (Berlin, 1955.

Archambault, G. *Justin, Dialogue avec Tryphon*. 2 vols. Paris, 1909.

—— 'Le témoignage de l'ancienne littérature chrétienne sur l'authenticité d'un περὶ ἀναστάσεως attribué à Justin l'apologiste', *R. de Philologie*, XXIX (1905), 73–93.

Bardy, G. 'Saint Justin et la philosophie stoïcienne', *R.S.R.* XIII (1923), 493 f.

Barnard, L. W. 'Hadrian and Christianity', *C.Q.R.* CLXV (1964), 277–89.

—— 'The Old Testament and Judaism in the Writings of Justin Martyr', *V.T.* XIV (1964), 395–406.

—— 'Justin Martyr's Eschatology', *V.C.* XIX (1965), 86–98.

Barthélémy, D. *Les Devanciers d'Aquila*. Supplements to *V.T.* vol. X. Leiden, 1963.

Bellinzoni, A. *The Sayings of Jesus in the Writings of Justin Martyr*. Harvard Thesis (1962).

Bethune-Baker, J. F. *An Introduction to the Early History of Christian Doctrine*. London, 1949.

Black, M. 'The Patristic Accounts of Jewish Sectarianism', *B.J.R.L.* XLI (1959), 285–303.

Blunt, A. W. F. *The Apologies of Justin Martyr*. Cambridge, 1911.

Bueno, D. R. *Padres Apologistas Griegos*. Madrid, 1954.

Campenhausen, H. von. *The Fathers of the Greek Church*. London, 1963.

Carrington, P. *The Primitive Christian Catechism*. Cambridge, 1940.

—— *The Early Christian Church*. 2 vols. Cambridge, 1957.

Chadwick, H. 'Justin Martyr's Defence of Christianity', *B.J.R.L.* XLVII (1965), 275–97.

—— *Early Christian Thought and the Classical Tradition*. Oxford, 1966.

Copleston, F. C. *A History of Philosophy*. Vol. I: *Greece and Rome*. Revised edn. London, 1947.

Cross, F. L. *I Peter: A Paschal Liturgy*. London, 1954.

—— *The Early Christian Fathers*. London, 1960.

Cullmann, O. *Baptism in the New Testament*. London, 1950.

Davies, W. D. *Christian Origins and Judaism*. London, 1962.

Dix, G. *The Apostolic Tradition of St Hippolytus.* London, 1937.
—— *The Shape of the Liturgy.* London, 1945.
Dodd, C. H. *According to the Scriptures.* London, 1952.
Dods, M. (and others). *The Writings of Justin Martyr and Athenagoras.* (Ante-Nicene Christian Library.) Edinburgh, 1867.
Elliott-Binns, L. E. *The Beginnings of Western Christendom.* London, 1948.
Enslin, M. S. 'Justin Martyr: An Appreciation', *J.Q.R.* xxxiv (1943–4), 179–205.
Every, G. *The Baptismal Sacrifice.* London, 1959.
Falls, T. B. *Saint Justin Martyr (in the Fathers of the Church).* New York, 1948.
Franklin, C. F. *Justin's Concept of Deliberate Concealment in the Old Testament.* Harvard Thesis (1961).
Gildersleeve, B. L. *The Apologies of Justin Martyr.* New York, 1877.
Goguel, M. *The Primitive Church.* London, 1963.
Goldfahn, A. H. *Justinus Märtyr und die Agada.* Breslau, 1873.
Goodenough, E. R. *The Theology of Justin Martyr.* Jena, 1923.
Goodspeed, E. J. *Die ältesten Apologeten.* Göttingen, 1914.
Hanson, R. P. C. *Allegory and Event.* London, 1959.
—— *Tradition in the Early Church.* London, 1962.
—— *Selections from Justin Martyr's Dialogue with Trypho.* London, 1963.
Hardy, E. R. *Faithful Witnesses.* London, 1960.
Harnack, A. von. *Die Ueberlieferung der griechischen Apologeten des 2 Jahrhunderts in der alten Kirche und im Mittelalter. T. & U.* i. Leipzig, 1882.
—— *Brod und Wasser, die eucharistischen Elemente bei Justin. T. & U.* vii. Leipzig, 1891.
—— *The Mission and Expansion of Christianity in the First Three Centuries* (E.T.). Edinburgh, 1908.
—— *Judentum und Judenchristentum in Justins Dialog. mit Trypho. T. & U.* xxxix. Leipzig, 1913.
Harris, J. R. *Testimonies.* 2 vols. Cambridge, 1916 and 1920.
Heard, R. G. 'Apomnemoneumata in Papias, Justin and Irenaeus', *N.T.S.* i (1954), 122–34.
Heinisch, P. *Der Einfluss Philos auf die älteste christliche Exegese: Barnabas, Justin und Clemens von Alexandria.* Münster, 1908.
Hermann, C. Fr. *Albinus. Prologus et Didascalicus (= Epitome). Platonis Dialogi.* Vol. vi. Leipzig, 1853.
Holland, H. S. 'Justinus Martyr', *D.C.B.* iii, 560–87. London, 1882.
Hubik, K. *Die Apologien des hl. Justinus des Philosophen und Märtyrers.* Vienna, 1912.

Hulen, G. 'Dialogue as a Source of Jewish anti-Christian Polemics', *J.B.L.* (1932), pp. 58–70.

Jalland, T. G. 'Justin Martyr and the President of the Eucharist', *Studia Patristica*, v (Berlin, 1962), 83–5.

Jeremias, J. *Unknown Sayings of Jesus*. 2nd edn. London, 1964.

Katz, P. 'Justin's Old Testament Quotations and the Greek Dodekapropheton Scroll', *Studia Patristica*, I (Berlin, 1957), 343.

Kelly, J. N. D. *Early Christian Creeds*. London, 1950.

—— *Early Christian Doctrines*. London, 1958.

Kenyon, F. 'The Date of the Apology of Justin Martyr', *The Academy*, XLIX (1896), 98 f.

Klausner, J. *The Messianic Idea in Israel*. London, 1956.

Kominiak, B. *The Theophanies of the Old Testament in the Writings of Justin Martyr*. Washington, 1948.

Krüger, G. *Die Apologien Justins*. 3rd edn. Tübingen, 1915.

—— (ed.). *Ausgewählte Märtyrerakten*. 3rd edn. Tübingen, 1929.

Lagrange, M.-J. *Saint Justin, Philosophe, Martyr*. 2nd edn. Paris, 1914.

Lebreton, J. and Zeiller, J. *The History of the Primitive Church*. E.T. 2 vols. (from French). Paris, 1934–5.

Lietzmann, H. 'Justinus der Märtyr' in Pauly–Wissowa, *Real-Encyclopädie*, x, cols. 1332–7. Stuttgart, 1919.

—— *Messe und Herrenmahl*. Bonn, 1926.

—— *The Founding of the Church Universal* (*The Beginnings of the Christian Church*, vol. II). E.T. London, 1938.

Lindars, B. *New Testament Apologetic*. London, 1961.

Louis, P. *Albinos, Epitome*. (Paris Thesis.) Rennes, 1945.

Manson, T. W. *On Paul and John*. London, 1963.

Martindale, C. C. *Justin Martyr*. London, 1921.

Moule, C. F. D. *The Birth of the New Testament*. London, 1962.

Otto, J. C. T. *S. Justini Philosophi et Martyris Opera* (Greek text and Latin translation). 3rd edn. Jena, 1876–9.

Pautigny, L. *Apologies. Textes et documents pour l'étude historique du Christ*. Vol. I. Paris, 1904.

Pfättisch, J. M. *Der Einfluss Platos auf die Theologie Justins des Märtyrers*. Paderborn, 1910.

—— *Justinus des Philosophen und Märtyrers Apologien*. Munich, 1912.

Prestige, G. L. *Fathers and Heretics*. London, 1940.

Preuschen, E. 'Die Echtheit von Justins Dial. gegen Tryphon', *Z.N.T.W.* (1919–20), pp. 102–26.

Prigent, P. *Justin et l'Ancien Testament*. Paris, 1964.

Purves, G. T. *The Testimony of Justin Martyr to Early Christianity*. London, 1888.

Rauschen, G. *Die beiden Apologien Justins des Märtyrers*. Kempten, 1913.

Richardson, C. C. (ed.). *Early Christian Fathers*. London, 1953.

Romanides, J. S. 'Justin Martyr and the Fourth Gospel', *Greek Orthodox Theological Review*, IV (1958–9), 115–34.

Sanders, J. N. *The Fourth Gospel in the Early Church*. Cambridge, 1943.

Schmid, W. 'Die Textüberlieferung der Apologie des Justin', *Z.N.T.W.* XL (1941), 87 f.

—— 'Frühe Apologetik und Platonismus', *Festschrift Otto Regenbogen* (1952), pp. 163 f.

Seeberg, E. *Die Geschichtstheologie Justins des Märtyrers*. Kiel, 1939.

Shotwell, W. A. *Biblical Exegesis in Justin Martyr*. London, 1965.

Sibinga, J. S. *The Old Testament Text of Justin Martyr*. I. *The Pentateuch*. Leiden, 1963.

Swete, H. B. *An Introduction to the Old Testament in Greek*. Cambridge, 1902.

Tarn, W. W. *Hellenistic Civilisation* (3rd edn. with G. T. Griffith). London, 1951.

Veil, H. *Justins des Philosophen und Märtyrers Rechtfertigung des Christentums*. Strassburg, 1904.

Vogel, C. J. de. *Greek Philosophy*. Vol. III. *The Hellenistic-Roman Period*. Leiden, 1959.

Warren, F. E. *The Liturgy and Ritual of the Ante-Nicene Church*. London, 1897.

Waszink, J. H. 'Bemerkungen zu Justins Lehre vom Logos Spermatikos', *Festschrift Theodor Klauser* (Münster, 1964), pp. 380–90.

Wendland, P. *Die hellenistisch-römische Kultur*. Tübingen, 1912.

Williams, A. L. *Justin Martyr: The Dialogue with Trypho*. London, 1930.

Witt, R. E. *Albinus and the History of Middle Platonism*. Cambridge, 1937.

Wolfson, H. A. *Philo: Foundations of Religious Philosophy in Judaism, Christianity and Islam*. 2 vols. Cambridge, Mass., 1948.

Ysebaert, J. *Greek Baptismal Terminology: Its Origins and Early Development*. Nijmegen, 1962.

Zeller, E. *A History of Eclecticism in Greek Philosophy*. London, 1883.

INDEX OF REFERENCES

I APOLOGY

GENERAL INDEX

Tannaim, 8, 24
Tarphon, R., 24, 39
Tatian, 4, 6, 12, 13, 62, 65, 101, 158
Tertullian, 4, 21, 22, 34, 45, 75, 135,
    140, 148, 153
Testimonies, 67–74
Theodoret, 172
Theodotion, 44
Theon of Smyrna, 10
Theophilus of Antioch, 4, 62, 85, 101
Thraseas, 132
Thucydides, 131
Timaeus, 35, 36, 83, 87, 104
Timotinus, 6
Trinity, 105, 106
Trypho, 13, 21–5, 39–44, 46–9, 52, 57,
    73, 118, 159, 160, 164, 165, 166
Trypho, Dialogue with, 21–6, 39–52

Ulpian, 174
Uncanonical sayings, 64–6
Urbicus, 17

Valentinus, 12, 54
Veil, H., 177

Verissimus, 14, 19
Vespasian, 5
Victor of Rome, 133
Vogel, C. J. de, 30

Waszink, J. H., 96, 98
Weber, W., 113, 115
Weidle, W., 135
Werner, M., 160
Westcott, B. F., 4
Whittaker, E. R., 29
Williams, A. L., 22, 23, 24, 108
Wisdom, Wisdom Literature, 86, 87,
    90, 91
Witt, R. E., 30, 31, 34

Xenophon, 56, 58

Ysebaert, J., 141

Zadokites, 51
Zahn, T., 177
Zebedee, 59
Zechariah, 48
Zeus, 48

Made in the USA
San Bernardino, CA
29 October 2013